Daddy's War

1 October 2009

For Miriam and Jimmy,
With fond memories of time
spent together this past
summer and with eager
hopes for more sharing soon!
Love,
Irene Kacandes

Daddy's War

[Greek American Stories]

IRENE KACANDES

UNIVERSITY OF NEBRASKA PRESS [LINCOLN & LONDON]

⊚

Acknowledgments for previously published
material appear on pages 351–52,
which constitute an extension of the copyright page.
All photos are the author's.

Publication of this volume was assisted by
The Virginia Faulkner Fund,
established in memory of Virginia Faulkner,
editor in chief of the University of Nebraska Press.

Library of Congress Cataloging-in-Publication Data

Kacandes, Irene, 1958–
Daddy's war : Greek American stories / Irene Kacandes.
p. cm.
Includes bibliographical references.
ISBN 978-0-8032-1933-5 (cloth : alk. paper)
1. Kacandes, John—Childhood and youth.
2. World War, 1939–1945—Greece.
3. Greece—History—Occupation, 1941–1944.
4. Greeks—Biography. I. Title.
D802.G8K24 2009
949.507'4—dc22
2008034279

For children of all times and places trapped in Somebody's War

[Contents]

[Illustrations]

[Abbreviations]

EAM   Ethnikó Apeleftherotikó Métopo
(National Liberation Front)

EDES   Ethnikós Dimokratikós Ellinikós Sýndesmos
(National Republican Greek League)

EKKA   Ethnikí kai Koinonikí Apelefthérosi
(National and Social Liberation)

ELAS   Ethnikós Laïkós Apeleftherotikós Stratós
(Greek People's Liberation Army)

UNRRA   United Nations Relief and Rehabilitation Agency

Daddy's War

[1]

Stalked by Daddy's War

Earliest Memories and How I Came to Face Them

When I was very young I knew things about my father that had no plot, no narrator, no audience. I don't remember being told these things. They were just there, like unwelcome relatives installed for the long haul, sponging off my parents and preventing our family from living completely in the present. They existed with a level of substantiality equal to that of my ancestresses who had thrown themselves off the cliffs of Soúli rather than be taken by the Turks and of my forefathers who had fought the Trojans. Whereas it was easy to want to make room in our crowded house for the heroines and heroes from Greece, it was a lot harder to live with the War Experiences. They took up space, had to be fed and placated. In Their presence one was supposed to be grateful and shut up. They had names like **trapped, abandoned, cheated, terrified, betrayed,** and **starved**. And they were barely kept in check by one called **saved**. It's hard for me to imagine that I could articulate the word "**trapped**" as a toddler—and besides, whatever I could say at that age would have been in Greek—but I feel sure I knew what It looked like and that It was living at our new house on Hawthorne Street. Even on moving day, as my older sisters Maria and Tina and I ran in circles from empty living room to dining room to kitchen and back to living

1. Kacandes children at the new house on Hawthorne Street, White Plains, New York, November 25, 1960. Left to right: Tina (Chrysoúla), Georgia, Maria, Irene.

room, They were leering from the corners. At only two years old, I was the slowest, and I was afraid They would reach out for me.

I can't recall exactly when or how these creatures began to accrue details for me. For as in the case of my earliest memories of Their presence, I don't remember being told stories about Them. So for years my father's past occupied part of my brain as barely perceptible vignettes that I would communicate now with something like the following associative word clusters:

trapped-greece-dictator-war
abandoned-streets

cheated-own house
terrified-messages-underground
betrayed-relatives
starved-death
saved-return to america

By the time I could read, the War Experiences began to circulate in my head as mini-narratives of whose relation to each other I was fairly ignorant. I suppose I could have told you that my relatives must have left America before they could have come back to it, but I never stopped to spell that out for myself, because no one ever asked me about it. Even though I believe I had ceased personifying the snippets of story by the time I reached school age—at least I wasn't as worried They would come after me—I was convinced that They still occupied space at our house and had something to do with the desperate way my father consumed food, the ignominy of his verbal castigations, and the capricious threats to take off his belt and beat us. I wondered if They were causing my mother's headaches and afternoon naps. I was pretty sure it was Their fault that we had to stay in the basement when we visited my paternal grandparents in Neptune, New Jersey, even though they had a beautifully furnished home on the first and second floors. We were told we weren't supposed to dirty the upstairs, but being in the basement had the quality of hiding, hiding from the War Experiences, I assumed. At the same time, I knew perfectly well, I wasn't supposed to ask my parents anything about Them. Similarly, I never questioned my three sisters about Them, even though these word clusters contained lots of mysterious and contradictory elements, and my sisters and I comforted and sustained each other by talking about everything else. There was only one place we felt safe and that was the closet in our bedroom—not to be confused with the closet in our parents' bedroom where our father's belts hung. We shut ourselves into our closet individually as needed and as secretly as possible, because if you got caught crying there you could get yelled at or worse.

I suspect that between the ages of about five and ten, I had an idea of the protagonists and basic plots behind Their presence. I will list those here in approximate, chronological order, though they were stored randomly in my consciousness. In trying to recapture here the form of these stories the way I knew I had them in my head as a child, I note immediately that some snippets come out in my father's voice:

Daddy, Yiayia, Aunt Pearl, Uncle Harry, and Uncle Nick went to Greece because Daddy was having trouble in school since his English wasn't so good. Pappou stayed behind to earn money. They got trapped by a dictatorship and the war and couldn't get out. When the war was over, they came back to the United States.

In Greece, Daddy went to a private boarding school that they closed down suddenly when the war broke out. He was wandering the streets of Athens by himself trying to earn money and find Yiayia.

Yiayia got kicked out of her house during the civil war because her brother robbed her. She had no place to go with the kids. They couldn't get money from Pappou. That's why Daddy had to earn money.

They were so hungry. They survived because there were so many dead people that they were always giving out that nice wheat stuff at church.

Daddy's grandparents were starving. One day his grandfather found the place where his grandmother hid the olive oil. He couldn't help himself. He drank so much olive oil he died.

Daddy ran messages for the Greek underground in the mountains because he was just a boy. The Germans didn't suspect him, but it was scary anyway.

When we got back Uncle Nick didn't know what a fork was.

They put me in second grade even though I was fifteen because I couldn't speak English.

We couldn't believe that they were just going to throw away the grass clippings. So we decided to collect the grass and send it to the goats back in the village. I was the one who knew the most English, so I told the guy at the post office what we wanted to do. They put me in the paper. This rich lady called Pappou and said, "I'll send your son to a good Christian school." That's how I ended up at Pennington Prep.

Now that I've reflected on it, it doesn't surprise me that some snippets are in my father's voice. I do have memories of trying to read the yellowed article about my father that appeared in the local Jersey newspaper in October 1945 and that was subsequently framed and hung in my grandparents' house. However, since part of what sticks in my head includes the cause and the consequences of the publication of that article, I am forced to realize that despite having no memory of ever being directly told or of overhearing these things, I must have been present at some recitals of them by my father.

As a consequence of simply growing older, my intellect developing, and having more contact with the outside world, my father's past took on more historical and narrative detail. I have vague recollections that I "explained" to people how my father had suffered, but I can't recall to whom or under what circumstances I would tell his story. I don't think my recitations were ever of the War Experiences as a single chronological tale, but these are all the narrative elements I currently believe I knew then and might have recounted to others as an adolescent:

When my father was young, his mother took him and his siblings back to Greece because he was having trouble in school in the United States. They were trapped by the Metaxás dictatorship and couldn't return to America. The war broke out. They didn't depart Greece until late 1945, and my father swore he would never return.

When the Italians invaded Greece, they closed down his school, and he was turned onto the streets of Athens. He started selling cigarettes. It took a while before he could earn enough money and find his way back to his mother in the village.

When the war broke out, the money his father had been sending couldn't get through any more, so they were really poor. As the oldest sibling, my Dad tried to support the family. He did anything he could to help them survive.

My father was from an area of Greece that was important strategically because it was near the Corinth canal, so there were a lot of Nazis there, and that's where the Greek resistance was born. He ran messages for the underground in the mountains.

My grandmother was thrown out of her own house by her own family. Greece had a terrible civil war.

There was dreadful starvation in Greece because of the particular timing of the start of the war. The harvest didn't come in, and the Greeks ate the grain, so there was nothing to plant the next season. My father watched his own grandparents starve to death.

So many people died and on such a regular basis that there were continual memorial services for the dead in the churches; my father and his siblings would go to every one so that they could eat the kolyva, the boiled wheat that is handed out to commemorate the dead. They would have starved without it.

When they got back to the United States none of them could speak English, and they didn't know how to use silverware, it had been so long since they had seen any.

There was an article about my father in the local paper, and a wealthy woman from Ocean Grove saw it and contacted my grandfather, saying that if his son were really serious about learning English, she would sponsor him at a private school. That's how he ended up at Pennington Prep and made it to Cornell University. He was the first person in his family to go to college.

My dad's war experiences were so terrible he swore he would never go back to Greece, and so far he hasn't.

To be sure, additional anecdotes were added to my pool of knowledge as events of varying importance occurred in the family. When my paternal grandfather died unexpectedly of a heart attack at age sixty-five on July 4, 1970, I was just twelve years old. But I remember well the brusque way in which my father threw us (now) six kids into the station wagon and the silence in which we made the long drive from Johnson City, New York, where we were visiting Uncle Alex, my mother's brother, and his family, to the Jersey Shore, where most of my father's family still lived. As is Greek Orthodox custom, there was an open casket at the funeral. My handsome grandfather lay there impeccably dressed and elegantly posed, but his skin didn't look right and his eyes were shut. I remember my grandmother screaming out to her dead husband over and over again throughout the church service: Γιώργιο, άνοιξε τα μάτια σου, άνοιξε τα μάτια σου! (George, open your eyes, open your eyes!) But most of all, I remember the stony monolith of my own still father, brooding at the periphery of my vision.

At some point in the days and months that followed my grandfather's death, two stories related to the War Experiences were whispered about and reached my ears. Someone recalled how my father was so upset with his own father when they got back from Greece in 1945 that he refused to address him with Μπαμπά (Dad) or even Πατέρα (Father), referring to him only as μπάρμπα, meaning literally "uncle," and often used to address any male older than oneself, related or not. I don't remember if I risked a direct question, but when my father's extreme moroseness in the wake of his father's death continued, my mother explained to me how sad he was that he had never had a chance to make it up with his father and that now it was too late. Furthermore, I learned that when my father went through his father's papers, he had found a bundle of letters that my grandfather had sent to the Red Cross and the State Department during the war, trying to locate his family. Until finding that correspondence, my mother explained to me, my father had believed that his father had simply **abandoned** them.

Autumn 1972 I was supposed to begin learning a foreign language. I decided to study German. I remember my motivation clearly: I wanted to do something different from my older two sisters, who had been excelling in French. German was being offered in our school system for the first time since it had been canceled during the First World War, and the teacher was a young, beautiful, tall, blond, blue-eyed German American woman. She let us call her "Frau" for short since her last name, von Burchard, was a mouthful—or maybe she just didn't want to hear us butchering its pronunciation. That same fall, the American Field Service decided to send my sister Maria, the oldest of us six siblings, to Hamburg, Germany. This foiled my plan to distinguish myself, but I continued with German anyway. My father didn't say a negative thing about either of his daughters' immersion into things German, and at some point, I realized that this was quite to his credit given his past. When I wanted to praise my father in the years that followed, especially to point out his open-mindedness, I would say:

Despite my father's war experiences he never got upset when I decided to study German or when my sister was sent to Germany as an AFS exchange student.

In fact, close relations quickly developed between all the members of Maria's host family, the Thiels, and my own, including among our parents, the War Generation.

In the summer of 1974 my mother took me and my younger sister, Georgia, to Greece. It was our first trip. We stayed for two months and traveled, among many other places, to Roúmeli, the area of mainland Greece where my father's family was from. While I remember being wowed by the countryside, especially by the ruggedness of Mount Parnassós, and being impressed by what good sense the idea of the Greek gods made in a place like Delphi, I don't remember feeling the presence of Daddy's War, except maybe a little during the suffocatingly hot night we spent in Chryssó, just below Delphi, in a mosquito-filled room at Theia Loukía's, my maternal grandmother's younger sister's house. She's a little crazy, my mother cooed to Georgia and me. Just be patient and polite. Looking back on it now, the significance of this trip lay not in my relationship to the War Experiences, but mostly in my realization that I wasn't as Greek as I thought I was, which in turn spurred my determination to learn the language properly, so that four-year-olds couldn't talk circles around me like they did in Gávrio, the village where my mother was born and where we spent most of that summer, on the Cycladic island of Ándros.

I did in fact become literate in Greek and made many subsequent trips to Greece, including one in 1984 when Daddy's War jumped out and grabbed me by surprise. I had already studied for one year on a Fulbright scholarship at the Aristotle University in Thessaloníki and had started a PhD program at Harvard in comparative literature, in order, among other things, to continue my study of Greek. Not only were my Greek language skills at their best, but I was finally comfortable with my double identity as someone who had grown up in the United States and simultaneously embraced her Greek heritage. I was taking a car tour with two of my maternal grandmother's cousins, Theio Níko and Theia Eléni, my mother, and one of her nephews, my first (maternal) cousin Nick, Uncle Alex's first boy, when we decided it would not be too much of a detour to go to the village in which my paternal grandfather had been born, Kolopetinítsa. Despite my trip to the region ten years earlier and my general interest in Greece and our family, I had never gone to this village. It felt like any connection we might have had to it had died with my grandfather, and even that connection was extremely weak. I couldn't recall ever having heard him talk about his natal village or the members of his family who had stayed in Greece, except for the occasion he refused to dance at my cousin Ted's baptism, because his sister—he had a sister?—had just died.

The only times I ever thought about this place were when I was explaining to someone the strangeness of our last name, and that anyone called Kacandes was sure to be from this village and was definitely related to me. When I was studying in Greece and would be asked about my origins, native Greeks would usually laugh and query: are you sure it's Kolopetinítsa? Confused and embarrassed and suddenly not at all sure, I would answer feebly, yes. One day someone finally explained to me that referring to "Kolopetinítsa" is like saying "Hicksville" or "Podunk" in English. Someone had made a kooky comedy called *Vacation in Kolopetinítsa*; though the movie didn't have anything to do with our ancestral village, the name serves as a cipher for the place that is the butt of all jokes about backwardness. Most Greeks don't realize there is a village that actually bears this name. The villagers even had the name changed to Tritéa to avoid the harassment.

Be that as it may, I had a closer connection to this place than anyone else in our little party during that 1984 excursion, so when we found the undistinguished village square and encountered a small group of villagers, it was I who began to talk. I announced that I was the daughter of John Kacandes and the granddaughter of George Kacandes, who had been born here. A tar-skinned, wiry fellow who could have been anywhere between the ages of forty and sixty took a step forward and said: Του Γιάννη του Κακαντέ η κόρη; Τον ξέρουμε! Κλέφτης είναι. (The daughter of John Kacandes? We know him! He's a thief.) I felt instantly wounded, then angry. The farmer went on, but I don't think I could hear him for the rush of thoughts I was having: Dad was here? This peasant doesn't have any understanding for a starving boy who was trying to feed his family during wartime?! I'm sure Daddy only stole when he had to. This guy is thinking about a few stolen apples forty years later?!

At the same time, there's no doubt that I felt anger towards my father too: stealing had not been a part of the War Experiences the way I had understood them so far. Though it was instantly apparent to me that my father might have stolen fruit—my American upbringing projected "apples"—or even other foodstuffs out of necessity and desperation, I know I felt vulnerable at that moment. What was I doing in this godforsaken place being exposed as the daughter of a thief? I have no recollection of how I moved from that scene to the next, but somehow I found myself walking with my mother down a narrow dirt street past mainly empty houses toward what was supposed to be my grandfather's house. Not really sure where I was leading us, I was relieved when two old women sitting in their courtyard returned my greeting and I could ask after the house. They wore long skirts, aprons, stockings, and scarves despite the heat. When they heard the name Kacandes they smiled, and I think it was only at that instant that I realized they both had bright blue eyes—like my grandfather and my own father.

The issue of eye color was a frequent topic of conversation—almost an obsession—among us when I was younger. Whenever I was asked

2. Unknown Kacandes relatives, Kolopetinítsa, Greece, July 1984.

to describe my family, my response was bound to include the following explanation:

My father is a light-haired and blue-eyed Greek. Yes, there are some. All of my siblings had light hair when they were young, except me. Many of our Kacandes first cousins have blue eyes, though all six of us, the John Kacandes kids, have brown eyes like our mother.

I remember being thrilled when I learned in high school biology class that Mendelian genetics held out the promise of blue eyes in the next generation, depending on whom we married.

The blue-eyed old ladies immediately claimed kinship to me, explaining that their mother had two brothers who had gone to the United States with my grandfather and my great-uncle Tom, that the four had quarreled and their uncles went to the West Coast where one was killed in a Prohibition era shootout and the other died without heirs. I'm not sure if I felt more relieved to have found sympathetic souls in this desolate alley or additional ancestors. I snapped a photo of them, and feeling the pressure of my relatives waiting back at the village square, my mother and I hurried on in the direction they had indicated.

Could this be it? The hovel we arrived in front of was tiny and looked even smaller because of the collapsed roof and walls. There was trash around. The only living things in sight were αγκάθια (thistles). It was hard for me to imagine anyone had ever inhabited this space, and yet it fit with the pervasive sense I'd always had that this village was a place to leave behind. Of course my grandfather had emigrated! The dwindling light only exacerbated my own desire to scram. When we got back to the square, my relatives seemed to have done fine talking to the natives, who had explained how sad they were because all the young people move away, leaving the elderly and the occasional grandchildren on a visit to populate the place. They were obliged by Greek custom to offer us something to eat: let us make you a frittata, they suggested. But I still felt stung by the "thief" comment, and didn't really trust their sincerity. Besides, the village looked so impoverished, I suspected they didn't actually have much extra food. I was happy to decline, get into my theio Níko's car, and descend to civilization on the coast. The villagers got their revenge for my violation of Greek hospitality rules, I thought to myself the next morning. We had been unable to sleep because of the quantity of mosquitoes buzzing around our heads in Galaxídi, the "civilized" coastal town to which we had retreated.

I don't remember much about when and how I related this incident to my father. It must have been in person, though, because I recall his smirk and snort when I reported that the fellow had called him a thief: so they're still thinking about that, eh? He seemed pleased with the report of the discovery of some kind of cousins, but the description I gave him of the two old ladies and their recital of their claimed connection to us didn't prompt any memories on his part. He was ignorant too of any cousins who had come to the States with his father and uncle, he assured me. This interaction, like the few other ones we had ever had about his past, ended quickly. I never followed up by writing to the old ladies as I had intended.

Two years later, in 1986, my father traveled to Greece. I don't know how my mother managed to convince him to go. We all believed he would truly stick to his oath to never return. Yet, the family was also relieved that he was finally going to go back. I don't think I would have been able to tell you why I thought it was such a good idea then, except that my mother had become more and more attached to visiting Greece, and Dad's going too would make it easier for her. In any case, I facilitated the trip by agreeing to take care of their two-hundred-pound dog Zeus, half Newfoundland, half black Labrador Retriever, 100 percent spoiled, for the period my parents would be away—not an easy task to combine with studying for my PhD general exams, I quickly discovered . . .

My mother and father started off their first joint European excursion—my parents had met in the United States—by visiting the Germans, Georg and Monika Thiel, the parents of the family my sister Maria had lived with more than ten years earlier. Mom and Dad thoroughly enjoyed their stay in Germany. My father raved about how clean the place was, how green the countryside. His reaction to Germany became the counterpoint to his reaction to Greece. I don't think anyone in my extended family living in the United States remembers anything about my parents' trip except that everything my father had to report when he got back was negative. He had taken hundreds of pictures to document the trash and the pollution. And his oral recitals confirmed his obsession: they had destroyed the country. Garbage, garbage, garbage. Everywhere you looked there was refuse: in the sea, in the valleys, in the city streets, in the village lanes, on the highway—absolutely everywhere. The only comments that occasionally broke the litany about how dirty Greece was, were about the suicidal Italian drivers. My parents had visited a cousin of my father's in Genoa on their way from Germany to Greece. Loukás Gerentés was the youngest of five children in a family I would later come to understand my family had been close to during the war years; the past aside, my father thought his cousin was out to kill him: "I had my heart in my throat every time we got in the car. I can't believe we're still alive." Sometimes a relative would try to persuade my father that he was exaggerating. Or they'd try to steer him to other topics by asking him about people or places he had visited. However, Dad was not to be dissuaded. The Greeks were lying, cheating thugs who had poisoned their own country. I even remember my easygoing Aunt Stella, Dad's brother Harry's wife, saying, "Oh come on, John. Enough! Could you quit knocking Greece for a few minutes?" For sure, I don't remember any signs of working through the past, unless one wants to interpret my father's rants as an implicit acknowledgment that the country had been at least physically beautiful during his childhood.

A personal crisis of my own was developing, and in January 1989 I moved out of the house I was sharing with my husband in western Massachusetts and into an apartment with friends in Cambridge. I didn't want to accept money from my husband, so I immediately searched for teaching assistantships. Asking around, I discovered that Erich Goldhagen, teacher of a popular general education course on the Holocaust and comparative genocide, had a particularly large enrollment that semester and needed additional TAs. Since my main area of study had been twentieth-century German literature and history, it seemed like a good fit. In any case, Professor Goldhagen took me on even though he didn't know me and the course was social sciences oriented. That semester, I found myself teaching two discussion sections of Goldhagen's Holocaust course and two for Richard Hunt's similarly well-subscribed lecture class "Weimar to Nazi Germany." I mention these teaching assignments because life can appear so overdetermined on occasion. Four sections was an unusual load for a graduate student trying to write her dissertation; and in my case, the burden seemed particularly heavy: Nazis, war, genocide, and death, all week, every week. I needed the money.

About a month into the semester I got a phone call from my sister

Georgia that in certain respects could be labeled life changing. At the least, it profoundly transformed what I thought I knew about the War Experiences:

Irene, you're not going to believe this. But last night Dad asked Tina and me if we wanted to go with him to the Jewish Community Center where he was going to give a talk. He was in a camp! They got hauled off as Jews because they were circumcised. They got taken to a transit camp. He talked about the filth and how they had to eat garbage to survive. The Nazis tried to torture him. But the Greek resistance liberated them, so they didn't get sent to Auschwitz. The survivors at the JCC find it too hard to talk about, so they asked Dad to do it.

Contrary to Georgia's expectation, I did believe it. I believed it immediately. It fit. I instantly decided we had the profile of a survivor family, which I happened to have just studied in the Holocaust class by reading a chapter in the path-breaking volume of Bergman and Jucovy, *Generations of the Holocaust*: the morose silences with the sudden violent rages; the unspoken and unchallenged prohibitions on asking; the drive for the children to achieve perfection; the shame and shaming. And yet, I don't remember that this news provoked an extended conversation between my sister and me. I cannot recall more than the brief facts that stuck in my head and which I have quoted above. I certainly didn't say anything directly to my father at the time, and it wasn't until years later that I asked Georgia and Tina more questions about what they had heard that night. Despite the fact that my father had given a public lecture, I was still operating under our childhood rules of engagement: don't ask our father to tell us things, even if you know he's told others outside the family.

My father was arrested as a Jew because he was circumcised? I accepted this right away, though it's not completely clear to me now why I did. As a family we never talked about anything related to bodies or sex except to be all four of us girls simultaneously lectured at when my older sisters were barely pubescent. Our mother sat silently at the table while our father threatened us that if we made the poor decision to have premarital intercourse, our parents would not help us out if we got pregnant. Sex was for marriage, he summarized. I remember thinking to myself: I haven't even thought of kissing a boy . . .

As far as I can recall, I had seen my father naked only once, sometime during my teen years when he opened the door after a shower as I was coming up the stairs that lead directly to the bathroom. I remember being royally embarrassed at getting a full frontal view, though it couldn't have lasted more than a second and neither of us said a word. At that age I didn't know how a penis with a foreskin would look different from a penis without a foreskin, and I was too far away to have detected the difference even if I had known what it was. On the other hand, though things related to sex were hardly a topic of open conversation in any part of my adolescent world, I realize that I knew that circumcision existed; that it was a Jewish practice; that my father and my uncles had been born in U.S. hospitals; that American baby boys were circumcised unless the family instructed otherwise; that I had changed my two younger brothers' diapers hundreds of times. Like so many other things in my life, I never put certain pieces of information or experience into dialog with one another. I knew and I didn't know that my father was circumcised. Or maybe, I knew and yet I could not have declared prior to Georgia's phone call: our father is circumcised.

For me, what I accepted at the time as "the revelation about my father" was mainly a relief. It seemed to explain so much about his difficult sides, about his rages, his overeating, about how we'd grown up almost relentlessly bombarded by criticism, about why the War Experiences had loomed so large in my life despite—because of?—never getting talked about openly. I thought maybe I could forgive him anything now, at the same time that I felt angry about his silence. Why hadn't he ever told us? Why hadn't he ever told me? Why did he always talk to strangers but not to his own family?

At the same time, I immediately began to feel confused about the professional work I was doing. Although I felt sure that my initial decision to teach those classes on the Nazi period and the Holocaust was based primarily on financial need and chance demand for teaching assistants, I had also quickly developed a short speech about how important it was for all citizens of the twentieth century to learn about the Holocaust, a speech I suppose I gave to the students in my discussion sections for starters, but which I have delivered in many other contexts since. I felt a determination to do this work precisely because I was not Jewish. But I'm the child of a survivor? I don't remember having had trouble taking on that mantle in some very private way to myself. And yet, I also recall wondering: Do I count as the child of a survivor? Does that invalidate my own work and the reasons I give for doing it? Was I interested in learning about and teaching the Nazi Judeocide because of a personal connection after all? I didn't think so. Still, it took me a long, long time to "come out" in my professional milieu as someone who was personally linked to the Holocaust. I continued to give my little speech about the importance of non-Jewish persons studying and teaching the Nazi Judeocide.

In the meantime, I was busy finishing my dissertation, applying for jobs, starting my poststudent career—and ending my marriage. I do not remember spending much time on the War Experiences, even with the spur of this unsettling information. I didn't think of the courses I was then developing and teaching myself on the Weimar and Nazi periods and on the Holocaust, nor even my new research project based on the Fortunoff Archive for Holocaust Video Testimony in Sterling Library at Yale University, as attributable to the news about my father. I still count that today as mainly correct. However, my research in the Fortunoff Archives did lead me to think: this is how I can find out more about what happened to him; I will get him to testify at Yale.

At some point in the early 1990s, I told my father about my work with video testimony, and I emphasized that the Yale archive collected all kinds of stories related to the Holocaust from eyewitnesses, for example, from rescuers, as well as survivors. "How about giving an interview? They'd be interested in hearing about your experiences in Greece. And after all, Yale's not very far away from here. You know the way by heart from visiting Peter [my brother who did his undergraduate work there]. They can even interview you in New York if you prefer." The response was not hostile, yet a bit defensive: "I'm going to write my own memoirs," he announced. "Great, Dad. That would be just great," I replied.

The only problem for me was, he never did.

I did not look for Daddy's War in the 1990s, but every once in a while, it would come looking for me. Maybe we were playing hide and go seek. I would look; it would disappear. I would find it and it would slip out of my hands again. Then I would try to hide, and it would find me when I didn't want to be found. Or perhaps the better metaphor is tug-of-war. When it would try to pull me toward it, I would resist with all my strength. And when I tried to muscle it toward me, it would obstinately hold its ground.

One such struggle occurred in March 1992. I had been invited to return to Cambridge from Austin, Texas, where I was holding my first job as an assistant professor, to give a seminar to the Modern Greek Study Group at Harvard's Center for Literary and Cultural Studies. I was flattered to be a guest speaker at the institution where I had felt so often humbled as a graduate student. Naturally, I was very nervous, too. I was trying out new material from a project I had just formulated on the influence of oral storytelling on literature, and many of my former teachers told me they would be there. My mother was in London for the birth of my parents' first grandchild. When my father offered to drive up from New York for the talk, I thought it would be nice to have some personal support, even though I knew I felt apprehensive whenever he made an appearance in my professional world.

Despite my not being as prepared as I genuinely intended to be, the talk went well. The audience seemed interested, and a lively exchange quickly developed after I finished delivering my remarks. When my father's hand went up a few minutes into the discussion period, my heart went into my throat. What could I do? He was sitting at the seminar table, too, and to not call on him would have been awkward. "Your talk reminds me of something that happened to me during the war that I haven't thought about for years," he began. Oh, no! I panicked, what's he going to say? My father continued:

One of my tasks when I was growing up in a really poor mountain village in Greece after the German invasion was to watch a herd of goats. Their favorite place to graze was in the village cemetery, because that was the spot where they could find at least a bit of green. When older women would come to the grave sites and talk to their dead relatives, usually about family news and village gossip, I would hide among the tombstones and try to overhear what they said. One widow came often, and she ran out of things to tell her dead husband. Around that time, the Nazis dropped leaflets on the village. The widow couldn't read, but she picked up a flier and marched to the grave of her husband and began to make up stories about the villagers. She went on like that for weeks, holding the flier in front of her. I couldn't read it either because it was written in German. But evidently it said that for every German found dead, ten Greeks would be executed.

A huge smile spread across my face despite the solemnity of the anecdote. Saved, I thought to myself. He hasn't embarrassed me. He got it just right. I don't remember exactly what I said out loud, but it must have been something about the profound intertwining of orality and literacy that the story reflected; the illiterate widow knows that paper "talks." I probably added that the graveside recitals illustrate how the spoken word can make people feel connected, even across the divide of life and death. Happy, I called on the next questioner.

It was with a lightened heart and genuine gratitude that I walked my father to his car when the seminar ended. Wasn't it more familiar, though, when the first thing he had to say to me was that I had better do something about my nose. What? "You'd better look in a mirror before you give your next lecture because you do something really weird with your nose, sort of screw it up and twist it to the side." I bit my lip and then tried to take a deep breath to counter the tension in my throat. "Oh, thanks for letting me know, Dad. And thanks for making this really long car trip to be here for this. You sure you're going to be okay on the ride back? I'm sorry about the mix-up of you not getting invited to stay for dinner." "No problem. I'll be fine." "Bye, Dad. Have a safe trip."

Despite the sting of "you're never good enough," sticking with me all these years, Dad's "death flier" story was a supreme illustration of the principles of conversation creating and sustaining relationship and of the influence of orality on literacy and vice versa that I was trying to analyze in those years. The widow not only believes her dead spouse can hear her and thus she needs new material each time she goes to his grave, but also, she knows the power of the written word, even though she herself is illiterate. I used Dad's anecdote when I rewrote the seminar material into a chapter of what became the book I wrote to earn tenure, *Talk Fiction: Literature and the Talk Explosion*. What strikes me about the whole incident now, though, is that yet again, I did not feel provoked into asking my father directly more about his War Experiences—or even about the anecdote itself: How did he find out what the flier said if it was only in German? Why on earth would it have been in German, anyway? Did the Germans perpetrate reprisals in his area? Did he know people who had died that way? Who was that widow? I never asked. And he never told me more about that incident.

It would be easy to put my wounded pride into concert with several other incidents that retrospectively, anyway, were pushing me away from dealing with Daddy's War. Although I was very stimulated by the research I had done in the Fortunoff Archives on Holocaust Video Testimony, around the same time I was ready to publish some of my initial results, Lawrence Langer's book *Holocaust Testimonies* (1991), about the archive and what he felt it taught us about memory, appeared to critical and popular acclaim. Although upon perusing the book I realized I had come to some different conclusions from Langer, it didn't seem smart to put more time into that endeavor. I was not confident enough to start a debate with such an established scholar, who, I had learned, held strong convictions about who was and who was not authorized to speak on the subject of the Holocaust. Would he consider mine a legitimate voice? I wasn't sure of his view, nor any longer of my own. So, I published one article on the topic and put the larger project aside.

My own authorization and desire to speak on the Nazi Judeocide was severely tested when I gave a paper in 1993 at the biannual meeting of the Modern Greek Studies Association on Primo Levi's perception of the Thessalonikan Jews he encountered in Auschwitz. I argued my main points primarily by doing a close reading of some passages in Levi's memoir, *Survival in Auschwitz* (1961), supplemented by the testimony of some Greek (Jewish) survivors I had listened to in the Fortunoff Archive and of course background historical research. I believe that at the time I was thinking of this work as just any other academic exercise; I was passionately interested, of course, as I always was in what I was presenting, but the topic was not particularly controversial in my view. I was wrong. Someone I didn't recognize, a nonacademic, a member of the local Greek American community, I was later told, stood up as soon as I finished speaking and accused me of falsely portraying the Greeks (read Greek Christians) as being antisemitic. Greeks hid Jews, he self-righteously asserted. They tried to protect them from the Germans, he went on. My mouth dropped open. That wasn't my point at all, I protested. I restated my thesis about Greek Jews being perceived and treated as profoundly Other even among Jewish prisoners in *Auschwitz*, and propitiously or unpropitiously, the discussion time allotted for my paper was over.

The issue of my supposed anti-Hellenism, however, was not over. I felt viciously misunderstood. During the banquet that evening, at which the conference participants were unusually just an addition to a local Greek community celebration of "Oxi Day," (October 28, 1940, one of two national holidays; it refers to the Greek government's purported reply to an ultimatum from Mussolini: Όχι [No], you Italians may not just march in and occupy Greece), I had no patience for the rhetoric of the after-dinner speaker and his longwinded praise of Greece as the cradle of civilization, despite what some academics might say about the role of Egypt. He went on to criticize Martin Bernal, the author of the study Black Athena, in quite a personal way, labeling him a Greek-hater. I knew Bernal's book was controversial and its thesis probably inadequately supported, but the context and tone of the attack were all wrong. I got up and left.

I wish I had put a lid on my own self-righteousness with that gesture, but the next day when we had our association's business meeting, I tried to make an apology on behalf of the American academics among us to our foreign guests for the patriotic excesses to which we had been exposed the night before. Little did I realize that nonacademics were at that meeting as well. An elderly man who identified himself as a doctor practicing in the San Francisco Bay area stood up and branded me as a disloyal Greek who had no business speaking on behalf of anybody. If the situation had been left at his public excoriation, I probably could have put it behind me more easily. However, in the weeks and months that followed, I started receiving at my office address copies of letters this man had sent to everyone he could think of who had something to do with Greek studies, in the United States and in Greece, identifying me as someone who should be excluded from the profession. I didn't think anyone I cared about was actually going to take this fellow seriously, but I felt stalked nonetheless. I doubt it is completely coincidental that I subsequently directed my professional attention more and more toward German and Holocaust studies and less and less toward Greece.

That redirection of my energies didn't spare me from the tug of Daddy's War.

A perhaps off-the-cuff, perhaps premeditated remark of a colleague one day in the halls of the German department along the lines that it was okay to teach the Holocaust every now and then, but he sure hoped

I wasn't planning to offer a course every year, fired me up. I don't know if my colleague was mainly motivated by what he thought could be "bad press" for the German department or if he was an antisemite at heart. In either case, his comment caused me to reaffirm and rearticulate the position I had adopted when I had first started teaching this material: that genocide was a particularly insidious crime even in the context of other forms of violence perpetrated by humans against humans, and that therefore every citizen of the twentieth century should learn about and struggle with the events we refer to as the Holocaust. I expanded my train of thought into an article-length argument about why and how we should approach the study of the Nazi genocide, putting my course syllabus and my own motivations for teaching such a course under scrutiny. My attempt to be as honest as possible necessitated mentioning the vexing issue of "pedigree" and admitting that "more unfortunately for my father than for me, I have that pedigree." When I heard about someone putting together a volume on Holocaust pedagogy, I decided I wanted to risk publishing this argument, and therefore, this personal admission. However, I didn't feel safe or comfortable doing so without checking the information with my father—something that, I mention again, I had never done in the by then five or six years that had passed since my sister Georgia had called me that night in 1989 with news of Dad's wartime arrest and deportation. Like many things related to the War Experiences, I don't remember much about the exact circumstances of my encounter with my father except that I printed out the relevant page of my article, placed myself between him sitting in his armchair and the television, held out the page, and asked, "Dad, do I have this right?" He tilted his head up and slightly back and raised both eyebrows the way he does when he's reading and presumably perused the following:

If I further reveal myself and tell you that I am not Jewish and my father was mistaken for a Jew because he was circumcised and that that was why he ended up in a Nazi deportation camp in northern Greece during the War, will it change one's evaluation of my right to speak?

Then my father calmly handed the sheet of paper back to me and answered, yes. I wanted to be sure. I posed another question: "So it's okay with you if I publish this, Dad?" Yes, came the monosyllable again. Interaction concluded. No additional information requested. None revealed. The poetic irony of the facts that the volume's editor had an accident and that that volume and therefore my article never appeared does not escape me now, though I felt more thwarted than amused at the time.

Whatever the smaller professional and personal frustrations of my life might have been in those years, I was thriving. I had been able to move on from my failed first marriage, fallen in love again, and landed a new job closer to my sweetheart, a job even more wonderful than my first one. I had made such close friends when I moved to Texas, I simply didn't expect the same good fortune when I moved back to the Northeast to accept a position at Dartmouth College, and yet that's what happened. I quickly became part of a large circle of colleagues who shared both their work and their leisure time. Although the move to Dartmouth initially put a halt to my Holocaust pedagogy—cultural theorist Marianne Hirsch and historian Leo Spitzer, two of those special colleague-friends, were already teaching a course on representations of the Holocaust, and theologian Susannah Heschel, who was to arrive shortly after me, soon added two of her own—it feels now like my move to Dartmouth sealed my eventual head-on confrontation with the War Experiences.

They made Their first appearance in Hanover on the third floor of unadorned, historic Dartmouth Hall, south side. I was speaking with Marianne in the perpetually dimly lit corridor outside the French and Italian Department about the usual mixture of comparative literature business, teaching, and gossip, and without me registering consciously that we'd turned to the topic of Marianne's research, up They surged into my throat and out my mouth, my nostrils, my ears. I felt like I was going to choke. "Postmemory," Marianne was explaining, . . . "term I've coined" . . . "parents' stories" . . . "traumatic experiences" . . . "so alive, so present for the children" . . . "children's own lived experience" . . . "overshadowed"

. . . "enormity of what their parents went through." I peered into Marianne's face more than a little alarmed. **trapped, abandoned, cheated, terrified, betrayed**, and **starved** were crowding around us, but I wasn't sure if she could see Them. Then again, I was afraid maybe she could see Them. "I—I know exactly what you mean," I stammered, despite not having consciously registered most of what she had just said to me. I do not recollect how we ended the conversation. I just know that I fled to my office and slammed the door.

I simply wasn't ready to deal with these revenants. Happy as I was about many things, I was still fighting my own demons that were blocking my way to tenure and starting a family—and I wasn't willing to consider that the two sets of ghosts were related. Concretely, the next years were filled with new and challenging experiences, like leading study programs in Germany and completing my first books. The tussles with my partner over making a commitment to parenting consumed me too. In 1998 my father suffered a major heart attack and had open-heart surgery a few weeks later. His illness stirred up various kinds of old grudges in the family, and I found myself acting as the main intercessor between him and the health care system and him and my mother for the first months after his attack. Still, as the decade came to a close and the new millennium began, I not only had completed a satisfactory amount of academic work, received tenure, and gotten married, but also my husband and I were trying to conceive, and I had drafted a new project on Holocaust testimony. Was I about to make my way back toward Daddy's War? I'll never know. Something happened that put my plans—my very life—into suspension.

Around midday on January 27, 2001, two of my closest friends, Susanne and Half Zantop, both professors at Dartmouth, were murdered in their home in Etna, New Hampshire. Their bodies were discovered by Roxana Verona, another close friend, when she arrived to have dinner with them that evening. For weeks not only their daughters, their families, and us, their large circle of friends, but also the greater Dartmouth and Hanover communities feared, grieved, and wondered. How could such a thing happen? Who could have killed such kind, generous people? Why? The police's apprehension of the two teenage perpetrators put an end to some of our most acute anxieties, however those arrests could not quell our incredulity nor lessen our distress over having lost Susanne and Half to a completely senseless act, strangers killing strangers for the experience of it and the fantasy of going to live in Australia as outlaws afterward.

Along with many others, I mourned for a long, long time. I grieved the violence of Susanne and Half's deaths, their lives cut off in their creative prime, the losses of the excellent guidance they had constantly offered me in matters personal and professional, their humor, their love for each other, their love for me. I grieved for my adopted parents.

I experienced the first months as a roller coaster of numbness and intense grief that alternated with persistent refusals to accept that my friends were dead. Especially before the suspects' arrest, I experienced near paralyzing bouts of fear. I despaired, bordering on panic, when confronted with my own amnesia of people and facts I had once known well. I moved through my daily activities, reduced to a minimum as they were, with an insecurity generated by never being able to anticipate what might trigger a bout of sobbing whose length and intensity I could not control. I think I felt the closest to insanity when I would look into the faces of people I loved and be overpowered by the conviction that they were going to die soon; sometimes I would break down weeping, sometimes I managed to hold myself together until the certainty faded a bit. Very little related to my teaching, research, or normal leisure activities could rouse my interest. My sense of the longer-term future had completely vanished.

Key to eventually moving on with my life was the patient and unqualified support of my husband, family, friends, priest, and therapist to just let me grieve as I needed to. I didn't try to rein it in. The result was a changed, but more knowledgeable self. I simply can't be in the world in the same way I was prior to experiencing my friends' murders, and some aspects of my transformed self, I now can see, helped prepare me for taking on Daddy's War.

The first change concerns a deeper, surely more personal understanding of violence. I was of course aware since my childhood in New York that homicides are not a rare occurrence in the United States. But I myself had never lost a loved one to murder before—only to illness. The act of taking someone's life became real to me in a way that it simply had not been before losing Susanne and Half. Having tried to play the scene of my friends' murders in my head over and over, I began to understand the human dimensions of it. Marks on the back of his hands revealed that Half had tried to parry the knife thrusts. Was he afraid or was the adrenaline so high he didn't feel fear? And the boy-murderers? I still can't conjure up for myself exactly what kind of state one is in that allows one to thrust a knife through the skin and into the body of another human being. Perhaps, though, it was the facts that the perpetrators of the Zantops' murders were so young, grew up in a town so very similar to the town I live in, and look like so many of the adolescent males with whom I regularly interact, that allowed me to comprehend, not just "know" in some kind of factual or philosophical way, that humans, not monsters kill. And though in order to be able to kill, perpetrators may reshape or downplay the consequences of their act, create a disconnection between what they are doing and their responsibility for it, or dehumanize their victim, part of what I felt I had learned was that none of those strategies should transform for the rest of us the tragic reality of humans killing humans. I needed then and I still need to witness to that tragedy.

At the point I was making these realizations, I had been researching and teaching the Holocaust for more than a dozen years, yet the quality of murder committed millions of times over in that genocide and in others also became known to me in a manner that it had not been before. During my first foray into the Fortunoff Archive a decade prior, for instance, I had studied the video testimony of Leon S. from Poland. I had viewed and listened to the tape of his interview scores of times. I could recite several sequences of it by heart. And there were many aspects of what Leon S. recounts that I felt I could understand, explicate, and pass on to others. Still, in the wake of Susanne and Half's murders I reexperienced a segment of that interview with an intensity, a level of cognition, perhaps even of recognition, that had never happened before. Leon S. is describing the family's deportation from his hometown. They are being herded into cattle cars. His infirm grandmother is in front of him. She requests assistance to get from the ground to the opening of the wagon. An SS officer standing near by offers to help. He moves closer. He takes out his gun and he shoots her in the back of the neck. Even now as I try to type these words I feel the heat of the bodies, I hear the voices, the shot, the profound silence in its aftermath. I experience the shocked disbelief and the raw fear that propels without volition Leon's own body up and forward into the car. Skin touching metal touching skin. Human skin of a human hand touching metal touching human skin of a human neck. I now know—in a way that doesn't just have to do with my brain—that humans kill humans by any number of means. I say none of this, of course, to minimize the historical, political, and social differences that can exist between murders, that do exist between the killing of Leon S.'s grandmother and that of my friends. I do not now know what Leon S. felt then. But I have always been uncomfortable with the rhetoric of the incomprehensibility of the Holocaust, and part of that discomfort concerns the distance we put between ourselves and the victims, ourselves and the survivors, ourselves and the perpetrators when we play the unknowability card. In the wake of the Zantops' murders, a certain gap between Leon S. and myself disappeared. I could move closer to him. In my heart I did move closer to him.

What exactly did my father see transpire in front of his eyes? What did it cost him? What did it cost us?

While I had been working on the problem of trauma and witnessing to trauma for years before the Zantops were killed, several aspects of that research also became newly comprehensible to me. For example, one of the points that professional trauma researchers like Jodie Wigren or Cathy Caruth and casual observers alike have emphasized, and which I had cited in my own analyses numerous times, is that not all individuals will react to stressors in the same way. Some witnesses to a terrible accident, for instance, may be able to move on with their lives in a healthy fashion. Others might develop symptoms of posttraumatic stress disorder. An early report in the wake of 9/11 published by Galea et al. in the *New England Journal of Medicine* in 2002 demonstrated that Manhattanites whose distress warranted psychotherapeutic treatment were an unpredictably heterogeneous group with highly divergent connections to the events and the victims of the World Trade Center attack. My observations of the Zantops' friends revealed a similar unpredictability in the identity of grievers and the manner and length of their grieving. I felt a need to suspend judgment about my own reactions and to extend this generosity to all mourners of that tragedy and others. While I felt sure that the War Experiences had left Their traces on each member of my father's nuclear family, I think my infantile naming of it as "Daddy's War" was on the mark. Somehow, my father was particularly affected by the Greek tragedies of the mid-twentieth century. Could I extend my generosity to him?

The emphasis of my research in the field of trauma studies has been on cowitnessing, the position of the sympathetic listener that enables the witness to recount the story of the trauma. In my processing of the Zantops' deaths, my grieving required some attention by professionally trained listeners, but I know that my recovery was also aided enormously by various informal settings in which I had amateur but compassionate listeners, individuals willing to be cowitnesses to my personal loss. Sometimes it pained me that I could tell certain people more easily than others what had happened and how I was feeling about it. I think this particular aspect of my grieving may have eventually pushed me to ask a different question about the War Experiences. Instead of demanding aloud or in my heart for my father to tell me what had happened, perhaps I could consider what he was in fact saying and to whom. I could ponder why he was comfortable talking to community members at the JCC—even with my sisters among them—and yet was unable or unwilling to raise the subject at home.

I gained these insights only slowly; they remained rather inchoate for at least two years. It was a different consequence of the Zantops' deaths that helped them come into focus for me so I could formulate an approach to Daddy's War. Though their deaths were clearly unexpected, they resulted in what I've come to think of as the Zantops' intended legacy to us: that we would be committed to one another as friends, as members of a true community. I remember once asking Susanne toward the conclusion of one of her own stints leading a Dartmouth foreign study program whether she was reluctant to leave Germany or if she was looking forward to coming back to the Upper Valley (the area in New Hampshire in which Dartmouth is situated and in which we both lived). Ah, she said to me in German, Berlin is great, but I can't wait to get back to my community, articulating this last word in English. In the course of the weeks, months, and, for some of us, years following the Zantops' murders, Susanne and Half's "community" has come together in various configurations, large and small, formal and informal, planned and spontaneous, to share our grief and commemorate our friends. Many of us have been comforted by these gatherings and the gatherings in turn have transformed some more casual relationships into deep abiding commitments. I think Susanne and Half would be happy about this.

Of the many blessings I received in the form of friends made through the Zantops it is my relationship to Marianne Hirsch and Leo Spitzer that is marked the most profoundly by this legacy. To be sure, the three of us were good friends before Susanne and Half were killed; however, in the immediate aftermath of the murders, we were together almost constantly. My husband and I were in a commuting marriage at the time, and I think it was in Marianne's and Leo's generous natures to keep a special eye out for me, knowing I would be spending a lot of time alone otherwise. Tragedy can push people apart, of course, but in our case I believe it might have made us even closer friends than we were on a trajectory to becoming. I need to mention Marianne and Leo here because more than any one else, they helped me approach Daddy's War.

For starters, they each made concrete invitations that furthered my work on the Holocaust: Marianne invited me to coedit a volume on teaching the representation of the Holocaust, where perhaps not incidentally, my admission about being the offspring of someone who had been in a Nazi camp first appeared in print. And Leo invited me to become the coinstructor of a course on the Holocaust that he and Marianne had developed and already taught several times, and which they were slated to teach again, when Marianne's schedule changed. Marianne's and Leo's own research had been inspiring me for years. I had learned of the concept of postmemory in conversation with Marianne directly. Around the time of Susanne and Half's deaths, Marianne and Leo had embarked on a joint research project investigating the Jewish community of the Bukovina (see Hirsch and Spitzer forthcoming), an area of the Hapsburg Empire, then in Romania and currently part of the Ukraine, where Marianne's parents had grown up. In addition to trying to document how that community was destroyed through the Second World War and the Holocaust, they have been exploring the forms through which the community survived in other places and in the memories passed on from parents to children. The way Marianne and Leo had been tracking their own emotional investments in the research instructed and inspired me. Being interlocutors for one another had built up my confidence to try similar work.

Most specifically, in fall 2003 Marianne asked me to contribute to a conference she was organizing with another friend of ours, historian Annelise Orleck, to be called "Contested Memories of the Holocaust."

Marianne had originally proposed we give a paper together, a version of the introduction we were preparing for our book on Holocaust pedagogy. But when she and Leo decided to present some of their work in progress on the Bukovina at that conference, she pressed me to give a new paper of my own. I remember sitting in front of my blank computer screen for hours thinking: Ugh, what can I propose? That request, I feel now, was the decisive push I needed from the outside to propel myself toward Daddy's War.

Not surprisingly, given our family history, I didn't—couldn't?—go in search directly. But I did commit to a new Holocaust project. (I had completely forgotten the previous one in the wake of the Zantops' murders; I cried when I bumped into that project proposal one day years later.) I was convinced at the time that I simply would never learn what had happened to my father. A satisfying surrogate activity, I reasoned, might be to find out how other offspring of survivors of the Second World War and the Holocaust had learned of their parents' experiences and what that knowledge meant to them. While there already existed voluminous writing on the so-called second generation, the "children of the Holocaust," as Helen Epstein had named them in her groundbreaking book of 1979, no studies—to my knowledge anyway—focused on the recital or the refusal of recital of the Holocaust experience by the parents to their offspring. How telling and being told is negotiated between survivors and their children would be my central concern.

The walls came tumbling down. I began to work with an intensity, with an energy, with levels of interest and actual joy that I hadn't felt in decades, maybe ever. I received each piece of information I gathered, each book I read or reread, each person who granted me an interview like a gift. Every respite I got from my teaching and administrative duties I would turn to this research. I would work for hours each day without ever consulting the clock. I made dramatic gaffes based on false assumptions, imprecise terminology, amateur interviewing techniques, projections of my own desires and needs. I gave a first paper at the "Contested

Memories" conference and then gave more talks, got feedback, corrections, advice, and tips. All of it felt like a blessing, a liberation, a vivification. Perverse that I emerged from mourning one tragedy by studying an even greater tragedy? Perhaps. But for me, turning back to the Holocaust signified a cessation to avoiding Daddy's War and therefore part of who I was.

To: georgia, peter
Subject: greetings and a request
Date: Wed, Mar 24, 2004 11:16 AM

Dear Georgia and Pete, my California siblings,

I would so love to just fly out and visit with you!!!! Alas, I am pinned down with several urgent writing projects, one of which, I'm really hoping you can take a few minutes to help me with. Here goes! Sorry if this seems sprung unexpectedly. I've been thinking about it for a long time, but only recently managed to get over my inhibitions and get going on it. (By the way, I'm only telling you two about it at this point; if you think Tom could handle it, let me know.)

One paper I am writing is to be on the topic of what children know or don't know about their parents' Holocaust experiences. Without boring you with the full proposal, my focus is not on what actually happened to people's parents, but rather on to what extent children know or want to know these stories, and how they feel about knowing or not knowing. What reasons parents gave for sharing information or withholding it is also of great interest to me.

It would be incredibly helpful to me if you could (independently) answer these questions in relation to our family. I have my own ideas, but I realized it would be much more helpful to me to hear your take on this before I share mine with you (or anyone else for that matter).

I realize that you are both very very busy and that these are emotionally laden questions that could be answered at great length, but if you feel you could give me a short answer for now, I would be so grateful! I also realize that some questions are more relevant for our situation than others, so just concentrate on the ones that make sense to you and put "not relevant" to the others, okay?

How would you describe (now) your father's relationship to the Holocaust? As a survivor? a refugee? someone who was persecuted? some other way? none of the above?

At what point in your own life exactly did you find out that he had a relationship to the Nazi persecution of the Jews in WWII?

From whom and how did you find this out?

Any recollections of how knowing about his experiences made you feel toward him? toward his family? toward yourself?

Did you make attempts directly yourself to elicit further information from him? from others? Why or why not? What information did you hope most to find out?

Do you recall having a sense of why you wanted to know what you wanted to know? Was there any information you were conscious of feeling afraid of finding out?

What has come of your attempts to find out about his experiences (so far)?

How did the information about your father's past of which you were previously unaware affect the relationship with your siblings and/or any other living relatives?

Anything else you want to share?

I am planning to use pseudonyms for anyone's story who comes to me in interview form (rather than published). If you don't feel you need anonymity, you could let me know that too. How does that sound?

Thanks a million for any length answers you have time to send back!

If you want to talk about this, just let me know when to reach you on the phone.

love, hugs, and kisses,

irene

And so it was that I finally began moving straight toward Daddy's War in March 2004, by asking the same questions of some of my siblings that I was asking of my other informants. I first approached Georgia and Peter, partly because at that point in our lives they had slightly less conflicted relationships with our father than our other siblings—maybe it helped that they both lived in California—and partly because I knew, or thought I did, something about what they knew about the War Experiences. Georgia, of course, was the one who had telephoned me that winter day in 1989 with information about Dad's arrest and deportation. And Pete had sent around an e-mail about two years prior to my own request for information, announcing that he had designed a Web site with a section where we could put up family stories. He had already entered some he knew about Dad during the war, he added. I was ashamed that I had never looked at Pete's Web site. I remember using the excuse to myself that I'm a technophobe and hardly ever consult the Net—which was and still is mainly true—but now I wonder if my never having looked at Pete's stories was more related to the fact that his request had come in the aftermath of Susanne and Half's murders, when I was still hiding from, among other things, the War Experiences.

Pete reacted to the urgency in my request right away. He assured me

Tom would be fine with the topic, so off went the same questions to Tom, the older of my two younger brothers. Tom too interrupted what he was doing to mail back answers. Georgia's followed a few days later. My siblings' e-mails astonished me in so many respects that I decided to sit down and try to write out a timed response to my own questions. I wanted to see if some of the unexpected elements in my siblings' accounts might be due to the medium and time pressure. Additionally, I was feeling a strong need to give something back to my siblings and my other interviewees for being so generous to me in sharing family stories and their emotions about them. To offer my own answers would function as a kind of explanation of the type of information I was trying to gather.

Comparing the responses of the four youngest of John Kacandes's kids schooled me in several important areas. For one thing, growing up in the same household and being relatively close in age didn't prevent us from having significantly different versions of Daddy's War. For instance, as Georgia told it in her e-mail, our father and his brothers were endangered by the Germans' discovery of their circumcision, but our grandmother was able to straighten out the mistaken identity of her children before they were sent anywhere.

What?

That's right: no deportation, no camp, no liberation from the camp in Georgia's 2004 e-mailed response.

But she's the one I got that story from.

Oh yeah, and no mention of ever attending a talk Dad gave at the JCC in 1989.

According to her questionnaire, she must have found out "in my teen years." (Georgia was twenty-nine years old in March 1989.) I was so incredulous that I dialed her, despite knowing she was very busy. "Sorry, Irene," she said gently but firmly. "I have no memory of going to a talk nor of telling you about it or Dad's past."

This interchange astounded me. An announcement that I could still hear reverberating in my head fifteen years later was completely erased from the memory of my sister, the messenger. From my earlier work on Holocaust video testimony, I was familiar with the frequent experience of witnesses remembering things during the course of giving an interview that they hadn't recalled previously. I've already recounted here my father's recollection of the incident with the widow in his village making up stories from the German fliers announcing retribution only when he heard me lecturing on the intertwining of oral and literate culture. What I had had no experience with, however, was the complementary phenomenon: being witness to interviewees forgetting things that they had previously claimed to know.

My instinct to try answering my own questions under time pressure demonstrated to me how easy it is to slip or provide contradictory facts about the past. At one crucial point in my narrative I referred to my father's mother as my "maternal grandmother," and a moment in which I recalled finding out about my father's deportation in my twenties is followed just two sentences later by a statement saying I was thirty at the time. Still, I didn't see how I could have invented the phone call with Georgia, nor how she could have forgotten it and Dad's revelatory JCC talk so completely.

Only slightly less disturbing to me from my siblings' answers was discovering that both my brothers remembered hearing about Daddy's War at a young age; I was disconcerted when I did the math and realized that I was still living at home then. Of course my brothers were young when they found out some things; as soon as we were capable of reading we all had had access to The Newspaper Article from 1945 about Dad; it hung in plain sight. No, I think what unsettled me was how much more my brothers seemed to have heard than we did. Plus, I felt really sad, like I had failed them, when I realized that they had never checked out these disturbing stories with us, their older sisters. The inconsistency didn't escape me. I knew I had never talked to my sisters about the stories I had had in my head growing up . . .

Before I recount how I finally got my father to give me an interview,

I need to mention another lesson from those initial solicitations of my younger siblings: we didn't just have different versions of the war, we also didn't share the same emotions about what Dad had gone through. Even though they each had reservations about the veracity of any specific element of the story as it had filtered down to each of them, Georgia, Tom, and Pete all had taken into their hearts the idea that our father had suffered during the war and that who he had become, including how he had treated us, had a lot to do with those hardships. I felt humbled and chided by the compassion my three younger siblings expressed with regard to our father's experiences. I wanted to believe that I felt something similar, but my own first attempt at writing out what I knew about the War Experiences betrays hints of anger that surfaced even when I was in professional mode interviewing nonfamily members or talking to other academics about my project. I have more than one recollection of the f-word slipping out of my mouth. Was I actually not able to stand close to Dad the way I thought I could to Leon S.? It turned out that it was going to take many more confrontations with **trapped, abandoned, cheated, terrified, betrayed,** and **starved** and making the acquaintance of some bogies I didn't know were from Greece, before I could overcome my fury and forgive my Dad for the specters he had saddled me with.

Having broken the unacknowledged oath of silence with at least some of my siblings, I knew the next thing I had to do was talk to my father. But how? Again, I borrowed from my official Holocaust project. I didn't have any delusions about being able to create a great work of art, a *Maus III*, so to speak. However, one of my informants had succeeded in getting her father's story on paper in a way that seemed feasible to me with regard to my own father and my own skills. Helen Gerzon Goransson is the mother of Jenny Goransson (one of the brightest students in the Holocaust class I had just taught with Leo Spitzer) and the daughter of Gittel and George Gerzon, survivors of the Nazi Judeocide. The Gerzon-Goransson family and story couldn't be more different from my own family's: Helen's parents were Polish Jews who had fled eastward, where they suffered terrible deprivation. And yet, by displacing themselves to the East and laboring in Soviet work camps, they escaped the Nazi sweep through Poland with its mass killings and deportations to death camps. Helen's father, again, in contrast to my own, talked incessantly about his experiences to his family, indeed, to anyone who would listen. In fact, Helen conceived of collaborating with him on a memoir, *Hand of Fate*, because she hoped it would exhaust his oral barrages (Gerzon and Goransson 2003). I asked Helen how she had managed to corral hundreds of anecdotes between the covers of a book. She provided her father with a cassette recorder and tapes, she explained to me, and told him to just talk. He complied. She transcribed what he had recorded, tried to create a chronological sequence out of it, and when she considered her father's story to be relatively coherent, to have a beginning and an end, she showed it to him. He made corrections and additions to the transcript and then kept sending her more stories, which she inserted into the existing narrative as best as she could figure out. She didn't think the final product was a great piece of writing, and it's certainly not how she would have done it herself, she told me in early spring 2004, but she is glad that *Hand of Fate* exists, her father is proud of it, and the family story has been documented for the younger generation. I saw Helen's point about the quality of the ultimate memoir, but I could only extol her, her patience, her determination, and the fact that she "got" her father's story.

A short while after learning about Helen's collaboration with her father I told my own father that if he wanted to record his memories about his life I would transcribe them, show him the transcript, and see that his grandchildren got it at the proper time in their lives. I think he heard what I had said, but he didn't react. His health was deteriorating fast. My mother was having a harder and harder time taking care of him. With the six of us spread out from Switzerland to London, New York, and California, it wasn't easy to give her the help she needed. The next time I ended up seeing my father was that September, when I cancelled a vacation of my own to give my mother a spell by staying in their home with my father for two weeks. My mother had finally agreed to hire someone to help, but that person would need some orientation. I would provide the transition, and Mom went to Greece for a month.

When I arrived in White Plains—before I had even had time to greet him—my father said to me, "Irene, when you get a chance, I want you to go buy me a tape recorder for that thing you talked to me about." "Great, Dad, only I don't need to go out, I have one here with me. I bought it for you." In the days that followed, it did not surprise me that every time I suggested I show him how to use the cassette recorder, he said he was too tired. At the end of the two weeks, when I couldn't delay my departure a single day longer, I essentially forced my father to listen to me explain how the recorder worked. He docilely pretended to be interested, but his eyes glazed over. I tried to stay positive. There's a cassette in there, Dad. Whenever you feel like it just push this button and speak, okay? Okay. It will even turn off by itself. Okay. And I'm leaving you a pile of blank cassette tapes right over here. Okay. In the months that followed—I visited even more often then than usual because of my father's continuing decline—the recorder was always in exactly the same place.

The next strategy I tried involved a certain amount of deception. I'm not proud of this fact. But I had become desperate by spring 2005. For one thing, it appeared that we might not have either parent around much longer. For another, my relationship with my father had become even more strained, and I felt the only way to put it on a different course before I lost him was to find out his version of what had happened during the war. This is what had made me desperate:

On January 2, 2005, my father and mother were returning to White Plains from a chiropractic evaluation of my father's back pains in Connecticut. As usual, Dad took the exit too fast, only this time he lost control of his beautiful new sky blue Cadillac. The car spun around, slid off the road and toward a rock wall. A tree just in front of the rock face stopped the spinning and probably saved my parents' lives. The Cadillac was totaled. The airbags had not deployed, and it is a miracle they survived. My mother's sternum was broken by the pull of the shoulder belt, and her upper body turned completely black from bruises. My father was not strapped in at all, and his head had hit the windshield hard enough to make a bowling ball–like impression. It appears that for once his large belly was an advantage, for it had broken the momentum of his upper body moving toward the windshield. Miraculously, no major harm had come to him, though he was rather scratched and sore. Of course, as the doctors in the hospital ran every test they could think of, they uncovered all his preexisting conditions: diabetes, diseased heart, high blood pressure, neurological and kidney damage, joint problems.

My parents spent a week in the hospital, or rather, my mother spent five days and my father stayed a week—which brings me to the second thing that had made me frantic about getting Dad's story. Tina and Tom, my siblings who lived closest and had attended my parents almost constantly during the first five days in the hospital, needed a rest. I could cancel some classes and stay a few days, but this was no long-term solution. Teresa, the person my mother had finally hired the summer before, was eager to help but was untrained, and in any case, not available full time. With our mother so badly injured she was unable to dress herself, it was crystal clear to us kids that she was incapable of rendering the kind of physical assistance she had been giving my father for years to facilitate his daily life: dressing him and pulling my father's over two hundred pounds into sitting position in the morning, or up and out of chairs during the day. Since his own banged-up condition had made him even less able to assist in those situations, we reasoned that he should go to some kind of rehabilitation center until he could regain some capability and my mother could heal and rebuild some strength. When I found out that the hospital was planning to release my father the day after my mother, I called the attending physician and explained that there was simply no one to take care of him. How could they do that? Oh, the doctor replied, he told us he has a full-time nurse and that his home is set up better than the hospital. Noooo, I moaned, he has an untrained cleaning lady who helps out for a few hours some mornings. Fine, we'll keep him here the weekend. Thank you, Doctor.

My father received lots of visitors, including me and Mom over the weekend, to whom he made it obvious that he was unhappy and eager to get home. When my sister-in-law and I showed up Monday morning to negotiate the transition to a rehabilitation center we were told at the nurses station that my father was going to be released to go home. How can that be? I queried apprehensively. He can't take care of himself and my mother is injured. I heard some murmurings in the back and then a social worker pushed herself forward. Well, she explained, when they came to evaluate him, he took forty steps unassisted. We can't authorize someone for rehab who's that functional. Now I was incredulous. Forty steps? My Dad functional? He hasn't taken more than ten steps at a time in months! The social worker seemed sympathetic but unflappable: What can I say? When we came to evaluate him for rehab he got out of bed and walked all the way down the hall and back by himself.

I then stepped into my father's hospital room. I'm not sure who was more furious at whom.

You witch! Why are you trying to keep me here?

Dad, I'm not trying to keep you in this hospital. I'm trying to get you some rehab. Mom's sternum is broken. She can't take care of you. Teresa's only there part time. I have to go back to work. So do Tom and Tina.

I don't need Mom to take care of me. I can take care of myself.

Take care of yourself? You can't get dressed by yourself. You can't get up or out of bed by yourself. What are you talking about?

Of course I can get myself dressed. It's just easier if Mom does it for me.

????

My thoughts went into overdrive: it's "easier if Mom does it"? You faker! I screamed at him in my head. I hated him at that moment. I hated him from the bottom of my heart. But this is what I said out loud:

Dad, when you go home you will *have* to do it for yourself. Mom can't touch you, do you understand that? She can't touch you without injuring herself!

No problem, he said defiantly.

Okay, here are your clothes. I'll wait for you in the hall while you get dressed.

As mad as I was, it was hard to hear him fumbling. Still, I was determined to call his bluff. I stared at the dingy wall in the corridor outside his hospital room and tried not to listen. If he could get dressed by himself, dammit, I was going to let him do it. And if he could not, well then, he'd better admit it right now.

Dad had his pants and shirt on—sort of. I straightened his clothes a bit, put on his belt and a jacket, and home we went. I won't describe the moaning as I helped him into the car. This had been the routine for a long time now, as was the constant directing about how to drive the car and which route to take. When my father entered the house, the first thing he did was tell my mother to take his jacket off. She took a step toward him. She can't touch you! I roared. Remember, Dad? I'll help you take your jacket off. I think he was so happy to be home he didn't retort.

Trying to get my parents to break their atrophied behaviors with each other in the next few days was one of the biggest challenges I have ever faced. My father continued to ask my mother to do things for him and my mother kept starting to comply. My terror that my mother would injure herself even worse by trying to help my father brazed me:

Mom, even if he has another heart attack and falls on the floor, you've got to call 911. Don't try to lift him. What will be will be.

Dad, you said you could take care of yourself. You've got to do that. Mom can't touch you for six weeks.

I wanted to take my mother home with me to New Hampshire, so that she really would be out of my father's reach, but she wouldn't budge. I had been blinded to the fact that the house itself had become a battleground for them. Neither was willing to concede the home territory to the other. Getting my mother to sleep separately upstairs was the only minor change I effected. With visiting nurses scheduled to come, Teresa's hours, and my siblings' continued visits, I let go; I had to get back to school, my husband, and my own life.

The long car ride north provided me with four hours of stewing time. As the monotony of the late evening highway conditions calmed me down, an odd remark of my father to my sister-in-law, who was working in the adoption field at the time, floated back into my consciousness. He had asked her if she couldn't do something to help me, something to help me adopt a baby. My sister-in-law had reported this to me as an infraction on my privacy, but once my anger at my father in general had subsided, it was actually his generosity that astounded me. After all, he had just had a major car accident. He had said this to her from an uncomfortable hospital bed. How did he make room for his infertile daughter's pain? What a conundrum he was! On the one hand he wishes for me something that I wish for myself, and on the other he assumes I wish him ill. His vicious tone of voice sounded in my head again: You witch! Why are you trying to keep me here? I was the betrayer; he the betrayed. Wasn't that an old positioning? Just like the narcissism. When one friend showed up at the hospital my father assumed the friend had read about it in the newspaper. It never occurred to him that the paper rarely publishes anything about nonfatal accidents or that perhaps his children had made an effort to let his friends know what had happened and had asked them to come visit.

And then there was the deception. My father had been lying about things for as long as I could remember. Still, insisting that I was under ten when we went to the drive-in or rewriting a paragraph in my college admission essay and then mailing it without asking me seemed a very different order of infraction from claiming incapacity so that others would do things for him. For starters, the kind of care my mother had been giving him was taking a huge toll on her, physically and mentally. She had raised six children and had cared for her own aged mother for decades. My mother also has diabetes and heart problems. It didn't seem fair that my father was letting her do things for him that weren't absolutely necessary. Even if he was as selfish as this made him seem, he was hurting himself: every physical effort he did not make on his own behalf was a lost opportunity for his muscles to be taxed and for his diabetic body to burn a calorie. He would complain constantly that walking was hard. But every step he didn't take made it harder to take the next one. My father was an educated man. He had been an athlete and a coach for decades. He had attended numerous seminars on diabetes and heart health. Why did this basic physiological principle of exercising one's muscles count for nothing with him when he needed most to abide by it? If he had been lying to his own wife about something as important as what he was and was not physically capable of doing, what else had he lied about and to whom? I couldn't consciously let myself articulate the possibilities then. But it was difficult not to suspect that at least some of them concerned the War Experiences.

For decades I had explained my father's obesity to myself and others by reference to the prolonged undernourishment he had experienced during the years he was in Greece. I remember during my adolescence when I had first tried to diet I spelled out to myself point by point what I figured happened for my father: ah, the moment his stomach gives off that hunger signal, it must trigger something in his brain that makes him panic about the possibility of starving, and he just can't tolerate that feeling for even a moment. So he gets rid of that hunger sensation immediately and eats. Naturally, I didn't think it was good that he was overweight and then became obese. And his diabetes was a nightmare; he progressed from one medication to the next to injected insulin practically faster than the doctor could write the prescriptions. Yet I felt I really understood how his eating disorder had developed and that that understanding in turn resulted in compassion and acceptance.

An analogous yet less lucid logic had been operative for me in relation to his other difficult behaviors; raging, shaming, ridiculing, withdrawing must be connected to the war as well, but I didn't know exactly how or why. As a child I had been terrified and confused by his behavior; how come everyone thinks he's a jolly man and a great teacher? I asked myself repeatedly. As an adult I carried the vague hope that if I could figure out what had happened to him, it would help me understand and accept him better. When I first got glimmerings of actually researching and writing his story I wondered if having his experiences related to him as a whole might promote his becoming whole again himself. I didn't make the connection at the time, but I realize now that there was a certain parallel to the magical thinking my friends and I experienced in the immediate aftermath of Susanne and Half's murders. Everyone I knew was desperately trying to figure out what had happened. We each seemed to share a fantasy that when we solved the case for the police, we would get our friends back. Maybe when I recovered my father's history, I could have my father back, the one who put in brief appearances every now and then, having fun with us at the playground or ice rink, defending us against the petty injustices of daily life, the one who was proud of our accomplishments even though he could never tell us directly.

But of course, both fantasies were just that, fantasies.

And anyway, after our confrontation in the hospital, I wasn't as sure I wanted to help my father. The idea that Dad's suffering was partly or even mostly made up clawed at me. And his stories about his past? Could Dad have lied altogether about having been arrested as a Jew because of his circumcision? That would confirm pathologies more perturbing than any I had thought of forgiving him for. How to get the story? I couldn't test its truth if I didn't actually have the story . . .

In the next months, I visited my parents even more often. Luckily, the news was good. With a diminution in how much she was doing for my father and with the passage of time, my mother was healing. And with temporary help from the visiting physical therapist, my father made some progress in basic physical activities like getting up and down out of a chair. There was a mini-détente at the parental home in White Plains. It reminded me of the brief period seven years earlier when my father was thriving physically, in the interlude between the subsiding of the pain of open heart surgery and his resumption of a sedentary lifestyle and destructive eating habits. The decrease in my own most acute worries for my parents' health and safety allowed thoughts of Daddy's War to come creeping back in. As with so many problems that lurk just below consciousness, one day an idea popped out—the duplicitous strategy mentioned above. On my 2005 Easter visit to White Plains I walked into the house equipped not only with my own tape recorder and cassettes, but also with maps of Athens and Greece. I announced to my father that I was planning to go to Greece in the summer to retrace his steps during the war. Could he please show me exactly where he'd been or at least where he remembered being?

That did it. That broke the wall of silence between us on this topic. On April 30, 2005, after some fifteen years of intermittent efforts to get him to give me an account of what had happened, he searched the maps and talked at me and my recorder for almost two hours, telling of various incidents from his family's arrival in Greece in summer 1937 to their departure in October 1945. Not in any coherent or chronological fashion, of course. Nor did he seem particularly happy to be talking to me. But tell me stories he did: stories about his experiences living in Athens cut off from his mother and siblings, selling cigarettes, working for the Italian and German occupiers, running messages for the Greek underground, and fighting with the British against the communist guerrillas for control of Athens after the war against the Germans was over. The conversation included a narrative of being arrested by the Gestapo as a Jew when he was alone in Athens, being deported with the Jews of Kérkyra via Thessaloníki to Yugoslavia, and being liberated by the resistance from a camp there and returned to Psarrós, the commander of EKKA, one of the partisan groups operating in Roúmeli, the area his family is from.

My struggle with Daddy's War had not begun on that day. But I finally had an interlocutor I could look in the face and interrogate. I transcribed and studied that interview and the half dozen with my father that followed, and in the next eighteen months I expended all the time, resources, and cunning I could muster to try to track the course of Daddy's War. I realized right away how much I did not know, including basic facts like the names of my father's grandparents—*paternal: Giánnis and Panagioú Kacandes; maternal: Harálambos and Asymoúla Tsíngas*—aunts and uncles—*father's father's side: Argyrí and Kondílo, in addition to the great-uncle Tom I knew during my childhood; father's mother's side: Despoúla, Giánnis, and Loukía*—and cousins—*Argyrí's son Thýmios, the cousin my father had the most contact with; Despoúla's oldest daughter, Zoé; Giánnis's daughters Chrysoúla and Ólga*—more distant and yet beloved cousins—*the entire Gerentés family, not just Loukás whom they had visited or Chémo whom I had known my whole life*—the dates of key events in their personal histories—*they left the USA on August 14, 1937; lost contact with my grandfather in March 1941, and finally got out of Greece on September 13, 1945*—as well as on the course of the war—*doesn't start in Greece 'til the Italians invade at the Albanian border on October 28, 1940; Germans invade April 6, 1941, and leave October 12, 1944*—Occupation—*divided between Germany, Italy, and Bulgaria; Italy controls Roúmeli*—and civil war in Greece—*not just the brutal communist-nationalist conflict that succeeds World War II, but three phases, the first and second of which occur during my family's Greek sojourn; dozens of groupings; alliances constantly shifting intra-Greece and between partisans and the Allies; main groups of resisters in our area: the communist affiliated ELAS, the originally republican and increasingly royalist EDES led by Napoléon Zérvas, and the noncommunist but motley 5/42 and EKKA, led by local hero and committed republican Demétrios Psarrós*—and the geography of Roúmeli—*dominated not only by Mount Parnassós, which made such an impression on* me during my first visit, but also a mountain named Gióna where Psarrós had had his headquarters.

To learn even more, I studied Greek histories, maps, and additional histories of the Holocaust, including the few that concentrated on the persecutions in Greece—*largest number of Jews deported from German-occupied Thessaloníki from March to August 1943; Italians refuse to cooperate; Athenian Jews mainly safe until Italian capitulation when Germans take over previously Italian occupied areas; Germans deport as many Athenians, Kerkyrans, and others as can spring–summer 1944, even as own position in country deteriorating.*

I interviewed my father's younger sister, Pearl, the only other person who had made that trip with him who is still alive—*good storyteller; knows much more family history than Dad even though she's younger; talked to each of her parents more.* I interviewed other relatives who knew my father and my grandparents, including my own mother—**Mom talked to her mother-in-law a lot; what a memory she has.**

I dug into my father's filing cabinets and discovered a very few documents related to this period in his life—*proof of my father's schooling, of my grandfather's attempts to find his wife and children, of my grandparents' claim on my grandmother's parents' house.*

I finally reread The Newspaper Article from 1945 about my father and compared it to what I'd been learning—**Dad already tailoring his experiences to his audience; his story compared to "Terry" and "Jack Armstrong" popular cultural icons of early and mid-twentieth-century USA; talks about arrest but not deportation.**

I found a photo album my father had put together in the late 1940s after his return to the States, while he was recuperating from knee surgery—*my grandmother sent scores of pictures to my grandfather before the war broke out; only two from during the war survive; many from after; sent photos function like letters; they're dated; Dad's captions from late '40s often contradict dates on photos.*

I located a correspondence log he kept from 1945 to '48 and queried him about the names I found there—**didn't put Greece behind him then;**

wrote to hundreds of people; he's forgotten most, remembers others; Mom re-members more; what luck! I can match some names in log to unnamed charac-ters in his stories.

Not least of all, I turned my own lie into a truth, and I went back to Greece in August 2005 and December 2006 to indeed trace as much of my father's peregrinations as I could—*long walk from his school to down-town Athens; cigarette factory located, police precinct not; how did he manage to travel between Athens and Roúmeli so often?* In Greece I contacted paternal relatives I had never met before—*some look like us!* I talked to strangers who lived in the area about their own war experiences, pursuing partic-ularly any events that seemed similar to ones my father told me he had participated in—*confirms likelihood of some stories; others not; people who stayed in Greece generally remember much more than those who left.*

Throughout this period of fact gathering, I continually compared each new piece of information and personal opinion to the ones I al-ready had. Taking stock in summer 2006, I realized that while I by no means could trace all phases of my paternal family's eight fateful years in Greece, I had indeed learned quite a lot about what had happened to them. Still, if I were a professional historian, I assume I would have been painfully frustrated: many of the crucial actors and witnesses were al-ready dead—*my grandparents and their siblings; my father's brothers, Harry and Nick;* much of the documentation didn't exist—*some local archives were burned or otherwise destroyed; some kinds of records were simply never kept in the chaos that was wartime Greece (for example, deportation records for Athenian Jews); and my father himself an inconsistent family archivist; found passport they went over on; not one from return.* Had I been a novelist, I felt certain I could have written a thriller or a gripping family saga. A Greek version of Maxine Hong Kingston's China Men (1989), I fantasized.

Sitting in the midst of my notes, tapes, transcripts, photos, docu-ments it seemed to me that though I am very much neither an historian nor a novelist, I needn't be despondent: what I had in abundance were stories, stories like why my grandmother might have left the United States to return to Greece with four young children and without her spouse, or how my father earned money to send back to his family in the village. I had, too, my own stories about who told these stories, how, where, and to whom. I, after all, had been trained as a narratologist, a professional analyzer of stories—I even had a subspecialty in stories of trauma, in particular of the Second World War and the Holocaust. What I needed to create, then, was a form to pass on the precious family stories now brought into the open and gathered together *and* the stories of getting the stories. I began to experiment. I wrote and rewrote. When I came up with pages that approximately resemble what you are reading now, I realized that such a book might be called a "paramemoir," a text that functions "alongside," "beyond," "aside from" and as a "substitute for" a memoir. For while *Daddy's War* has some of the characteristics of memoir, that is, according to Webster's, "a narrative composed from personal experience," it also contains analytical components.

Though both the narrative and analytical dimensions are in evidence throughout this book, storytelling dominates chapters 1, 2, and 5, and analysis preponderates in chapters 3, 4, and the epilogue. In this first chapter, "Stalked by Daddy's War: Earliest Memories and How I Came to Face Them," I have attempted to reconstruct my childhood conceptions of my father's experiences in Greece, to trace how those memories changed over time, to convey my growing sense in adulthood that I would need to actively pursue further details about those wartime events if I wanted them to play less of a role in my life, and to recount the research and interviewing I undertook over the last several years that led to the writing of this book. Keeping an epistemological space open for the difference between what occurred in the historical past and what one thinks happened in the historical past has been an important dimension of this work for me. Even what I have written here in chapter 1, I realized, is not what I actually thought or felt as a child, teenager, young and then middle-aged adult, but rather is my recollection at this point in time of what I thought I knew in earlier periods of my life.

This distinction is important for reading the next section of this book, "Recounting Daddy's War: Family Stories." Chapter 2 consists of various anecdotes I heard while interviewing relatives about family history, and most specifically about what happened to my father, his siblings, and his mother from 1937 to 1945, as they tried to cope with separation from my grandfather and to survive the Italian and German invasions and occupations of Greece, and the first two rounds of the Greek Civil War. By relaying narratives in as close to the exact manner as I received them and by juxtaposing stories about the "same" events to one another under a topical heading, I provide through chapter 2 a kind of "brain scan" of family memory, that is to say, a sort of simultaneous view of how certain past events are present today (more exactly, between 2004 and 2006) in the memories of a large number of family members of two generations. These stories add a bit to what we know about how civilians survived the war, occupation, and civil war in Greece, but most of all, they demonstrate what individuals think they remember and how easily the storage of memories can be and usually is transformed by subsequent experiences and information. To this end of recording the family memory scan and learning about how memory functions, you will notice that for the most part, I do not correct during the interview what I myself sometimes already knew to be incorrect assertions.

This family memory scan is then read by me, the narratologist daughter/sister/niece in chapters 3 and 4. I've grouped in chapter 3, "Analyzing Daddy's War: Insights from Established Theories," insights I gained about the family stories by considering them in light of established theories of oral storytelling, memory, and trauma. I have placed ideas for extending or modifying available theories that were inspired by the Kacandes family stories in chapter 4, "Grappling with Daddy's War: Speculations for Extending Theories."

Having analyzed and grappled with our family stories using my professional tools, I put my heart back into the equation and try again to "stand next to" my father, the way I related here I have tried to stand next to Leon S. and other victims of tragedy. Drawing on a concept I originally borrowed from psychoanalyst Dori Laub and developed in terms of reading literature in my first book, *Talk Fiction*, in chapter 5, "Cowitnessing to Daddy's War: An (Im)Possible Recital of What Might Have Happened," I try to "cowitness" to my father's trauma, by narrating to him what I now think happened to him between 1937 and 1945. I then reflect on how this entire process of remembering, researching, and writing has affected me in the epilogue, "Surviving Daddy's War," to complete the narrative of how I have indeed survived Daddy's War. Over the course of the whole book, I hope to have relayed poignant stories, conveyed some information about the Second World War in Greece, and contributed to current conversations about storytelling and memory.

[2]

Recounting Daddy's War

Family Stories

In this section I have organized the stories I heard when I asked family members between 2004 and 2006 what they thought had happened to my father and his family during their stay in Greece from 1937 to 1945. In order to achieve the "scan" of family memory I explained at the conclusion of chapter 1, I am presenting these anecdotes to my readers in as close a form to the way I received them as possible. That is to say, where I received written replies, I have reproduced here that writing. And where I received oral recitations, I have reproduced the way that speech sounded during interviews and is recorded on tape. Thus I have included hesitations, false starts, back-channeling ("uh-huh"), hedges, repetitions, and so on, because the kernels of additional, alternate, or contradictory stories are often to be located in such comments and sounds. To those who have never read transcribed speech, it might be helpful to think about what your eye is reading as a play script: the cues are given for where to pause, falter, and restart, or rather, where I or my interviewees did pause, falter, and restart. Nevertheless, this transcription style can be misleading: transcribed speech often conveys an exaggerated inarticulateness or at best inelegance on the part of the speakers, whereas in point of fact almost all of my interviewees are highly educated, and most transcribed spoken discourse bears some of the same characteristics readers will notice in these stories. Additionally, though, these stories' structures are highly marked by Greek oral storytelling style (a topic I will address more fully in chapter 3). For those who have never been exposed to Greek storytellers, I suppose the most prominent characteristic is the rambling, or as my Swiss husband puts it: "Greeks tell for the sake of telling." I did not try to reduce the meanderings of the stories I received, though I did obviously decide in the case of written and oral communications, where an anecdote begins and ends.

Also toward my goal of tracing how stories travel through and metamorphose among family members, I have included my early memories of specific stories for comparison's sake; they can serve my readers as an approximate summary of my knowledge when I started conducting these interviews. My childhood memories appear here, as they did in chapter 1, in bold letters for my earliest memories, or, as I would like to call them borrowing from my friend Marianne Hirsch, my postmemories, and in italics for my incipient narratives. Readers will thereby notice that as a child I did not have any awareness whatsoever of some of these topics. The introductions to each story and anything placed in square brackets stem from me, the adult compiler of these stories.

1

Immigration and Return or How George and Chrysoúla Met, Married, Ended Up in the United States, and Chrysoúla Left for Greece Again

Daddy, Yiayia, Aunt Pearl, Uncle Harry, and Uncle Nick went to Greece because Daddy was having trouble in school since his English wasn't so good. Pappou stayed behind to earn money.

The cultural commentator and Holocaust scholar Eva Hoffman wrote about her own childhood: "In the beginning was the War." In my case,

I would say that: in the beginning was the Trip to Greece. I knew very little about what had preceded the fateful trip to Greece that my father's nuclear family, minus his father, embarked on in 1937. For instance, I had heard almost nothing about my grandparents' youth or how they had met. There was a large photograph of their village wedding hanging in their house—and after their deaths in our own. I know I spent a lot of time staring at this picture as a child, but I never remember asking about it, though at some point someone must have told me the scene was in Chryssó, near Delphi. This added to its mythical aura: set in a steep village street, with a church and houses lining the sides, the handsome couple was in the center with the musicians and children in front of them, and all the other villagers lined up behind them. It was paired with a studio wedding portrait, taken post facto in the United States, in which my grandfather looks devastatingly dashing and my grandmother very fashionable in her midcalf-length 1920s gown, but too serious, making her appear a touch scared, to my mind. As a young child I never created a narrative for myself about how they got from their wedding day in Greece to the United States and then my grandmother to the point of departure back to Greece with the kids. As a middle-aged adult, I finally asked.

1a

This story was told to me by my aunt Pearl Veronis, my father's sister, and the only other person who is still alive who experienced with him those eight years in Greece from 1937 to 1945. I drove to her house in Lancaster, Pennsylvania, on December 27, 2005, specifically for the purpose of getting her view of certain pieces of family history. My aunt is a tall, slender, very attractive older lady whose blue eyes and distinctive nose particularly resemble her father, my paternal grandfather George Kacandes. At the time of our interview, she was doing radiation therapy as follow up to breast cancer surgery. It being Christmas season, she had just come from a church service in honor of Saint Stephen, the

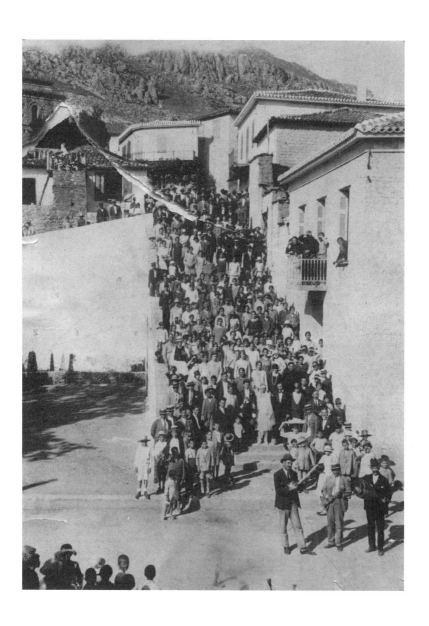

3. Village wedding of Chrysoúla H. Tsínga and George J. Kacandes,
Chryssó, Greece, June 14, 1928.

4. Studio wedding portrait of George and
Chrysoúla Kacandes, Newark, New Jersey.

first martyr of the Church, and her children and grandchildren popped in and out of our conversation in person or by phone. We were seated at her kitchen table eating delicious avgolemono soup (Greek style chicken soup with egg-lemon sauce) and spanakopita (Greek spinach pie). She's a good cook, like her mother was. Most of the interruptions and the comments about the food are edited out of the story. *Yiayía* (γιαγιά) and *Pappou* (παππούς) are terms for "grandma" and "grandpa," respectively. *Theia* (θεία) and *Theio* (θείος), "aunt" and "uncle." We mention Chémo, a member of the Gerentés family I spoke of in chapter 1, who is a cousin on my father's mother's side and the only one of those five siblings to spend her adulthood in the United States.

IRENE: Aunt Pearl, how is it that Yiayía and Pappou came to the United States?

PEARL: Well, Pappou's father had died from a massive heart attack when he was thirty-three or thirty-two. He was John, your father's namesake. So, honey, he died and then my uncle Tom, Pappou's older brother, came to America and went into the restaurant business, and he married Aunt Helen, who was one of his waitresses. She was only sixteen. When the news got back to my grandmother, my namesake Panagióta, Panagioú her name was—once I met her, I always used to complain to my mother that I wasn't named after her mother, instead of my father's; Panagioú was a real strong, stern woman—

IRENE: You know, Theia Chémo was just telling me the same thing. I guess Panagioú was living with her daughter Kondílo in Itéa before and during the war and mother or daughter would come to the Gerentés house and help with the housework. And Chémo remembers Panagioú combing her hair. Panagioú would yell at her: don't you move. And she would comb out the knots and it really hurt Chémo, who would cry, but she couldn't say anything for fear Panagioú would become even more rough.

PEARL: Chémo is right: Panagioú was a tough lady. So, when the news got back to her about my uncle Tom, she claims that from her crying, she lost her eyesight, that's how upset she was that my uncle would marry a ξένη, a foreigner—and it's true that when we met her she couldn't see out of one eye. Uncle Tom was very sensitive to his mother's pain, so he sent Aunt Helen to Greece for two years, where she lived with my grandmother in the village, learned her Greek and how to cook, and then came back to America. Well, by that time my father, George, was old enough to come to America, and Uncle Tom and Aunt Helen took him in, and my father really became her guardian, her companion because Uncle Tom worked round the clock practically, so he would give my father money and say: take her to New York, take her to the shore, Asbury Park, to Belmar. My aunt Helen adored my father. Of course, my father was also working in the restaurant, and he really wanted an education. He begged my uncle. But my uncle wouldn't give him the time off, so my father would sneak out and go to night school without my uncle knowing about it. That's how Pappou learned his English and became so, so Americanized. In the meantime, my father also falls in love with a woman here, and when my uncle sees this happening, he's devastated. He didn't want my dad to repeat what he did with marrying a foreigner and breaking their mother's heart, so he paid my father's expenses, packed him up, and sent him with the very first AHEPA excursion to Greece.

IRENE: AHEPA [American Hellenic Educational Progressive Association, founded 1922], that's a philanthropic organization started by Greek immigrants in the United States, right?

PEARL: Yes, Pappou went on their first excursion to Greece in 1928 with his best friend, Tom Zévas. He went to see his mother, whom he hadn't seen since he was eleven years old. He had been gone from her more than half his life. To stay in touch with her sons, my grandmother had decided on a plan to write them letters. She herself was illiterate. So she went to the priest in the neighboring village of Chryssó and asked him to give

5. Earliest known photo of George J. Kacandes (right), in America, pictured with unidentified family friend, believed to be taken in 1918 when George would have been thirteen years old.

her a young person who could write letters for her to her sons in America. You see, she wanted to write them her complaints and other confidential things, so she couldn't make this request of anyone in her own village. Well, the priest found my mother. She was the second daughter in the much beloved Tsíngas family. I mean my maternal grandfather

6. Harálambos Tsíngas (left), with his first grandchild, Zoé Paphíli (center), and unknown friend (right), probably 1931.

Harálambos, my brother Harry's namesake, was an angel. And my grandmother Asymoúla—that's who Yiayia named her first daughter after, the baby who died—well, she was a wonderful person too. You know that my mother lost a child, right?

IRENE: Yes, I did learn that, but only very recently. Yiayia herself never told me about it, although we talked often—

PEARL: I'm surprised she never said anything to you, because every time we went to Newark, she wanted to go to the cemetery.

IRENE: This Asymoúla was born right after my dad, right?

PEARL: Yes. First there was your father, then came a daughter. Yiayia named her after her mother. The baby became ill and Yiayia and Pappou called the doctor. She was only three months old. And they called the doctor. And he came to the house, examined her. And then honey, when he gave my mother a prescription—which you know, my mother didn't speak a word of English at that point—the prescription he gave her, instead of putting down "three months" he put "three years old." And the second teaspoon my mother gave her, she found her dead in the crib.

IRENE: Aunt Pearl, are you sure it was the doctor who prescribed the wrong dosage? I had heard it was a Greek neighbor who read the label to Yiayia and told her the wrong thing, and that that was why my grandmother resented her so much, on top of her suspicions about the relationship she had to my grandfather . . . I think I heard that from both my mother and aunt Stella.

PEARL: Oh yes, I'm sure it was the doctor, Irene, because of what happened next. So, they searched for the prescription. And my father—I had such admiration for my dad even though I know he made my mother's life miserable. All those years I adored him. He was really my best friend. And that's why I think I have a good marriage and a good relationship with men, because I had a great father and wonderful brothers who respected me a great deal as the only girl in the family. And then of course

7. Asymoúla Tsínga, née Kózari (left), with her older sister.

marrying just such a great person. Well, anyway, and my father, honey, they went back and they found the prescription. And my father was kind enough to say, he would not get the doctor's license taken away; he said, "All I want him to do is to pay to have the baby buried." And that's what happened. He never lost his license. They buried the baby somewhere in Newark and my father told my mother that the past was the past. She had a child to look after. And she should think about the future. Every time we went to Newark, my mother wanted to go to the cemetery. But my father wouldn't let her.

IRENE: Wow!

PEARL: Oh yeah. It was so traumatic for my mother.

IRENE: I bet.

[Arrival of Pearl's youngest son, Luke, with his youngest child, Panagióta, named after his grandmother, the person I'm speaking with, as she is named after her paternal grandmother, one of the people we were just speaking about. After hellos, I return us to the previous topic.]

Aunt Pearl, I think you were telling us about your maternal grandparents and how our grandmother met our grandfather.

PEARL: Pappou Harálambos and Yiayia Asymoúla, they were truly holy people. Our grandmother took care of everyone in the village: when they died, when they married, baptized their children. She washed their bodies, dressed them. Our grandfather Harálambos, he was very special too. The village of Chryssó has two churches, one in the upper part of town and one in the lower. You know that right?

IRENE: Right. They lived across from the lower one . . .

PEARL: Yes. My grandparents lived right across from Saint Nicholas church, the one in the lower part of town. Every morning my grandfather would take his children into the church. They would light the vigil lamps, say their prayers, and then go to their work. My grandfather was a shoemaker—

IRENE: You know, I just learned that from my dad, who said he was really good at it. Dad remembers that his grandfather would go down to the πανηγύρι, to the fair of Ághios Giánnis [Saint John] in Itéa and take orders to make shoes. Dad said there were a lot of refugees there from Smyrna who came to the area after the Asia Minor disaster.

PEARL: Right, our grandfather was an excellent shoemaker, and our grandmother was a homemaker; our mother became the υφάντρια, the weaver. She was weaving since the age of eleven. She did all of the προίκες, the trousseau, for all of her sisters.

IRENE: I don't know if they were part of her dowry, but we have several of the blankets that Yiayia wove. When we were kids we just thought of them as heavy and scratchy, but now we treasure them so, that they were made by her.

PEARL: I'm glad you have those. And my theia Despoúla from Galaxídi, she was the seamstress. She did all the beautiful κέντημα, the needlepoint, and my theia Loukía, who was the youngest and a little spoiled, she was doing just odds and ends around the house. And their brother Giánni was a spoiled brat who just did whatever he wanted to. So anyway, my mother was picked by the priest. And my paternal grandmother, Panagioú, had all these letters written to her sons in America by my mother.

IRENE: You know, that's a special story for me, Aunt Pearl, because at the end of my life—that was an interesting slip!—towards the end of Yiayia's life, when I had finally learned Greek properly, she and I corresponded. We exchanged several letters in Greek. I had planned on asking her about the war years and how she learned to do all the things she knew how to do, like make her own soap, her own yogurt, her own rosewater, but unfortunately we didn't get that far. She died so quickly after her diagnosis of cancer. I have always treasured those letters, but I'm going to treasure them even more now. I didn't know that writing letters had played such a critical role in her own life. Speaking of that critical role, Aunt Pearl?

PEARL: Well, when my father went to Greece with the AHEPANS in 1928 his mother told him: before you leave again, you are marrying this woman. And that was my mother. You know, my father, he left when he was eleven; he had very few memories of Greece, the village, even of his own mother. When he went back in 1928, it was amazing that he was obedient to her. It reminds me a little bit of Jesus when His mother tells Him at the wedding at Cana to make the wine into, uh, the water into wine. Woman, my hour has not come. And yet the mother says: do what He says, bring the water, because He will do it. I mean there was no doubt in the Virgin Mary's mind that her son was going to be obedient to her. And I think of my father doing exactly that when my grandmother insisted that he had to marry my mother. And within months, honey, they made the arrangements. They got married. This *koumbáros*, their best man, was ready made. You know, a good friend of Pappou's. And then they came to America together. As for my mother, well, she already knew a lot about my father from the letters that had been dictated to her, but my mother never wanted to come to America. She was in love with a little boy—a young man in the village.

IRENE: Ooohh. I'm sorry to hear that. I know my other grandmother also was not allowed to marry the man she fancied. She and my grandfather Psomás were completely wrong for each other. They had such different personalities: she was so serious and devout. My mother told me her father was a jokester who loved to have a good time.

PEARL: Well, when I say Yiayia was in love with a young man, I don't really mean love. You know, they would pick olives together. They liked each other. Yiayia's father never intended to send his daughter away from the village, but here was someone who wasn't demanding a dowry and who could provide for his daughter. And he still had one unmarried daughter at home. They knew my paternal grandmother from the letter writing, and of course, everyone fell in love with my father when they met him, he was so handsome and charming. So my grandfather agreed to the marriage. That's the way things were done then.

8. Engagement portrait of Chrysoúla (standing center) and George (standing left), spring 1928. Also pictured are Panagioú Kakandé (seated left), Asymoúla Tsínga (seated right), and unknown man believed to be the couple's *koumbáros*, Efthémios Zévas (best man; standing right).

Still, whenever my mother fought with my father she would say: "I didn't want to come to America. I didn't want δολλάρια, dollars. I wanted to live a simple life." You know, when Yiayia died, she was with me. I had her wallet and I opened it up and inside was this beautiful song:

[Pearl starts to sing in Greek.]

Μη με στέλνεις, μάνα,	[Don't send me, momma,
στην Αμερική	to America
Γιατί θα μαραζώσω	Because I will whither;
Θα πεθάνω εκεί	I'll die over there
Γιατί θα μαραζώσω	Because I will whither;
Θα πεθάνω εκεί.	I'll die over there.
Δολλάρια δεν θέλω	Dollars I don't want
Δολλάρια δεν θέλω.	Dollars I don't want
Ψωμί, ελιές και λάδι	Just bread, olives, and oil
Και κείνον π᾽αγαπώ	And the one I love;
Ψωμί, ελιές και λάδι	Just bread, olives, and oil
Και κείνο π᾽αγαπώ.	And the one I love.]

That poem was in her wallet and she used to sing that.

IRENE: Wow! When did you hear that from her, already as a little girl?

PEARL: Yes, she used to sing that and I learned it from her. She had a very hard life, sweetheart. You have to remember, when our mother came to America, she was very much the village girl. Even though Chryssó, where she grew up, was a little more sophisticated than the village Pappou was from, than Kolopetinítsa, she followed traditional ways. She had very long hair, an extremely long κότσο, plait. And uh, they had to live with my theio Tom and my aunt Helen when they came to the United States as a young married couple, because my father never owned anything. And my aunt was very cruel to my mother. She hated her, because she had taken away her boyfriend. She related to my father more like a boyfriend than a brother-in-law, because she was a young woman, much younger than my uncle, and my father had been her companion, he did anything she wanted to do. This was a good excuse for my uncle Tom. He didn't have to be bothered and could work all the time. She only had one child to look after, my cousin John. So when my mother came, honey, Helen was so cruel to her. She's the one who got my father to make my mother cut her hair off. It broke her heart. She was such a village girl. That's one of the main reasons Yiayia went to Greece honey, because of that cruelty.

IRENE: Aunt Pearl, it is so helpful to me that you are able to fill in some of the background about our grandparents, I don't want to make you late for your radiation treatment, though.

PEARL: It's okay, honey. I've got a little more time.

[My cousin Luke and his daughter say goodbye.]

What were we talking about?

IRENE: You were still telling me about Yiayia. You were sort of talking about why Yiayia decided to go to back to Greece in 1937. By the way, how did you get from Panagioú to Pearl?

PEARL: When I was born in Newark, my mother's Jewish friends came to see the baby and they asked her, what's her name? And my mother said, Panagioú. No, no, no, they told her. You have to give the baby an American name. Yiayia was puzzled and she said, well you name her. And they said, call her Pearl. So that's how I became Pearl Kacandes. My mother always had a very special relationship with the Jews.

IRENE: Our grandfather too.

PEARL: My father admired the Jews, but my mother liked them, because she lived with them in Newark. They were the only kind people to her. The Greeks were jealous of her. Because by that time, you see, there were some Greek women around, and they would have liked to marry my father. He was so handsome and fun and so Americanized. That's why when my father decided that my mother should take us to Greece, my mother didn't mind leaving Newark.

IRENE: Aunt Pearl, a few minutes ago you cited Aunt Helen, Tom's wife, as being cruel to her new sister-in-law and also that the Greek women of the Newark area were envious of Yiayia. Jealousy is a powerful emotion to be sure, but it seems a little extreme to me to deal with it by moving to Greece with your four children and leaving your husband behind.

PEARL: Well, I know it could sound extreme, but the jealousy was too. My aunt was so angry at my mother that she put mothballs on the couch, and I ate them thinking it was candy. I had to have my stomach pumped. So, there were a lot of reasons: there was the death of the child, which really took a toll on my mother. My father didn't want my mother to ever think about it again. He would not take her to the cemetery to visit. She never really got a chance to mourn that child. They were having children much too close together; after Asymoúla died, Harry was born, and then I just a year and a half later, and my father was overwhelmed. In fact, with Nicky, my father wanted my mother to have an abortion. Pappou just went crazy. He knew he couldn't afford to have another child. But my mother refused. She begged Saint Nicholas, because he was her favorite saint, that if my father would let her have the child and it was a boy, she would name him Nicholas. And that's what happened. See, Nicky's named after Saint Nicholas. So, they were struggling financially. And my mother missed her family terribly. That's why when my uncle John [my grandmother's brother] was so cruel to us during the war, it hurt even more. My mother loved him so much that she had gathered up clothes in America and sent them to him, even though she and my father didn't really have much in those days.

IRENE: So, there really were a number of reasons that Yiayia and Pappou or Yiayia or Pappou made the decision to take you all to Greece: their physical separation would serve as a kind of automatic birth control method, making sure no more children were born; Yiayia could protect you and herself better from your jealous aunt and neighbors; and she could visit with her own family, whom she was missing terribly.

PEARL: Right. So, my father said to my mother, go for two or three years, and that's a long time. I'll work around the clock, and when you come back, we'll have enough money to have our own home. All that was very encouraging to my mother. And that's why she went.

1b

My father has very few memories of his life before leaving for Greece in 1937, even though one might think he'd have some, given that he was already seven when they left (he was born on December 8, 1929) and that as the oldest child and a first-born Greek son, one could assume he was treated royally—perhaps even more protectively after my grandmother lost her first daughter. The following story came to light on April 2, 2006, addressed to me and my first cousin, Nicholas John Kacandes, the only son of my father's youngest brother, Nicholas. Because naming children is such an important topic in the previous segment—and as it will turn out for this book as a whole—I mention here that this cousin's naming did not follow standard Greek custom: normally a child would have his first name come from a grandparent and a middle name from his own father. I don't know why my uncle Nick decided to name his only son after himself, but I do know that his middle name derives from a deal my uncle made with my father. Since they both had sons at the same time, they each gave their sons the other's first name as a middle name. Hence, as a sixth child, my youngest brother is named Peter (after Pétros Tsardákas, a man who had helped my dad during the war) and Nicholas (after my uncle, but conveniently that was also my maternal grandfather's first name). My cousin Nick had called me when he heard I was working on family history and told me he was interested in getting some of my father's stories on videotape. The interview took place in my parents' living room in White Plains, New York. I had driven down from New Hampshire, and Nick had driven up from the Jersey shore; he still lives in the area where our fathers grew up. I've edited out many of our queries, because they were just too frequent. My father didn't really "tell us" anything; rather, we and my mother, Lucie, had to pull the words from his mouth. He wasn't very interested in talking that day.

IRENE: Dad, we're trying to establish the context in which your trip to Greece took place, and I'm wondering if you can share with us any memories you have about growing up before you left the United States. I know you were young—only seven years old when you all departed—but you might remember something about where you lived, your school. Do you remember your first day at school? Or maybe the birth of any of your siblings? Of your sister Pearl or your brother Nick?

JOHN: Nick was born in 1937.

IRENE: Right, Dad. Do you remember anything about your life then? Where you lived, for example?

JOHN: Irvington, New Jersey. I remember the house and everything. It was a two-family house. We lived upstairs. It was on Spring Street.

IRENE: Did your uncle Tom and aunt Helen live in the same house?

JOHN: No, but I used to go over to their house. Uncle Tom would give me a quarter and I would go to the movies, buy ice cream and everything. I liked the movies.

IRENE: Do you have any other memories of your early childhood in New Jersey? Maybe about your school or your friends?

JOHN: I was very delinquent apparently, and the threat was that my father was going to send us to Greece. I was the scapegoat. One incident I remember. I don't know if I stole it or what. I took some kind of a bicycle.

NICK: Uncle John, you mean you were hanging out with a bunch of kids and you rode somebody's bike home?

JOHN: I really don't remember.

NICK: What did you like to do? Who was your best friend?

9. John G. Kacandes, American boy, ca. 1936, New Jersey.

JOHN: I used to like walking along the railroad tracks. There were rail-road tracks. I don't remember any friends with me. One of the things that made my father very angry was that I picked up some money. And I heard him or my mother coming and I flushed it down the toilet. Five dollars. Back then that was a lot of money.

NICK: Where did you find the money?

JOHN: In my father's pocket. He used to sleep late. He worked all night. He woke up. When he found out, he gave me a good spanking, and again, the threat was to send us all to Greece. My father wanted us to learn Greek.

LUCIE: John, how about that story you used to tell with Lincoln's statue in Newark?

JOHN: There was a statue of Abraham Lincoln and I had a knife and I was trying to cut off one of Lincoln's fingers. A neighbor saw me and told my parents. I got in big trouble for that too.

IRENE: I'm confused about the language thing. All these years, I thought your father sent you to Greece because you were having trouble in school since your English wasn't so good, and now you're saying he wanted you to learn Greek. Didn't you all speak Greek at home?

JOHN: I don't remember what they spoke, but I don't remember speaking that much Greek. The plan was for us to learn Greek and then for my father to come over and decide whether we were staying there or coming back.

1c

Despite learning that a number of immigrant families or members of families actually went back and forth often between the United States and Greece during the early twentieth century, I still puzzle over the issue of why my grandmother took her four kids to Greece in 1937. I tried asking one other eyewitness of sorts, Chémo Glynos, née Gerenté (on the forms of Greek family names, see appendix A), a woman who knew my grandmother in Greece during the war and interacted with both my grandparents in the United States after the war but who did not experience them during the early years of their marriage. I drove to Chémo's house in Oakhurst, New Jersey, on December 26, 2005. My brother Peter drove my parents in their car and I rode in my own, since I was going to continue on my journey to Aunt Pearl in Lancaster, Pennsylvania, from there. It was my father's first trip to Jersey in more than a year because of the car accident he had had that previous January and his subsequent driving restrictions. Prior to the accident, and especially prior to the death of his brother Harry in fall 2003, my father would visit the

10. Studio portrait of George J. Kacandes, dandy.

area where he grew up often, even if he only wanted to stay an hour or so and the trip took two and a half hours each way. During this excursion, he seemed happy to see his cousin and her husband, who used to visit my parents regularly before their own old age prevented them from driving north to see my parents. Chémo is about five years older than my father, but at present, she is in significantly better health. I waited to pose certain questions until my parents and brother had departed. This was one of them.

IRENE: My grandmother was older than you, but you saw her during the war years in Itéa and you talked to her a lot in the postwar years in

New Jersey. Did she ever say anything to you about why she returned to Greece in '37?

CHÉMO: Well, my aunt always said ότι ο θείος ήθελε να μάθουν τα παιδιά ελληνικά [that my uncle wanted the kids to learn Greek]—that they went for that reason. But I think your Yiayia had a lot of problems with your Pappou. He didn't behave himself the way he should have. For what reason, though, I donna know.

To this day, no one in the family is willing or perhaps able to say whether my grandfather did or did not have affairs. We all agree he was a handsome man who enjoyed dressing well. The next group of stories concerns a different kind of cheating.

2

The House in Chryssó or **cheated**

Yiayia got kicked out of her house because her brother robbed her during the civil war. She had no place to go with the kids.

From the time of my earliest memories I had some sense of an injustice done to my grandmother in Greece around the issue of a house. Very early on in my own life, the idea that this had something to do with the civil war was added to the disconnected narrative elements in my head. (I remember reading about the American Civil War as a young child and learning that "civil war" meant that sometimes brother fought brother. I believe that's how "her brother" entered the jumble in my mind, because otherwise I do not recall knowing at that age anything about my grandmother having a brother.) I know now that that connection is false in relation to my own family. The house troubles had nothing to do with the Greek Civil War. Still, the fact that something that was told to me that helped me make an association between the house and the civil war shows how much the house in Chryssó is connected to intra-familial strife.

Of the four Tsíngas children of my grandmother's nuclear family, I feel like I always knew that her sister Despoúla (b. 1902) was definitely the oldest and her sister Loukía (b. 1908) the youngest. My grandmother claimed to be born in various years: 1903, 1904, 1905, and 1908. On some documents like her Greek identity card, it looks like she changed the "3" to an "8." However, since none of his children remember when my great-uncle Giánnis, John, was born—though they did tell me that he had a twin who died—I couldn't be sure who was the older of the middle two children (many of Chryssó's town records were destroyed in the third round of the Greek Civil War). After questioning my father and my aunt again, they seemed to share a vague memory that my grandmother was older than my grandfather, who always listed his birth year as 1905. At this point in my research I finally discovered the Greek passport with which my grandmother was able to leave Greece in 1945; it did indeed list her birth year as 1903. Even though I now feel confident of my grandmother's birth year, I spell out these difficulties because the issue of age may have affected her relationship to her husband, and because birth order was certainly a factor in the distribution of family resources in the Greece of her youth; to a lesser extent it remains so to this day.

I never met my great-uncle John for reasons that will become more apparent as these family stories unfold. However, I did meet my great-aunts Despoúla and Loukía in 1974 on the trip to Greece I took with my mother and sister Georgia when I was sixteen. I remember being astounded at the beauty of Theia Despoúla's blue eyes. About Loukía, I only remember a lady in black whose affection toward us seemed awkward and insincere to me at the time. I felt a little scared of her. The fact that her house and the room my sister and I tried to sleep in were suffocatingly hot and filled with mosquitoes didn't help endear her to me. The house in question in this set of stories has been boarded up and abandoned since Loukía's death in 2001.

11. The house in Chryssó as it appeared in 2006.

This story was told to me by my aunt Pearl in the same interview mentioned in the previous section. It did not pop out as a story unit by itself but was embedded in the longer sequence explaining why my grandmother ended up going to Greece: she missed her family so much.

PEARL: That house was my mother's προίκα [dowry]—even though my father didn't want a προίκα.

And a few minutes later . . .

PEARL: My father bought that home, and he permitted my grandparents and my theia Loukía to live in it. So when we went there during the war, honey, we went to Chryssó, that's where we were living. But my mother and Theia Loukía never got along. Theia Loukía was a very demanding person. We left and went down to Itéa for two reasons. My mother went down because it was near the sea and she was hoping the sea people would give her some fish for her children, and also because people didn't know her in Itéa, like they knew her in Chryssó, so she could go around begging for food, without being embarrassed and without embarrassing her family's name of Tsínga in Chryssó. So, um, that home belonged to us, and when my mother went down to Itéa she rented a home for us, a lovely home, which during the war years the landlord could not get rid of you because if you didn't have money to pay, there was a law that you could stay indefinitely until the war was over and that's the way we ended up being able to stay there.

The following story was told to me by my own mother during the occasion of her first visit to me in Berlin, Germany, my adopted home, a city I know better than any other. There had been many discussions about my parents' visiting me there during my frequent stays over the decades, but none had ever materialized. In October 2005, with my brother Tom able to stay with our father full time, our mother finally made the trip. I hadn't seen my mother since my own trip to Greece to research this book two months prior, so I was eager to share my discoveries with her. I had barely allowed her to get over jetlag before I started asking for her version of some stories I'd heard for the first time in Greece that year. I remember feeling bad about just jumping in with these stories and questions, but luckily I did, because we only had two days of fun before the phone calls started coming from the United States that my father was having another health crisis. My mother stayed the programmed number of days, but her peace of mind was gone.

My mother was my paternal grandmother's first daughter-in-law and the only one of the eventual three who had grown up in Greece. My mother stayed in my paternal grandparents' home in New Jersey for several months before my parents were married in 1954, and we visited them frequently during my childhood. Whatever tensions there may have been between mother-in-law and daughter-in-law—and my oldest sister claims there were many—my grandmother talked to my mother a lot. When I recently blurted out in sheer admiration to my mother how amazing I thought it was that she could remember so many names of my father's relatives and friends from stories she had heard in many cases literally forty to fifty years before, she told me, "I was young and interested." This is what my mother told me my grandmother had told her about the house in Chryssó. I was fascinated by how my mother immediately segued into a story about my father that I had never heard before and how that in turn led her to explaining to me a big difference between her experience of wartime Greece as a child and my father's. It is not irrelevant that my mother is a middle child and three and a half years younger than my father.

LUCIE: Yiayia and Pappou didn't have a lot of money in the thirties, but

12. Earliest surviving photograph of Chrysoúla Kacandes and her children after their August 1937 arrival in Greece, presumably in courtyard of rented home in Itéa. Left to right: Harry, John, Pearl, and Chrysoúla, who wrote to her husband that their baby son, Nicholas, was asleep when the photo was taken.

Pappou sent money to Yiayia's parents to fix up their home in Chryssó. The idea was that whenever Yiayia would get there, the house would be hers. But her parents wanted to marry off her younger sister, Loukía, and so they gave Loukía the house as a dowry. When Yiayia got to Greece in 1937, she discovered that the house wasn't hers. So she went down to Itéa and rented a house where they lived okay. First they lived in one house, then in another. Your father went to live for a while with his theia Despoúla, his mother's older sister, in Galaxídi, the next town over from

Itéa. Her husband was a master carpenter, and your father was enamored of him. But they couldn't take care of—they just couldn't take a kid in.

IRENE: You mean, Dad would have liked to learn carpentry?

LUCIE: Yes, but they wouldn't keep him. Their primary concern was their own family. I didn't feel that when I was growing up. We could go to any relative's house and it was home. Well, Theia Despoúla was taking care of her mother-in-law and of course she had her own children.

3

School Closing or **abandoned** and **trapped**

Daddy went to a private boarding school that they closed down suddenly when the war broke out. He was wandering the streets of Athens by himself trying to earn money and find Yiayia.

Like the image I had of my grandmother being physically turned out of her own house, for years I had a picture in my mind of my father as a boy being pushed out of a school building and having the door locked behind him. The idea of the war in Greece starting suddenly has a basis in historical fact. But what really terrified me as a kid was the idea of my father being completely cut off from his own family and having to find his way back to them from a chaotic urban space; I had been in New York City enough times to know I wouldn't want to be lost there or left alone. When I finally got my father to talk to me directly about his stay in Greece, his school and how it closed was the first topic I pursued with him.

3a

The following story came out Easter weekend 2005 in the first interview I got my father to give to me about his wartime experiences. We were sitting at my parents' dining room table with a huge map of Athens that I had had put on poster board to use in teaching my Greek language courses and that I was hoping would now stimulate my father's memory. My mother was going back and forth between the dining room and the kitchen. We started out by spending a lot of time trying to locate "the school," which turned out to be called Χατζηκωνσταντίνου (Chatzikonstantínou) and to be, alas, just out of range of what was included on the map we had in front of us. After telling me about the great view from the school and about playing hooky with his friend Giórgios Papandréou, my father started to narrate the end of his school days, which led him to a variety of other topics, jumping chronologically. Since this was the very first time he had ever agreed to talk to me, I mainly tried to just keep the conversation going, but I note now my repeated efforts to get him to tell me about the closing of the school. The way I phrased the questions reveals the version of the story I had in my head from early childhood. We both had plenty of historical facts wrong. I had not yet done any reading up on wartime Greece and was going by accumulated (and imprecise) knowledge.

JOHN: So I spent three years there 'til the American kids started to leave, come back to the States because of the war. It had already been rumbling and by the time . . .

IRENE: So there were other Greek Americans there?

JOHN: Oh yeah, most of the students were Greek Americans.

IRENE: That's interesting. I don't think I knew that. So they started to go back home . . .

JOHN: The big, the big—I don't know where my address book is—

IRENE: It's okay, Daddy. Let's just leave that for now. I'll make a list of questions and we'll try to look all that up later.

JOHN: Sakellaríou is the big name . . .

IRENE: And who was that?

JOHN: During the war he was head of third police precinct; Tríti

13. Believed to be portrait of Sakellaríou,
head of the Fourth Police Precinct in Athens,
Greece, during the occupation.

Septemvríou [Third of September; name of a street in central Athens].
He had a niece [John coughs] in the school, and she got out; she got back
to the States. Her uncle more or less looked after me when he realized
that I was trapped there. Her uncle had a big job during the occupation.
He was captain of a precinct and at this precinct off Plateía Káningos—
between Káningos and Tríti Septemvríou was the police station [plateía
means "square" and "Káningos" is a proper name]. And underneath
there were the cooks, and then they had a room where they had me and
the assistant cooks. There were two brothers, Leonídas and Pantelís.
    What were their last names, Loukía, you remember?

LUCIE: Andriótes . . .

IRENE: What?

LUCIE AND JOHN: Andriótes; they were from Ándros.

JOHN: They were from Ándros. Their father was a captain from Ándros. Well anyway, so . . .

I lived with them in this little room until the big changeover took—until the communists [took over] the area and then the next day, the British with the nationalist troops took over the area.

IRENE: Okay, but now you're talking about way towards the end of the war . . .

LUCIE: 1944 . . .

JOHN: Huh?

IRENE: The British didn't come into Greece until much later. Right? You know what, Dad? Can I just pick up a few other issues? You know, when you were going to this school, Uncle Harry was school age too. Was he going to school in Itéa? He was going to some δημοτικό [public; referring here to elementary school] in Itéa?

JOHN: Yes, δημοτικό in Itéa.

IRENE: And Aunt Pearl was too young?

JOHN: Well, maybe she was in school, too. Uncle Nick was too young.

IRENE: So what do you remember about the day they actually dissolved the school? Were you just kind of going along . . .

JOHN: The school? No . . .

IRENE: How did that happen that?

JOHN: I think probably that probably Italy had started the war in Albania and, um, when we got to—

When my mother got notice to report to the American embassy, whatever date they invaded Greece, I don't know . . .

IRENE: October 29, 1940, yup?

JOHN: And then we, we were already on our way to Athens to leave with the last of the Americans before the German occupation. But we got as far as Θήβα—Thebes is a big city before Athens . . .

IRENE: Yup . . .

JOHN: —and from those plains we watched the Germans parachute into Athens . . .

IRENE: Uh-hum; you actually saw that yourself?

JOHN: Oh yeah.

IRENE: Now how did you get back to Itéa? What point did you go to Itéa?

JOHN: They had these buses.

IRENE: I'm still trying to get to the moment when school kind of stopped; I mean what . . .

JOHN: Well, when the school stopped in Fáliro [area of southern Athens where the school was located] . . .

IRENE: They just announced to you? Go home?

JOHN: My mother withdrew me στο-στην Ιτέα [to Itéa]. And then we were—they were bombing the port of Itéa with Stukas, and so we went up to Kolopetinítsa to stay in my father's house. So we spent a couple months up there in Kolopetinítsa.

3b

The idea that my grandmother had actually come to Athens to retrieve her son made, of course, much more sense than the idea that the school just shoved a ten-and-a-half-year-old child out the door at the announcement of war—although that probably happened in various places, too. This freed me up to wonder when my father actually did leave school. During the interview with my father described in 1b, my mother responded to a query my cousin Nick made about how my father got back and forth between Athens and Itéa with an additional comment that offers not only a different date, but a different reason for the conclusion of my father's private schooling.

NICK: How did you get back and forth between the village and Athens? Did you go a lot?

LUCIE: You didn't just go back and forth on a whim. It was a long distance. Every few months. In 1940 his mother didn't get the money [from her husband in America], so John had to leave the school.

4

Mountain Stories *or* Message Runner for the Greek Underground *or* **terrified**

Daddy ran messages for the Greek underground in the mountains because he was just a boy. The Germans didn't suspect him, but it was scary anyway.

If there is a single pervasive image from the war that circulates in my extended family, it would probably be of the young Kacandes boys roaming the countryside near Delphi. My aunt Stella, Harry's wife, put it to me this way in August 2005: "Harry was left to run—literally." Harry and Stella's only daughter, my cousin Dina, had expressed a similar sentiment to me several months earlier: "They were still kids, running over the hills like they could dodge death." Run they did, sometimes openly, often surreptitiously in the hills and mountains that surround the lóngos, the sea of olive trees that spreads from Delphi in the north through Chryssó, to Itéa on the coast in the south. Mount Parnassós (1,915 meters) dominates. An even taller mountain named Gióna (2,510 meters) looms to the north and west.

In the early years of the war, my father traveled through this area selling the fish he was given as pay for helping with the catch. My uncle Harry spent a lot of time in the hills watching sheep. I wonder if my uncle Nick did something similar when he was older toward the end of their stay. Both Uncle Harry and Uncle Nick had passed away years before I began this project: Nick, the youngest, in 1992 to cancer, and Harry, in 2003, succumbing to pneumonia after years of successfully dealing with his heart condition. Nick, according to his children, never talked about his years in Greece. However, Harry, like my father, hoped to write his memoirs one day; in the course of my research I found out that he had also tried to recruit several family members for the task. I wonder what would have happened if he had asked me? When my aunt moved out of the house she and Harry had shared for decades, she found dozens of notebooks with a single sentence or sometimes two of reminiscences. What Harry did manage to complete before dying was a personal map of the area indicating not only the towns and homes of people they knew, but also the location of various skirmishes with the occupiers. To me the map demonstrated how intimately Harry knew the area as a child traversing these hills on foot and how strong the memories of it were for him to the end of his life.

It turns out that even the women in the family traveled through this area alone. Above all, my grandmother would crisscross the region trying to sell or barter the items she had woven on her loom. When food became particularly scarce, my aunt Pearl was sent to live with a family in Livadiá, so she would have had to travel through from southwest to northeast and eventually back when my grandmother became deathly ill. A first cousin on the maternal side, Zoé Paphíli—Zoé was born to my grandmother's older sister, Despoúla, one year before my father—would travel, taking food from the village Tolophónas near Eratiní, where her father was trying to make a living during the war as a carpenter and jack-of-all-trades, down the hill and along the coast to her paternal grandmother in Galaxídi, just to the west of Itéa, and also on the Corinthian Gulf. Zoé told me it would take her eight hours to walk one way.

Having traveled these hills and mountain roads myself now, though mainly by car, I am even more astounded by these stories as an adult than I was as a child. The terrain is very steep and the rock is often precariously loose. The sun is unrelenting in summer and the cold is piercing in winter. Having now also studied the history of the war and occupation, I can only marvel and give thanks that none of my family was killed on these treks. The area was filled with Germans, then Italians, then Germans again. And from late 1941 on, those outsiders were being stalked by Greek resistance fighters of various political convictions ranging from ardently royalist to committed republican to fiercely communist. A small number of British commandos also infiltrated the area, trying to support the resisters in their efforts to disturb the occupiers and their supply routes.

4a

In addition to the backdrop—and sometimes foreground—of danger, I am struck that family members always seem to have been alone when they were traveling through the hills. One story that could be considered an exception occurs in a segue my father made from talking about grazing his own sheep in the mountains to going to the *lóngos* itself with his brother Harry. This is the only time my father talked to me about "the mountains" and "arrest," so I begin with this story, which came out in the same interview referred to in 1b and 3b; my father, my mother, my cousin Nick, and I were present. Note that the "them" at the conclusion refers to those who ran the jail, the local Greek collaborationist police. Chémo is the cousin of my grandmother who narrates in 1c and the third child of the Gerentés family mentioned several times previously.

IRENE: You once told me a story about being in Kolopetinítsa, Dad. Was it goats or sheep you had?

JOHN: I had my own sheep. I remember, I had the largest ram in the area. We used to make money off him. When we were getting ready to leave [in 1945], I gave it to my uncle. I didn't want to slaughter it. I had raised them up. Wherever I went, so did the sheep. My uncle had promised to

14. John and Kítsos, the ram, Easter 1945, Itéa. Also
pictured are (left to right) Panagioú, Pearl (with local dog),
Chrysoúla, and Harry and Nick with the sheep.

send us feta cheese here to America, until he decided one day that my ram took my sheep and some of his and jumped off a cliff—my uncle claimed the sheep committed suicide!

LUCIE: —So that he didn't have to send him anything more. Well, he never sent him anything anyway.

IRENE: Dad, where did you take those sheep so they could eat?

JOHN: To the mountains.

IRENE: You could go wherever you wanted?

LUCIE: There were free spots that belonged to everybody.

IRENE: Did you come home every night or would you go for several days and then come back?

JOHN: Did you ever see my father's house? How was it?

IRENE: It was small, but there were two parts. And one part was for the animals. The sheep stayed on the ground floor.

LUCIE: There was a μαντρί [madrí].

JOHN: Τι λες; [What are you saying?]

LUCIE: Ξέρεις τι θα πει μαντρί; [Do you know what madrí means?]

JOHN: Of course.

IRENE: Εγώ δεν ξέρω τι θα πει. [I don't know what it means.]

LUCIE: Μαντρί, sheepfold. The animals did not always sleep in the house. In the winter they stayed there to keep the people warm, but most of the year, they stayed outside.

IRENE: Did every family have animals, Dad?

JOHN: Most people did. Not everybody. See, Greece is very hot. We used to go to the λόγγο [lóngo] to stay cool at night.

IRENE: I know lóngos can be a place name, but what is its common meaning?

JOHN: You slept in the woods. Lóngos. That's the area from Itéa to

15. View of the *lóngos* from Delphi toward the Corinthian Gulf.
Identity of shepherd and exact date unknown, by 1930.

Ámphissa. It's covered with olive trees. We would pick up the olives that had fallen.

IRENE: I don't know what that's called in Greek, but there's a really great word in English for it. Gleaners. Those are the people who come after the harvest and are allowed to pick up what was left behind. So, did you do that, Dad? Was that hard work?

[Lucie comes back with the Greek–English dictionary.]

LUCIE: *Lóngos*: wood, grove, thicket, forest.

JOHN: It was hard work because they had police guarding the property.

NICK: So one of you would play lookout and the other would pick things up?

IRENE: Is that something you and Uncle Harry would do?

JOHN: I remember one time they caught me and they threw us in the jail. The jail was at Chémo's house.

IRENE: Oh yeah?

LUCIE: The jail was downstairs.

JOHN: No, upstairs was the jail. Downstairs were the αποθήκες [storage areas]. My aunt used to cook for them.

LUCIE: She always gave you something to eat.

NICK: Who got caught more, you or Uncle Harry? He was the lookout guy?

[No response. Long silence. Irene introduces a new topic.]

4b

During my childhood, I never remember hearing anything about picking up olives or about my father or uncle going to jail. But as I recounted in chapter 1, I had been confronted with the idea that my father might have stolen things to feed himself and his family when I finally visited the birthplace of my grandfather, Kolopetinítsa. I was almost dumbfounded when my cousin Dina, Harry's only daughter, reported a very similar experience that had happened to her when she had visited Itéa with her older brother, George, in other words, different protagonists, different place, different year, same accusation. At the time Dina recounted this story to me, I was visiting her in her home in Watertown, Massachusetts. It was June 2005 and I had just come from visiting a close friend who was dying of AIDS. I was about to visit another close friend who had recently received a diagnosis of advanced lung cancer. As if that wasn't enough of an emotional load, it was the weekend of my twenty-fifth reunion at Harvard. I had decided I couldn't handle the official reunion events, but I was scheduled to have brunch with my former roommates and their families. My hours with my cousin were a welcome reprieve from the stress. I had explained my family history project to Dina, and my question about how much she knew about what had happened to our fathers launched this series of anecdotes. For the record, Dina is one of the many blue-eyed Kacandeses. Her brother George is darker like me. Amalía Tsakíri and her husband were Greek immigrants to the United States from the same area as my grandparents in Greece, but they had emigrated before the war. They were close friends of my grandparents in New Jersey in the postwar years.

DINA: I had been to Itéa with my grandmother Pantages [Dina's mother's mother] in 1972. She said: I can't take you back to the USA without having taken you to Itéa, otherwise I'll get hell from your grandmother [our fathers' mother]. The next time I went was with my brother George in 1983. We get out of the cab and there's this guy standing there. George—who spoke pretty good Greek at the time—says to him: Do you know where the house of Amalía Tsakíri is? And without blinking, the man says to George: you're the son of Harry Kacandes. Now you know that George doesn't really look like my father. It turns out the guy was a childhood friend of my father's, and he showed us where Yiayia had lived.

IRENE: Oh yeah? I've never seen the house.

DINA: You know how those houses have these basements; well that's the kind of thing it was. Then another guy comes over. He says: What a thief your father was! George says: Thief? You're kidding me. My father wasn't a thief; they were hungry! When my dad heard this story, he said how they were eating olives that were on the ground. Of course those trees belonged to other people, but they only took what fell. This guy was looking at George. I was thinking to myself: He should have been looking at me! I'm the one who looks like a Kacandes! What are you doing calling my father a thief?

Well as a male child—all three of them were mischievous. It was the kid side of it.

IRENE: It's funny you should put it that way, Dina. When I asked my sister Georgia what she knew about our fathers in Greece, she told me that your dad had told her quite a bit about my dad and about his misadventures as a sneaky little boy. I remember she added that she could really relate to that, since she had a sneaky little boy of her own to look after these days.

DINA: [starts laughing] Yeah. Her Johnny fits the profile. To me, the interesting part is that kids in general can turn so adult when they have to, and yet even under the most extreme circumstances, they can also do something that is so kidlike.

4c

I do not remember ever hearing a story directly from my father about running messages for the underground, even though that story is part of my earliest set of knowledge about my parents. Some of my siblings, though, do remember occasions in which this activity was recounted by my father, though as two of them attested to me very clearly, they were rarely the intended addressee for the stories. The following version comes from my brother Tom, the fifth born John Kacandes child, but the first son. I still remember the day Tom was born. My father had gotten my mother to the hospital in the early hours of the morning, and he had returned home immediately since his four daughters were home alone. We were sitting at the breakfast table waiting for my father to serve us poached eggs—the only thing he knew how to make—when the phone rang. I can repeat my father's end of the conversation as if it were last week, even though that was forty-five years ago and I was one month shy of turning five at the time: "It's okay, Doc, you don't have to lie to me. I love girls. I got four sitting right here. Is she healthy? Does she have ten fingers and ten toes? How's Lucie?" Then there was stunned silence. As if in one motion, he hung up the phone, turned off the stove, scooped up all four of us, and threw us into the car. I remember sitting with my sisters in the parking lot of White Plains Hospital waiting for our father to come back—this was long before the days when siblings could visit newborns. My father finally had his son. We were excited, too, but I don't remember the emotions as purely joyful. It was pretty impossible to mistake the royal reception for the son. As it turned out, Tom didn't have an easy row to hoe. I guess maybe Dad had had too much time to think about what he'd be doing if only it were a son he were raising instead of girls . . . This story came to me from my brother Tom via e-mail in 2004 when I had first decided to try to research what children know about the traumatic pasts of their parents. The extract below was in response to my question: "From whom and how did you find out what you know?"

> [Tom's written response:] Multiple sources: Uncle Harry and Aunt Stella. I definitely asked him [our father] about it during this period [sometime between age eight and twelve] and got some small amount of information. [. . .] I already knew something about how Dad had fought with the King George guerrillas and run messages for them through the mountains near his village as a boy my age. I was already running competitively for several years (from the age of seven, strictly speaking) and this was a point of connection with my dad, who coached track at

the high school and encouraged me in it. He had made a comment that he had been seven when the war started and how I should appreciate the track meets he took me to because at that age he had hiked for miles to go to work, miles to go for food, and had run bare foot through stones at night to "avoid the German soldiers." I had seen his black beret from his teenage association with Montgomery's British troops. All this information was so sketchy that even today I do not trust what I "know" about any of it, because so little came from him directly and the information was almost never directed at me. If he told me tomorrow it was something completely different, I would believe him.

<h2 style="text-align:center">4d</h2>

Our oldest sister Maria, three years my senior, not only remembers a lot of stories related to our father being in the mountains, but also the occasions on which Dad recited them. In late December 2005 this businesswoman sister flew from her home in London to join me in Washington DC, at the annual conference of my professional association, the Modern Language Association, where she was invited to speak about negotiating strategies for women. I took the opportunity of being alone with her during the long car ride from the conference to my parents in White Plains to ask her too what she knew of our father's experiences in Greece. (I had not queried Maria when I first launched my Holocaust generations project in spring 2004 because she was dealing with major health issues in her own nuclear family.) The following excerpt, I noted when I did the transcription, was related to me as we were driving up the New Jersey Turnpike. We had been on this road together scores of times before as children, on our way to our grandparents and other relatives on the Jersey shore.

MARIA: You know, I remember stories about him living in caves and walking miles and things that happened in villages; soldiers—how many times did you hear the stories about cigarette marks or burns or the scars on Daddy's arm and where they came from?

IRENE: Wow! This is really helpful to me, Maria, because, actually I never heard that story until I started doing this research; Tom and Pete had heard it, but I have no conscious memory—I don't remember hearing the story.

MARIA: I heard that story so many times, hundreds of times growing up.

IRENE: And every time it was different?

MARIA: Something happened to him, but exactly what happened—and it wasn't something nice. I think the retelling of it was to exorcise the ghost and part of it was a way of getting attention and sympathy. Now as an adult and as a parent of children—the fact that he was so desperate for feedback—because I can remember some of the contexts. Now with my adult critical judgment, I would say you wouldn't launch into that kind of story. And the other thing was Dad would tell that story about scars whenever he wanted to say how good life was for you; he wanted to make you feel guilty for what you had; appreciate what you had; that was the only way he knew how to do that: "but for the grace of God you could be suffering there too"; "not everybody is as lucky that they don't have those kinds of people lurking about them, trying to steal their food." I think most Greek people—and I don't know nearly as many Greek people of that age as you do—but all of the ones I know, all have an unbelievable relationship to food.

Χόρτα was a big thing. [Hórta is a general word for edible green grass vegetables, like dandelion leaves. They are normally boiled and eaten with lemon and olive oil—if you have them.] We ate a lot of hórta as kids, especially in comparison to the average American diet.

It was almost Jewish in its nature, that the home becomes the church where the stories are told; the religion is inculcated in you that way. And to me now that's what it feels like. You were being educated into this religion because those stories were always told in the home. And I cannot to this day eat bitter green vegetables without being flooded with memories of Dad telling those stories.

IRENE: Whoah! You were not alone—I mean you were alone just for one year; then Tina was there, I was there, but I could never say what you just said. I have big lectures in my mind about eating food: "eat every scrap on your plates!" but I only remember that being related to the war in the most vague way.

MARIA: "All we had to eat was hórta for weeks and weeks and weeks." And "that's when you need to appreciate what grows in the ground and can keep you alive."

IRENE: [laughing] Do you not like hórta? 'Cause I love hórta.

MARIA: And so do I; the older I get, the more I enjoy the taste.

IRENE: So there was the scar; there was eating hórta that triggered story telling.

[...]

MARIA: I remember being told about Daddy carrying messages; I was there, but not as part of the audience, as parked in the back of the room, as being babysat for. He was carrying a message from one village to another; they hid him somewhere behind a door. Nazis came. They dragged everyone outside; shot them all, and then went away. And then Daddy made his escape. And he shit in his pants he was so scared.

IRENE: Interesting detail . . . [pause] So he was hiding behind a door? That's also a story I've never heard before. Do you remember other people's reactions to these stories?

MARIA: He always got a huge amount of sympathy: "it's amazing you survived"; "look at how well you survived." My observation as a kid was less about the information, but rather that he would launch into these stories when he needed some kind of pumping up.

IRENE: You remember having that thought?

MARIA: Very distinctly.

Even given the many recent times I have talked to my father about the war, I have never heard from him directly about his activities for the underground. He does possess a document in Greek dated "25 October 1946" that states that he "served as a guerrilla in the National Resistance group of the 5/42 Evzone Regiment" and that, following that group's dissolution, he worked with "secret armed organizations on behalf of the Allied armies." The document is signed by a man named Efthémios Dedoúsis, who in the document itself is identified as "captain and now representative [to the Parliament]" and who my father described to me as "the commanding officer of 'Psarroú' [the 5/42 regiment]."

JOHN: Dedoúsis was such a popular hero in our area that he was elected Congressman. This guy was a very famous hero because the Germans had captured him and had taken one tooth at a time out of his mouth.

When I found this document along with two British ones from 1945 attesting to my father's service for the 50th Royal Tank Regiment of the British Army, I asked my father about them all. Although Dad had referred often to his "discharge papers," and the testament from the British Captain Bond was quoted in the 1945 newspaper article about my father, I had never seen any of these documents before, so I was particularly excited to hold these pieces of paper in my own hands. They seemed like my first direct connection to History, to Dad's role in History. However, I was also intentionally trying to distract my father with my many questions and my attention to each detail in the documents, because my mother had left earlier that morning for London to visit my sister Maria and her family, and about an hour after my brother had dropped her at the airport, we heard the news that the London subways and buses had been attacked. It was July 7, 2005.

Proving that he had worked on behalf of the Allied cause in the Second World War had become critical to my father in the mid-1950s, because, as he told me on that July day in 2005: "I didn't want to go into ROTC." I certainly understand his reluctance to serving. The ROTC stood between him and his diploma, and a new phase in his life: he had met my mother, gotten married, and they were expecting their first child. I'm still not sure to this day why the British documents weren't sufficiently impressive proof to the ROTC at Cornell that my father had fought in the war, but they were not. Perhaps because they were literally produced in wartime and therefore didn't have any fancy stamps like the postwar document from Greece? In any case, it quickly became clear to me the day I found the file with the documents and asked my father about them that the Greek document served an almost fetishistic function for him.

JOHN: That was the only living proof [of my involvement in the resistance] besides my relatives, you know, my cousins who took me up there.

I was a little disappointed, but not completely surprised, when I showed the document to friends in Greece and they told me similar ones were produced by the kilo in that period, often attesting to resistance that was not actually waged by the individual possessing the document. I do not doubt that my father had some type of contact with the guerrillas. One day after my 2005 research trip to Greece I showed him a book about Psarrós's partisans. Dad looked at a list of participants and immediately pointed to two names he recognized. I have not been able, however, to verify any details about what he did or saw "up there."

5

Family Deaths and Near Deaths during the Occupation or The Evil Uncle or **betrayed** and **starved**

They were so hungry. They survived because there were so many dead people that they were always giving out that nice wheat stuff at church.

Daddy's grandparents were starving. One day his grandfather found the place where his grandmother hid the olive oil. He couldn't help himself. He drank so much olive oil he died.

If the single pervasive image of my father's family during the war is of running through the hills, the single dominant legacy would be an obsession with food. Observing her Holocaust survivor parents, author Lisa Appignanesi describes "the ardour with which they ate" and "an unstoppable hunger as if food were a novelty which might disappear at any moment" (1999, 19). I have quoted my sister Maria's realization in the previous section, that all the Greek people she knew of a certain age had an "unbelievable relationship to food." I am certainly aware of my own embarrassing obsession with getting my share. I remember reading a newspaper article in the 1980s that reported that Greek babies were the fattest infants in Europe. The researchers had traced the phenomenon to the parents' and grandparents' memories of undernourishment during the war and occupation. Even if the money my grandfather was sending my grandmother from the United States had continued to get through, procuring food would have been a daily challenge for my family. There was a whole series of problems caused by the occupation: for one thing, the Germans and the Italians (and I assume the Bulgarian occupiers as well, though I haven't read anything about this directly since the Bulgarians simply expelled as many Greeks as they could from their occupation zone) requisitioned food, regardless of the needs of the local population. The Greek partisans sometimes were, sometimes were not, more compassionate in their own demands on the locals. For another, the occupiers and the puppet Greek government handled distribution incompetently, so even when there was enough of a certain foodstuff in one region, it didn't mean the people who needed it in another region could get it. As my father's schoolmate Evgenía Argyríou had told me, the Itéa area was drowning in oil. Still, getting wheat for bread was expensive. Additionally, inflation was rampant, aggravated to the point of near financial chaos and collapse by *Besatzungskosten* (occupation costs) (Clogg 2002, 121). As my father colorfully put it when he got back to the United States in 1945, "it took a car to move your money." Of course, no one he knew had a car; he had already juxtaposed his Greek experiences into his American environment.

In the Itéa area gold sovereigns and olive oil were the basis of the economy. The gold sovereigns entered mainly through the British operatives in the region buying off silence and cooperation from the locals. An older Greek friend of mine from the town of Galaxídi, where Zoé's family was settled, claimed that virtually every Greek there was receiving such "cooperation" payments from the British. The black market flourished in Roúmeli, as it did all over Greece. Because my grandmother didn't have either form of "currency," she had to barter her household goods and beg. When I traveled to this region in 2005, numerous people I spoke with, related to my father's family and not, kept repeating two refrains: Υπέφεραν πολύ [They suffered badly]; and Τους δώσαμε φαΐ εμείς [We gave them food]. When I would ask specifically about the deaths of my great-grandparents, each speaker insisted to me that it was impossible they had starved. No one here died from starvation, they kept saying. That's not what I have heard from my own family.

5a

The story I must have been exposed to as a child was related to me again by my mother recently when I reported to her about my informants in the Itéa area saying it was impossible that my great-grandparents had starved to death.

LUCIE: His wife had already died of hunger. Somehow he got hold of some oil. I don't know where or how much, but τον εθέρισε.

IRENE: What does that mean?

LUCIE: It cut him down. Like the wheat during harvest. The oil overwhelmed his system, and he died immediately.

5b

The following story comes from a telephone call I made to my father's first cousin Zoé, née Paphíli, in Greece in July 2006, because I hoped she, as the oldest grandchild, might remember how her grandparents

Tsíngas had died. I had not yet had the chance to meet Zoé in person, but my father had fond memories of her, and one day when I was with him in White Plains, we called her in Athens, and I introduced myself on the phone. She was very friendly and lively, and her memory seemed to be much more intact than my father's, even though she is a year older and was fighting cancer. My second conversation with her, as the previous one, took place entirely in Greek. When I described my project and its challenges to her, she told me without hesitating:

ZOÉ: Ότι σου λέω είναι αλήθεια. [Whatever I tell you is the truth.]

I didn't mention to her what I'd been told by others until after I heard her version. I asked her how her maternal grandparents died. Without a second's pause, she answered:

ZOÉ: Πεινούσανε. Από την πείνα. [They were starving. They died from starvation.]

I then told her the story I had heard the prior summer from her first cousin Ólga, her uncle John's youngest child, born 1940, that their maternal grandmother Asymoúla had had some kind of operation, that it had gone badly and that she had died, probably from an infection, and her husband Harálambos then died shortly thereafter from grief. Zoé responded again, without hesitation:

ZOÉ: Εγώ δεν έχω ακούσει τίποτε για μια εγχείριση. [I never heard anything about any kind of operation.] Πέθαναν από την πείνα. [They died of hunger.] Ο Παππούς ήτανε κόκκαλο. [Grandpa was skin and bones.]

It was only then that I mentioned how many times I was told in summer 2005 that the area had enough to eat during the war and that nobody died of hunger. She shot down that generalization immediately.

ZOÉ: Σχεδόν όλοι είχανε δυσκολίες να βρούνε αρκετά να τρώνε. [Almost everybody had troubles finding enough to eat.] Πολλοί γέροι πέθαναν από την πείνα. Αλλά οι νέοι πέθαναν πιο πολύ από τη φυματίωση. [Many older people died from hunger. But the young ones died more frequently from tuberculosis.]

5c

My aunt Pearl gave me much insight into the extremity of the search for food experienced by our family during the occupation. In this short sequence from the long interview I did with her in December 2005, one sees a whole range of possible reactions to another's suffering: generosity, exploitation, indifference. From the recitals of my aunt and of my father that follow, I finally understood as an adult why I believed from earliest childhood that there was an "evil relative" who had done harm to my family. This excerpt from my interview with Aunt Pearl includes and is embedded in stories of sexual exploitation of female members of my family, a topic I take up explicitly later (section 7). My aunt was probably seven to eight years old during the events she recounts here. Itéa is downhill from Chryssó.

PEARL: My mother would send me to ask this male neighbor for food, and the only way he would give me anything was if he used me a little bit, not to a great degree, but just I mean fondling me. I hated him, and I would beg my mother not to let me go, and I couldn't tell her what was happening to me, because I knew we were starving and we needed food. If it wasn't for Chémo's family [the Gerentéses], I mean they always had enough and Voúla her sister—we were much closer to Voúla than we were to Chémo and she was the oldest one and she was a wonderful woman, and she would sneak olives and olive oil you know for us to—

They all, everyone knew in Itéa we were starving, and Yiayia and Pappou [meaning her maternal grandparents, my great-grandparents], honey, they both died within twenty-two days from starvation. You know my mother's parents both died from starvation?

IRENE: Well, you know, Aunt Pearl, that's what I heard, and one of the things that was very surprising to me when I went this summer [2005] was that everybody denied that, that particular piece. They didn't deny that Yiayia, my grandmother, suffered very much. They didn't deny that—

PEARL: Yeah, but who, honey?

IRENE: Well . . .

PEARL: Pappou's family, Pappou's family? They weren't my mother's were they?

IRENE: No, no, I can tell you exactly who.

PEARL: Tell me.

IRENE: From two different sources. One source was in Chryssó; I don't know what her maiden name was, unfortunately. Her married name is Kontagiórgou, and she is definitely older than you are. I think she's younger than Yiayia would have been if she were alive and, uh, and they and other sources I asked said nobody starved in that area.

PEARL: Wow . . .

IRENE: That was one thing. Then another source was a woman, I'll give you her exact name because I'd like to know what you know about her. I asked Theia Chémo too.

PEARL: Yeah, what did Chémo say? Now, she would know.

IRENE: Her name was Evgenía Argyríou.

PEARL: Yeah.

IRENE: She's Daddy's age. She was born the same year as Daddy. She also insisted that no one starved in the whole area . . .

PEARL: Including my mother?

IRENE: She kept insisting that there was lots of food. She kept saying: Υπέφερε. Υπέφερε πολύ αυτή η γυναίκα. [She suffered. That woman suffered a lot.] But she also kept saying: Τους δώσαμε εμείς να φάνε. [We, we gave them food to eat.]

16. Portrait of Giánnis (John) Tsíngas, sent by him
to my grandparents in the United States in 1930.

PEARL: That's the pride, honey.

IRENE: I know. I know. It's so interesting. Everyone claims to have given you guys food. And the other people of course were—and this is harder I'm sure for you to hear—but I made contact for the very first time in my whole life with Ólga and Chrysoúla, Uncle John's girls.

PEARL: You know, Chrysoúla, now, she was named after my mother.

IRENE: Yes! Oh yeah.

PEARL: That's how much her brother loved my mother until he turned his back on her. He was—

IRENE: Right . . .

PEARL: He was in the black market. He had all—honey, your dad—I don't know if he recalls this story—but your dad, who really lived in Athens most of the time, he would come to visit us, and he came when Pappou was dying, my mother's father, and my Pappou said to your dad, he went up to Chryssó to see him, he said to your dad: Πήγαινε στο γιο μου και πες του να σου δώσει ένα ποτηράκι κρασί και ένα κομμάτι ψωμί να φάω πριν ξεψυχίσω—πριν πεθάνω. [Go to my son and tell him to give you a little glass of wine and a piece of bread for me to eat before I expire—before I die.] And your dad went down to Uncle John's and asked, and you know what his response was? Να πας και να πεις στο γέρο· Εδώ πεθαίνουν οι νέοι και θα φοβηθούμε τον γέρο να πεθάνει; [Go and tell the old geezer, here the young people are dying, and we're going to fret about the old man who's going to die?] And your brother—your dad came down, went up and told Pappou. And his last breath was taken cursing his son. It was very sad. My mother was furious at John, at her son, for going back to her father and giving that message. So honey, they were suffering.

IRENE: That's what I always heard, Aunt Pearl . . .

PEARL: And the suffering, honey, that came to Yiayia and Pappou would never have happened, but they lived with Theia Loukía. So they would take the food away from themselves and give it to Theia Loukía and her children. See, they lived with them.

5d

My father has revealed his recollections of the famine and its effects on his family in little snippets of conversation and in various forms. In the first extended conversation I had with him on April 30, 2005, I found out for the first time that he did not witness the "great famine" of 1941–42 in Athens, where, as I had learned as a teenager from historical sources, people literally were dropping dead in the street from starvation and

17. Chrysoúla at her loom with her children, taken in
their rental home in Itéa, August 1940. Left to right:
Nicholas, Chrysoúla, John, Pearl, Harry.

which I had long assumed—incorrectly—he had personally seen. He
told me, rather, that at that point in the war he was in Itéa:

IRENE: So, in the village do you remember some situations where it
was particularly tight, or could people usually manage to just eat
something?

JOHN: Oh sure, it was very tight—are you kidding? Yiayia used to have to sell her ρούχα [clothes, clothing] from the αργαλειό [loom] that she used to make; we had πεντέξι μπαούλες γεμάτα ρούχα [five–six chests filled with clothes] that she had made all during you know the three years that she was there, that was her ambition. All of that, we sold one piece at a time, για λάδι, για— [for oil, for—], whatever it . . .

IRENE: Whatever it was.

JOHN: Yeah.

5e

When I began to pursue more consciously my family's wartime stories, I realized both that I didn't have a clue who the mean relative from my early memories actually was, and also that in that first long interview of April 30, 2005, such a relative did not make an appearance in my father's narration. So on July 7, 2005, I asked my father about it point blank:

IRENE: So, Dad, who was the relative you hated so much?

JOHN: My mother's brother, John Tsíngas. His daughter lives in Itéa [now], across from the [can't make out word]. He was a black marketeer. He had lots of dealings with the Germans and became rich off them. When my mother was very sick, she needed ενέσεις [injections], and I went to my uncle John. He had pictures we had sent him of the *Morro Castle*, that's a luxury liner that had burned off the coast of New Jersey— he had a calendar of it from us in his store! He told me whatever he had είναι για τα παιδιά μου, όχι για τη μητέρα σου. Γιατί να έχει έρθει χωρίς τον άντρα της; [It's for my children, not for your mother. Why did she come without her husband?]

5f

I received a very similar version of events about a year later when I posed a different question to my father:

IRENE: Was it obvious during the war who was doing the black market?

JOHN: My uncle was the worst one of all. My mother got very sick. I'm trying to think what she had. She needed injections. During the war period these things were very very expensive. I remember going to him to—I'm trying to think. I don't remember whether it was pneumonia or what. My uncle, who at that time still had his store decorated with a photo of the *Morro Castle* cruise liner, which caught fire at Asbury Park, he had those photos in his store. I asked my uncle John: Θα μας δώσεις τις ενέσεις που χρειάζεται; [Are you going to give us the shots that my mother needs?] And he answered: I'm not going to punish my own kids by giving you something for free. [short silence, big sigh] I'm trying to think who ever helped us.

5g

When I asked my aunt Pearl how my grandmother managed to get better, she said:

PEARL: Oh, people came and brought food. But my uncle John—when your dad appealed to him for help, he said: Ας πεθάνει αύριο! [Let her die tomorrow!]

6

The Vellisários

The *Vellisários* was a traditional Greek caïque captained by a Greek man named Pétros Tsardákas (a.k.a. Captain Pétros) and requisitioned by the Germans during the occupation. My father crewed on this boat for a period of several months in what I'm fairly certain must have been 1943. I don't recall being told anything about the *Vellisários* when I was young, although I've had so many indications by now that I must have been an auditor to certain stories, even though I don't consciously remember hearing them, that I don't exclude the possibility that I had heard some version(s) of this tale too. Its themes of danger, near death, and being saved were definitely elements of (other) stories I thought I did know. Furthermore, the coprotagonist, the owner of the *Vellisários*, Captain Pétros, was the only actor—other than my father, aunt, uncles, and grandparents—in any of these war stories with whom I actually had had contact during my childhood. Pete Tsardákas and his wife, Marge, visited us in our home in White Plains, and we sometimes went to their apartment in Far Rockaway, New York. In 1967 Tsardákas baptized my youngest brother, who was given his name, Pétros. Even though we saw Pete and Marge often throughout my childhood, they seemed to me like they belonged to another world. Marge made her own clothes, and I remember being fascinated by the mannequin set to her exact measurements which stood in her sewing room. Marge and Pete were older than my own parents; they dressed fashionably, in a manner that I didn't recognize anyway; Marge died her hair jet black, wore a lot of make-up, and had plucked eyebrows; Pete was perpetually tanned. They didn't have children of their own, and while they did converse with us kids, the message was often one I couldn't or didn't want to relate to. Somehow they always managed to make clear that they had money and we didn't. I remember in particular one lecture from Uncle Pete that made me really angry: he told us that we'd better watch our weight, because as girls, the only chance we had in life would be if we were attractive and could marry men who would take care of us. Being beautiful is the only important thing for women, he warned us. I don't remember how old I was at the time—probably between eight and ten—but I can still feel the combination of self-consciousness, embarrassment, and fury his words provoked in me. Sometimes I think I started to gain weight around that age just to spite him. In any case, and most fortunately for us, our parents held different beliefs about girls; all four of us daughters went to college and have careers.

6a

Given that he was named after Tsardákas, it didn't surprise me that my brother Peter was the only one of my siblings to volunteer a story that included the ship. Actually, the "story" is more of a fragment in a list of vignettes about our father he had heard at some point or other and which Peter sent to me in the 2004 e-mail when I launched my project on children of survivors' relations to their parents' stories. Peter felt he didn't know much about my parents' wartime experience—though he would have liked to know more, adding that he had heard some stories from people outside the family and had also tried to elicit information from my parents directly. As I mentioned in chapter 1, Pete had once dedicated a part of his Web site to family stories, but none of us had responded by adding to or modifying its content.

[Peter's written response:] [. . .] our father was working on a freighter that was sunk by an Allied sub and he was saved by my godfather for whom I am named. What are the details of that? Again, it's all just little pieces here and there with no continuity. I understand that these memories are painful for them and they don't want to talk about it, so I have never really pushed it, but it also leaves me feeling very unsatisfied.

6b

In the first long interview I had with my father (Easter 2005), he told me a relatively great deal about the *Vellisários* and his time on board. I had a lot of trouble following my father during this part of our talk. Looking back on it now, I see that my confusion partly had to do with the fact that I had never heard anything about his experiences on the ship before, partly because we were trying to locate actual sites on the map in front of us, and partly because I couldn't follow the associations my father had in his own mind between sending money to his mother, the ship, and working for Pete Tsardákas's mother. I eventually figured out that his time as a crewmember began when Pete bumped into him by chance while my father was in Piraeus trying to find a caïque to ship paper currency he had earned from selling cigarettes to his mother in Itéa. Pete, according to my father, was surprised to see him, because he had assumed that my father and his family had left the country when the war broke out. My father then joined Pete and worked on his boat. Once, when the boat was docked in or at least was located near the dock in Piraeus, a larger boat near it was bombed—presumably by the Allies—and my father was hurt in the explosion. After being treated at a hospital, he evidently spent time recuperating at the Tsardákas home and working for Pete's parents. That sounds rather clear, I believe; however, this is how the actual interchange between my parents and me unfolded:

JOHN: Wha—what was happening was I was selling cigarettes . . .

IRENE: Right.

JOHN: . . . in Athens. Now I remember. And uh, every so often I tried to send money to my . . .

IRENE: Your mother, right . . .

JOHN: To my mother in Greece—in Itéa. And they had to be σε σακούλες μεγάλες [in big sacks]; I mean potato sacks . . .

IRENE: The cigarettes or . . .

JOHN: No, the money, the money. With the German occupation . . .

IRENE: Oh, the money, that's how you disguised it?
   [The next lines overlap, all three of us talking at once.]

LUCIE: No, they were devalued . . .

IRENE: Oh it was so devalued, oh, okay . . .

JOHN: With the German occupation you couldn't deal with Greek money . . .

IRENE: So the money was so devalued that you had to, what it really was—sent in big sacks . . .

JOHN: Yeah, by the time it got to Itéa, they rolled it up and lit the fire.

IRENE: Uh-huh.

JOHN: Anyway during one of those times, [pause] I was going to Piraeus to find a καΐκι [caïque] to send the money and . . .

IRENE: Oh, that's how you sent the money? Okay . . .

JOHN: And out of this area στο ρολόι [at the clock] I don't know where it would be.

What's on the other side [of the map]?

IRENE: This is Piraeus. Somewhere on this side. This side of the port I think, Ma, has changed a lot, right? Because it's big ship yards now that maybe were not so big before?

LUCIE: Where is the—if you can find where the train is . . .

IRENE: Which train? The train that comes from Athens?

LUCIE: The train that comes from Athens. "Rolói" is very close by, they must have the train marked—

IRENE: That's a train; I don't know if the subway's on here . . .

LUCIE: "To Rolói" is somewhere down here.

JOHN: It was down by the water.

IRENE: It was close to the water, okay.

[There follows more wrangling about who's reading the map best.]

IRENE: This area was called Rolói, like a clock?

JOHN: It was a seaman's clock, rolói, in front of a church on this side . . .

IRENE: Okay.

JOHN: And one of my trips to send the money to Itéa, Captain Peter jumped out, yelled my name. This is Tsardákas—

IRENE: Yeah.

JOHN: —and he thought we had left; he thought we had gone back to the U.S. He used to come with his father's kaḯki [to Itéa] and load up ελιές [olives]. But the kaḯkia during the war, they were taken by the Germans, so they were manned by the Germans. Well, so, as soon as he found me he-hi-his family lived in Kallithéa [a nice area of Athens, toward Piraeus]. So for a—for a while I was selling cigarettes, working for his mother, carrying her groceries basically; they had their own big house. His brother was a doctor and so on.

IRENE: Can we pause just for a second to find that? I know I know Kallithéa, but I can't remember where it is. Is that on the coast this way, Ma?

LUCIE: It's on the coast before Fáliro; around Fáliro . . .
  [More tussling about the location.]

LUCIE: Check around Palió Fáliro towards the city.

IRENE: Oh, here it is, Dad.

JOHN: What?

IRENE: See, Kallithéa. So they lived over there somewhere.

JOHN: Yeah, near the train station.

LUCIE: Στην Οδό Καλλιρόης . . . [on Kallirόis Street . . .]

IRENE: What was that near, Ma?

LUCIE: When I went back in '67, I went to—to find them, but they had moved.

IRENE: You found the street?

LUCIE: I found the street and the house and everything, but there were—nobody was there from the family.

IRENE: Well, anyway, it was over there. Maybe I can look for it after. Kalliroi?

LUCIE: Kallirόis . . .

IRENE: —was the name of the street. [turning to Dad] So you lived with them for a while . . .

JOHN: Who's them?

IRENE: With um, Pete Tsardákas's mother.

JOHN: Yeah. But still, my base was still in Piraeus.

IRENE: So you were talking about this one particular time when you were trying to send money to your mother—

18. John Kacandes, μούτσος (ship's boy)
of the *Vellisários*, Patrás, 1943.

JOHN: Uh, yeah, and I uh, that, Tsardákas saw me, and he thought that we had left for Greece . . .

IRENE: For the U.S.?

LUCIE: For the U.S.!

JOHN: So, when I told him what was happening, that I was trying to sell cigarettes to support my mother and all that, he says, uh, you come with me and you'll make more money. He was captain of this Greek ship that was manned by a crew of Germans and Greeks.

IRENE: And he was actually the captain?

JOHN: He was the captain.

IRENE: That's very interesting.

LUCIE: Of the *Vellisários* . . .

JOHN: *Vellisários* . . .

IRENE: That was the name of ship?

JOHN: Yeah, and our destination was Corfu, all the way up to Kérkyra and down the coast and Piraeus. ["Corfu" and "Kérkyra" are two names for the same island.]

IRENE: Uh-huh. So, the Ionian sea?

JOHN: Yeah. And it was during that—we made three or four trips by— During that, uh, time that, uh, the Americans and the Greeks had invaded Italy. Because we made two attempts from Kérkyra to run the sea and find the Americans, but our engines conked out, and the German patrol boats brought us back in, so we never made that escape.

IRENE: You mean you were going to try to go to the other side?

JOHN: Oh yeah. Yeah. Well anyway, so, I was with Captain Pétros at that time, and as I said I lived in their house, because in a bombing raid on Piraeus, our boat was anchored next to a bigger boat, and by the time I could get to the land, a barrel had fallen off and taken off part of my toe. So, now I'm walking from Piraeus heading for— [looks to Lucie] Πως το λένε το νοσοκομείο πίσω από τον εθνικό κήπο; [What's the name of that hospital behind the national garden?]

LUCIE: Ερυθρός Σταυρός; [Red Cross?]

JOHN: No, no.

LUCIE: And the other one is Πολιτικό [Politikó]—

JOHN: Politikó, yeah . . .

LUCIE: —Ευαγγελισμός; [Evangelismós?]

JOHN: No, Πολιτικό νοσοκομείο [Politikó Hospital]. His brother was a surgeon there.

IRENE: Whose brother?

JOHN: Captain Pétros's brother.

IRENE: Captain Pétros had a brother who's a surgeon?

JOHN: Yeah, he educated him. And they cut off the rest of my toe.

IRENE: So you succeeded in getting to the hospital?

JOHN: Yeah, and it was during that time that I must have stayed at his house, doing things for his mother.

IRENE: The brother now? Or, no—

JOHN: At the Tsardákas's home in Kallithéa. Okay, now, so what else?

IRENE: There was an experience that you were telling me about of trying to send money to Yiayia; one particular experience . . .

JOHN: Well, that's when he discovered me.

IRENE: Oh, okay, so you associate those two events—

JOHN: He was in one of those yards there and he saw me and that's when he realized we never got out of Greece.

LUCIE: That's when he stopped selling cigarettes του μπακάλη [tou bakálee; the grocer's cigarettes (way they were referred to)], because he went on the boat.

IRENE: Oh, okay.

JOHN: Yeah. I did—I made three or four trips during the war, Athens to Kérkyra.

IRENE: Right.

6c

Toward the end of that same interview, Captain Peter's boat came up one more time, in the context of me asking my father how he traveled between Athens (Piraeus) and Itéa during the war. When he told me the bus would sometimes take as long as three days to make the trip, I responded:

IRENE: Really? Wow! Was it also possible to go by boat, or was that too dangerous?

JOHN: Oh, no it was po—but uh, again, it had to be a boat that had clearance from the Germans to be operating, because they controlled the seas. You see, like Captain Pétros's boat was his boat, but they manned it, you know.

IRENE: So, do you think—I mean, I know he did a lot for you and he's a friend—but do you think in that context he was viewed as a collaborator?

JOHN: Who?

IRENE: Uncle Pete—because he had the permission from the Germans?

JOHN: Oh nooo, because he was trying to protect his property; he was grabbing as much as everybody else was grabbing at the time. Are you kidding? When—many many times when we were out in what we called open waters—when we weren't afraid of the German torpedo boats, we used to give the guerrillas the ammunition we were carrying for the Germans. We were a supplier of ammunition from Athens to Piraeus, I mean from Piraeus to Kérkyra. Sure, he used to give away a lot of stuff. In fact, uh, we purposely, or he did, not I, put the boat aground στο Μεσσολόγγι [in Mesolóngi] so that we wouldn't have to go back to Patrás and load up with German ammunition, you know? Yup; he was quite a guy.

6d

I don't know exactly when or how my paternal grandmother's profound faith in God was forged, but I myself witnessed her devotion as a child. When we stayed with her in Neptune, New Jersey, as young children, she would take us to every service that was offered in the Greek Orthodox church in Asbury Park, the next town over. She didn't drive, so if my grandfather wasn't around—and he usually wasn't—we walked to church. She would always try to get us a ride home, but often we walked back, too. I can still see the route in my head today. Sometimes certain street corners of that walk appear in my dreams. It used to seem endless, but it turns out it's less than two miles one way. When I interviewed my aunt Pearl in December 2005, she gave me some further insights into my grandmother's faith. She told me that during the war, my grandmother's constant prayer to the Panagía, the Mother of God, was to intercede for her with our Lord, and that if He would bring her children through this war and back to the United States, He should please take her life. I guess she even prayed this out loud, for my aunt told me she was terrified to return to America because she was certain her mother would die the moment they arrived. My grandmother's faith was so strong that she remained positive her children would survive the war despite all the hardships she and they endured. She believed this even in the face of the numerous times she was told one or the other of them was already dead. At least one such incident involved my father. Here is the way my aunt Pearl told me the story of my father and the *Vellisários*. Πρόσφορο (*prósforo*) is bread offered for Holy Communion.

PEARL: One day when they were close to the large harbor of Piraeus, the ship was bombed. You know when the ship was bombed there was a container, a tank or something, and the ship was going down and your dad dove into the water. And this oil tank just rolled down on the ship and it caught his foot just when he was diving into the water, and you know three of his toes were hanging. I mean he lost a lot of blood. The people that found him described that to my mother. Honey, your dad had been taught to swim by Pappou at the YMCA in the United States before we left. So, see, he was able to save himself by swimming to shore despite being wounded in the foot. When he collapsed near the chapel of Saint Nicholas, he prayed to the saint: please, Saint Nicholas, please let someone find me, and my mother will bake you πρόσφορο [prósforo]. Well, when they told Yiayia that the ship your father was on had been blown up, and there were no survivors, she didn't believe them. She went to Athens immediately and looked in all the hospitals for your dad. When she found him, he told her of his promise to Saint Nicholas, and she fulfilled it.

IRENE: Oh, I remember her prósforo well. It was so delicious.

PEARL: See, she just refused to believe that her beloved eldest son could be dead, and she was right.

6e

Over the last two years I was able to gather one more story about my father's experiences on the Vellisários. This story came from my mother and was recounted to me when the two of us were far away from my father, from the United States, and from Greece. It was during her first and only visit to me in Berlin that my mother remembered something my father had told her during their first years together in the mid-1950s.

LUCIE: . . . the other thing was when he was with Peter Tsardákas on his kaïki, and they went to Kérkyra and these islands up there, and he, uh, told me that, uh, the Germans that were occupying the vessel were, uh, people—The young men would go and sell their sisters so they can get some food, some oil and bread and whatever—

IRENE: The guys on the boat?

LUCIE: To the guys on the boat. Those guys, most of them, were very young, in their teens, I mean late teens, eighteen, something like that. But they would, uh—The brothers would go and offer their sisters to the Germans, so they can have, to survive!

IRENE: Daddy told you that?

LUCIE: Μούλεγε ότι ήτανε τόσο δύσκολα τα πράγματα εκεί επάνω στην Κέρκυρα. [He told me things were so difficult up there in Kérkyra.] Και δε θυμάμαι. [And I don't remember.] Στην Κέρκυρα νομίζω πήγανε. [To Kérkyra I think it was they went.] Και [And], you know, είχανε μεγάλη πείνα [they had terrible starvation]. Και οι αδελφοί πήγαιναν τις αδελφές για να— [And the brothers took their sisters in order to—] So I don't know how the transactions were going. Τους πήγαιναν σπίτι; [Did they take them home?] Τι κάνανε; [What did they do?] Δεν ξέρω. [I don't know.] I never asked those things.

Αυτό του είχε μείνει πολύ. Στο μυαλό του. [That stayed with him deeply. In his head.] You know. [Mom's voice is loud and high pitched when she quotes the next words of my father:] Can you imagine? he used to say to me. Can you imagine?

I had never heard this story before. However, when my mother related it to me, I could imagine the situation—and not just because of my book knowledge of starvation and German atrocities committed in Greece and other occupied territories . . .

7

Rape. Rape? Chrysoúla and Loukía and Pearl and . . .

It must have begun at some point. I must have begun on some specific day, month, and year to worry about being raped. When was it and why did it start then? I was young, very young—but not so young that I wasn't allowed to walk home from school or to downtown and back by myself. I'd be walking alone along a street, and I'd be worried that some man would jump out from behind a bush. I didn't know what would happen next, but it would be bad: he would "rape" me, it would be scary, and my life would be changed forever. At some slightly later point in time I began to connect the act of rape with the act of making love. I'm sure that at that age I still didn't know what either really involved, but I knew that somehow the "making love" part was nice, even beautiful, and it was done with someone one really liked; the "rape" part was hurtful and frightening, and it was done by a stranger. For sure by the time I was twelve, but I suspect at an even younger age, this "knowledge" was apparent in a prayer I recited to myself whenever I was walking alone, especially if it was getting dark: "Please, dear Lord, please let me make love before I am raped."

It took many years before my brain registered that the "*before* I am raped" part of my mantra revealed a certainty that this disaster would befall me. Even when I learned as a teenage feminist about the horrific statistics on numbers of women who *are* raped at some point in their lifetime, I had to admit that my attitude toward rape as a child in a peacetime suburban setting was peculiar. I finally began to wonder about who made the little girl I once was so afraid of rape and so certain that it was bound to happen to her. Or maybe it's more accurate to say that I finally let myself be conscious of the fact that it was my father who had instilled this fear in me. I was already in my early twenties when I began to be sure that my terror had something to do with my father's War Experiences in Greece. I hypothesized that he must have seen someone whom he loved be raped. The idea of this was so painful to me that for years after I had made this connection, I never allowed myself to think of who it could have been. (Note the absence of a family story about rape among my earliest memories related in chapter 1.) It was only as a middle-aged adult, when I very intentionally started to piece together what had happened to my father during the war, that I let myself put names to the possible victims of the rape I now assumed my father had witnessed: Was it my grandmother? Was my grandmother raped by Germans? by resistance fighters? by a local taking advantage of her status as a woman living without her husband? Was it my aunt Pearl? Oh, my God, she was only a little girl! Had my father seen his own sister raped? Could it have been another female relative? Was my father himself raped? He was young and small, too.

I now realize that, in a loose emotional sense, it was all these scenarios, and that in a strict factual sense it may have been none of them. My mother's hesitation about where the sexual transactions between the locals and the Germans took place when the Kérkyrans pimped their sisters for food (6e), makes me wonder how much my father saw or heard beyond the initial bargaining at the docked caïque *Vellisários*. I have already reproduced above my aunt Pearl's recounting of being sexually abused by an older Itéan before he would give her the handout her mother had sent her for (5c). I am certain my father (as my grandmother) must have been completely unaware of that situation, for the shock and disgust my father communicated to my mother years later at the idea of some Greek brothers exchanging their sisters for food indicate to me that he was sensitive to the vulnerable position of the women around him. If he'd known what was happening to his own sister, I suspect he would have intervened immediately by preventing my aunt from begging, for sure, but also possibly by trying to do harm to the perpetrator. Over the course of my research I was confronted with the particularly disastrous combination in Greece of traditional cultural attitudes toward women and the sexual violence of war. It appears that my great-aunt Loukía suffered the worst and the longest from this poisonous mix, but my grandmother and my aunt Pearl did not emerge unscathed either. Here are some other stories that, in combination, help me understand better another dimension of my family's fight for survival.

7a

The hours I spent with my aunt Pearl in December 2005 revealed a number of relevant pieces of information. Perhaps because I had met each of them only when they were at an advanced age and I was young, I was a bit surprised, though not astonished, when my aunt repeatedly related how attractive the three Tsínga girls, that is, my grandmother and her two sisters, were. I recognize now that emphasizing beloved individuals' beauty is a regular feature of Greek storytelling, as is exaggerating any physical feature that is associated with being lighter, whether in hair, skin, or eyes.

PEARL: The people in the village of Chryssó were jealous and angry at the Tsínga girls because they were beautiful and they had all married "out." My theia Despoúla had married a carpenter and gone to Galaxídi. My mother had married, of course, my father, someone from Kolopetinítsa, who took her to America. And my theia Loukía married a man from Itéa.

7b

Their attractiveness and the facts of their marriages were a distinct liability for all the Tsínga girls, but most problematically for my grandmother during the war. I would have been more confounded by my aunt referring to her mother as a ξένη (foreigner) if I hadn't read Nicholas Gage's Eléni. There, Gage explains very clearly and poignantly that even Greek women who barely ever left their native villages, like his mother, became labeled as "foreigners" and "Americans" by virtue of the fact that they had married someone who had gone to the United States (1983, 40). Here is how my aunt Pearl described the situation of her mother, my grandmother Chrysoúla.

PEARL: My mother suffered so much, Irene, during the war years because she was a very attractive woman, she had three young children, and men were really after her. I mean, mind you this, because she was a ξένη [foreigner]—she was an Αμερικανίδα [American woman], they wanted a relationship, so they could destroy her reputation. So my mother feared every male that came to our house. As a matter of fact, honey, her cousins would come down from Chryssó, down to Itéa, because I was

19. The Tsínga girls in traditional Greek dress, probably early 1920s. Left to right: Despoúla, Loukía, Chrysoúla.

always at home—I was like a little mother, because my mother had to go out begging, and your father was in Athens so he wasn't available from a young child—so I was home taking care of Nicky and Harry. And even though I was younger than Harry, Harry was completely dependent on me. I mean I had no childhood at all because of Harry, I took care of him all the time. So, I stayed at home. So my mother would get these cousins that would come down from Chryssó and she would give me the tray. Never invited them in the house. She would have them sit in the— στην γιάρδα [in the yard; n.b., not standard Greek], you know sit outside and she would give me the tray to go serve the γλύκο [sweet], you know, the Greek coffee or something. And I would say to her: Μαμά, έχουμε ωραίο σπίτι, γιατί να μην έρθουνε μέσα; [Mom, we have a nice house, why shouldn't they come in?] And she would say: Όχι παιδί μου, όχι, όχι! [No, my child, no, no!], and she was afraid, honey, that people in Itéa didn't know these were her relatives, and if she brought them in the house, the next thing you would know, someone would go up to Kolopetinítsa and tell my mother—my grandmother that her daughter-in-law had a man in the house. It was terrible, honey, the reputation; she feared everyone.

7c

This story, also told to me by my aunt Pearl at the kitchen table in her home in December 2005, immediately followed the anecdote related in 5c above, explaining how her maternal grandparents had sacrificed themselves by giving the food they should have eaten themselves to Theia Loukía and her children. *Eirene mou* means "my Irene"; the possessive with a first name commonly functions as a form of endearment in Greek.

PEARL: Theia Loukía was the most beautiful woman you can imagine. Blue eyes, blond hair, she was very attractive. She was married to a rather nice man. He was a—he was from Itéa. You know, they had the, uh, two children together, Asymoúla and Giánni. And then of course you heard the story that Theia Loukía got pregnant with a German when he—

IRENE: Well, that's interesting too. I heard a different version of that story.

PEARL: Oh, nooo. That story, honey, I know very well, because you know, honey, we lived in Greece for two years, 1959–61 [the "we" here refers to Pearl and her husband, Allen, who studied theology in Greece during the early years of their marriage]. So we were going to Chryssó, all our vacations. When Niko was born, when George was born, and there I went to show off our children. And also Allen fell in love with Chryssó. It was very different than Crete [where his family is from], he just found mainland Greece very attractive to him. So, honey, when my, this is—I'm not saying my aunt gave her body or anything. She was raped by a German. See the Germans, honey, would come. Even in Itéa. There was a time, Eirene mou, that my mother had thirty Germans living in her house. She used to shut her bedroom door and put the μπαούλα [trunks] on top of each other that they would not break down the door and rape her and do harm to her. She washed for them; she cooked for them. And so they did the same thing in Chryssó. When they went, they went to Theia Loukía's home, and I'm sure somebody forced themselves on her and got her pregnant. So she was pregnant with Elefthéri, who was born, uh, very end of the war. Elefthéri. She named him Elefthérios because of the victory, ελευθερία [elefthería; freedom, liberation]. And when my uncle got the rumor that his wife was pregnant, he knew that it wasn't from him. He was up the mountains fighting the guerrilla—fighting with the guerrillas, fighting the Germans. And he came down, honey, and he took the son, Giánni, and he left Asymoúla with my aunt and left her. And this boy was born.

7d

My aunt then relayed that the "consequences" for my great-aunt and her children lasted for decades afterward.

PEARL: When we went to Greece [in 1959], I never told my husband any of these stories about my family. I wanted him to meet my mother's sisters, my mother's nieces, nephew, her brother Giánni—whom I disliked a great deal—but I didn't tell him any of the stories. So here my husband went to Chryssó, we stayed with Theia Eléni [a beloved first cousin of my grandmother, who never left Chryssó], it was Easter, and he fell in love with this Elefthéri. He was about fifteen years old. So, he said: O

Ελευθέριος θα με πάει [Elefteris is going to take me] and he's going to take me, show me the village. 'Cause I had—Niko was just a month old. So I stayed home with the baby at Theia Eléni's. He went, he came back. Allen was white as a goat—ghost. "What happened, honey?" "Pearl, tell me the story of this boy! They were throwing lemons at him, they were throwing tomatoes! They were calling him a bastard, μπαστάρδικο!" That was his reputation. My aunt had to live with this, honey. And when we— we heard it, Eirene mou, we were—Allen was devastated. We were very poor. We lived on seventy-five dollars a month. We had a scholarship, a Taylor scholarship from the archdiocese. So we had very little. We lived with another couple. Who were also staying in the same apartment. So when I gave birth to Niko we couldn't all live together, and we eventually rented a two-room apartment on the Leofóros Alexándras [Alexandra Avenue], and we had a lot of help from people we knew from America. They were studying at Harvard when Uncle Allen was studying at Holy Cross. So they welcomed us in Greece. And they're the ones welcomed us, who took care of us. Showed us a lot of hospitality. So anyway, we brought Elefthéri to Gr—to Athens. And Allen—he [Elefthéri] loved cars, and Allen put him in a, um, a school where he became a car mechanic. And after he became a car mechanic, he went to Germany, and he loved it there. And he was—his mother thinks—It was a glorious period in my aunt's life. Because finally she could show all these village people: this comes from the bastard. This is what my son is doing. This is how he loves me. And then, Eirene mou, he was in love with a young woman in Germany, and one night they were all driving, I guess they had been drinking, and they had a car accident and they all died except he. And the woman that he was in love with, he was going to marry, she died. And then, honey, he almost lost his mind. So he went back to Itéa—to Chryssó and lived with his mother. Well, at that point, he became very abusive with her. So Theia Loukía lived a dreadful life. I mean, it was. And then of course her daughter, Asymoúla, got cancer and she died to cancer.

IRENE: I was told she was hit by a bus.

PEARL: No, he was. No, he was hit by a bus. He eventually committed suicide. He went down to the πλατεία [town square] in Chryssó—she might have too. Maybe that's how she ended her—she—she worked in Delphi. As a matter of fact, Venus and Vicki, our two good friends, our dearest friends, every year they went to Delphi and stayed a month. And they stayed at the Hotel Amalia, and one time Asymoúla heard they were American women, and she said, I have a cousin and an uncle and an aunt, cousins that live in America. We think he's a priest. And Vicki said, well, that's my priest [meaning Allen Veronis, Pearl's husband]! And they fell in love with Asymoúla. So, she could have been hit in Delphi by a bus, but Elefthéri was definitely hit by a bus.

7e

The following version of what happened to my great-aunt Loukía was told to me by a Greek, a friend of a friend, a gentleman from Chryssó just a touch older than I—and therefore someone who didn't experience the war himself. I had first asked him in a general way, as I had asked about half a dozen other people in the region, about rape during the war. The unanimous response, like the response I got to my question about starvation, was "No one was raped here." Not by the Germans? "No." Not by the Italians? "Definitely not." By the resistance? "No way." I then asked him specifically if he knew anything about my theia Loukía being raped. He did not. But he asked his elderly mother the next day, and the essence of what she said to him, and he then to me, I repeat below. I had received the story in Greek, but am quoting here the English version I gave to my aunt Pearl after hearing what she had to say on the topic (7c and 7d). The story I relate offers a different set of reasons for why Loukía would have been ostracized by the villagers. It then triggers further remarks from Pearl both about Theia Loukía as an outcast during and after the war and about the paternity of her children.

PEARL: Now, has your dad shared that Theia Loukía was raped?

IRENE: Well, he never said that to me. Okay, he never said that to me. But my suspicion was always that someone in the family—that he had seen someone raped. Or at least that he had lived it very closely. Okay? But when I asked in Chryssó about Theia Loukía, they told me something very, very different. So I just want to tell you what they told me.

PEARL: Tell me.

IRENE: They told me that her husband decided, volunteered to go to Germany to work during the war, once the war had started. And the Germans recruited workers all over Europe—so, factually, that's easy that that might have happened. So he actually left the country and went to Germany to work. So, she was left by herself, and I was told just with John, just with the one son. And then—and I'm just repeating what I was told—I don't know the truth of any of this. Then I was told, she took a lover, she took a Greek lover. And by that lover she conceived the other children. Both children are by the lover. And that when her husband heard about it, he came and got his son and left her.

PEARL: That, that's a very inaccurate story. Mainly because my aunt was hated by everyone in Chryssó.

IRENE: Not everyone. I'll tell you about someone else who loved her very much. But I under—what you're saying.

PEARL: Because, honey, because of what had happened to her, she was always an outspoken person.

IRENE: Well, people are always jealous of beautiful people too.

PEARL: Well, that's very true. And I think too. My mother was very cruel to my theia Loukía too. Because like I said, she was attached to this cousin Eléni, attached! So, whenever we went to Chryssó—because we wanted to go as children—she would always make us go visit and stay with Theia Eléni, always. That's, that's—and we wanted to see Theia Loukía when we went to Greece [1959–61]. And I stayed with Theia Eléni too with a baby. And Theia Loukía, she came to Eléni, whom she didn't like very much because Theia Eléni was a very proper person, embarrassed at Theia Loukía's behavior. She [Eléni] was a very quiet person, very quiet. She never had children with her husband. So they lived a very comfortable, very good life. And he had some relatives himself. But her relatives would have been my relatives. And Theia Loukía would have been her first cousin too. So when we went there [to Theia Eléni's], honey, she [Theia Loukía] came and she yelled at me and cussed me out: Why was I following another tradition—another generation of going to Theia Eléni's house instead of her house? She wanted me to go to her house. And I never even thought of going to Theia Loukía's! I mean it was just—I just knew Theia Eléni's home as a very comfortable home, I knew I could have a baby there. I'd have all the attention and luxury and all that. And I really didn't know my theia Loukía all that well. Because my mother resented her so much, that I had those awful feelings about her. And yet when I met her that time and the trips we made in those two years we lived in Greece, I really fell in love with her again. And I felt sorry for her. And then when I met Elefthéri—Isn't that an interesting story? Honey, if you would have met those children! Asymoúla [Loukía's daughter] was the image of our family. I mean she really looked like my grandmother. She took her name too. And I loved Asymoúla.

IRENE: Oh yeah?

PEARL: She was a very soft, kind person. She reminded me a lot of my Yiayia. And Elefthéri was a typical German—Of course having a mother who had blue eyes and blond hair and a German father, he was a typical German. I mean his build, his looks, everything. So it was—It could have been that he [Loukía's husband] went to Germany. All I heard as a child was that he went up to the mountains to fight against the Germans. But he could have been in Germany and not up in the mountains. And—but—the girl was definitely his child. And the reason he left her is because she was a girl and he didn't want the responsibility. And then he remarried in Itéa another woman and he had a couple children. And

I wish that I had been in contact with my cousin John, her [first] son, just to—I often wondered, as he got older: Why he didn't make a contact with his mother just to know who she was and—

IRENE: Again, I can only say what people told me. But you know that it's Ólga [Uncle John Tsíngas's youngest child] and her husband who took care of Theia Loukía at the end?

PEARL: I asked about that. I was very happy to hear about that. Who did I ask recently? I had no idea what had happened to the house or anything and someone told me that she had left it to Ólga.

IRENE: Well, it's interesting, because what Ólga said to me is, you know, and everyone's trying to save face and this that and the other. But what Ólga said to me was that by her opinion even though she sacrificed the years of her life to take care of Loukía—and I got confirmation from several people that she and Kóstas [Ólga's husband] really did take good care of Theia Loukía at the end—but in any case, that Ólga felt that the house belonged to John, because John was the only living child of Theia Loukía. She said she tried desperately to get in touch with him as it became clear that his mother was going to die. He never responded. She told him about the funeral. He did not come to the funeral.

PEARL: So she [Ólga] knew where he was?

IRENE: And she told him about the funeral. He never came to the funeral. And now, she says, "I don't want the house." I mean, she has her own house! You know. "I don't want the house, but it has to be taken care of." And you know, she does not have children—Ólga. She has a very nice husband, I have to say. Very nice straightforward man, simple people. And they have no children.

PEARL: Oh, and they have no children.

IRENE: So I think—my—just trying to, I think I'm a pretty good reader of people's personalities. When I met her this summer. You know, I understand how she needs to protect her father, and you know the image of her father with our family. But, in terms of Theia Loukía, she said, that house by rights belongs to John. But somebody's got to take care of it and you know—

PEARL: I'm surprised John didn't respond. Because you know they just jump at those opportunities.

IRENE: I know. Usually they jump at those things.

7f

The irony of that particular house being abandoned, having no one who wanted to claim it, didn't escape me. The topic of family houses came up when I talked to my father's cousin Zoé, the oldest of her generation. She, like her cousin Ólga, has no children of her own. She seemed to be wistful when she said that her grandparents' house in Chryssó, the one that passed to Theia Loukía and then to her cousin Ólga, is κλειστό [closed]. But when I tried to probe further on the topic of her mother's sister, she wouldn't say a thing.

IRENE: Θα σε ρωτήσω κάτι πολύ ειλικρινά, Θεία. [I'm going to ask you something very frankly, Auntie.]

ZOÉ: Εντάξι. [All right.]

IRENE: Τί έγινε με τη Θεία Λουκία; [What happened to Theia Loukía?]

ZOÉ: Δεν ξεύρω, δεν ξεύρω. Δεν ξεύρω τίποτα. [I don't know, I don't know. I don't know anything.]

7g

After all the stories I'd heard about women in the war, and specifically about my great-aunt, including my father's interjected fleeting remark— "Did she have two husbands or what?"—from my own perspective today, it seems to me that whether Theia Loukía became pregnant by a German or a fellow Greek, her contemporaries considered it voluntary, and therefore shameful. Zoé's silence itself adds to the picture of the legacy of war for my family. In the context of coming to this conclusion, I am therefore perhaps even more grateful now than I was the day I met her το Παγωνίτσα Σκούρα (Pagonítsa Skoúra), a widow in Chryssó whose view of Theia Loukía didn't have anything to do with the begetting of her children.

It was a hot, sunny day in August 2005 when I finally went in pursuit of family history where it had happened. I had driven myself to Delphi in a rental car very late the night before, and after a horrible night of sleeplessness in the Hotel Zeus, I headed down the mountain to Chryssó. I just followed the road signs, not having preserved much of a memory from my visit there with my mother and younger sister, Georgia, more than three decades prior. I pulled the car over in a part of the street that seemed wide enough to let someone drive by should another car arrive in this desolate location, and got out. It was very hot, even though it was only midmorning. I wrote in my journal: "I don't know a soul here. I have no connection—I feel no connection here. What am I doing?? It's blasted hot. I'm covered in flies." There were very few people in sight. An area that looked like the outside seating area of most Greek tavernas but less appealing was entirely deserted. Three older men sat on flimsy chairs in front of some unidentifiable kind of store. An elderly woman dressed entirely in black was sweeping opposite my parked car. I decided to ask her about the church, because at this point I couldn't even recognize the street in front of the church from the photograph of my grandparents' wedding. The widow seemed happy to speak with me. I didn't have my cassette recorder with me, so I summarized as much of our conversation as I could remember in my journal an hour later while sitting on a comfortable, clean, cool terrace at the quay down in Itéa. This is part of what I wrote on Wednesday August 17, 2005:

> Παγωνίτσα Σκούρα. [Pagonítsa Skoúra.] She was a seamstress. Learned how to sew locally. Then went to Λαμία [Lamia, a city almost directly north of there, on the road toward Thessaloníki] to apprentice to a professional who was so good she went to

London every year to work for the fashion shows. Has two sons, 37 and 29. Husband just died. A first cousin too. She said they just had a program at the local school about the history of area. She wanted to go but because of death of her first cousin she didn't. She said: This is a small place; they can criticize you. It was very quickly said. But the whole scene was so clear to me in those furtive words. Life of a woman around here! Turns out she knew Theia Loukía. Said she sewed for her. Talked about her two children and losing them both. I don't remember what she said about the boy. But she said the daughter was hit by a bus right in the village. She didn't know exactly how it happened. She kept saying what a tragedy and how Theia Loukía died a little later. The house is opposite the lower church not the upper one near where we were standing and that it was κλειστό [closed].

I tried to figure out from her which church could be the one where Γιαγιά + Παππού [my grandparents] were married, but couldn't really discern. She said both were used a lot. She had baptized her kids in the upper one.

She loves plants and was pruning this one pathetic flower which she said the Δήμος [municipality] had just cut as they were cleaning the streets. It wasn't even in front of her house. I told her Γιαγιά [my grandmother] loved plants and flowers. She kept saying how clean Theia Loukía and her daughter were. How nice they kept things. Thought went through my head about contrast between this woman's praises and my own vague but negative memories of her; the mosquito-infested sleepless night I spent in her house as a sixteen year old; how Georgia and I felt imprisoned. Dark airless room. We couldn't wait to get away. I really have no memory except the dark interior of that room. It's extremely recently that someone told me Theia Loukía was raped by the Germans and shunned as a result by the whole village.

"Family Archaeology." No knowledge or sympathy on my part when I first met her. In any case Παγωνίτσα [Pagonítsa] had genuinely fond feelings for Λουκία [Loukía]. She kept wishing she could offer me something, a γκλυκό, ένα ποτήρι νερό [sweet, a glass of water] and kept gesturing to her appearance after cleaning all morning. I had her point out her house to me and told her I would knock if I passed by again. It was a genuinely pleasant interaction. I was happy to speak with her after how weirded out I was by being there. I wished I had asked her if she knew anything about my great-grandparents starving to death, but it didn't occur to me at the time. She checked for me by the way, but said church was closed up. I wanted to light a candle for Γιαγιά [my grandmother].

8

Body Marks and Mistaken Identities *or* Arrest and Deportation

As much as rape was lurking in our family history and as much as the idea of rape affected me personally at a young age, it was actually the story I had learned very much later in my life that pushed me to actively pursue Daddy's War: that my father and his brothers were mistaken for Jews because they were circumcised, and that they were in the process of being deported when they were liberated by the Greek resistance from the transit camp in which they were being held. I recounted in chapter 1 how I heard this story on the telephone from my younger sister, Georgia, in early 1989 when I was thirty years old and what some of the immediate consequences of hearing it were for me. In the last two years I have been able to gather versions of this story from everyone in my family, including my father. I pass them on below in an approximate chronology of when they were first heard by that person. In other words, my oldest sister, Maria, remembers hearing versions of this story and reading the 1945 article about my father from a very young age, at least by first grade, so probably by 1961. Therefore, I begin with what she told me. I then proceed to my brother Tom, who said he had heard about this part of my father's history when he was in seventh grade, which would be in 1975; and so on. I'm passing on the stories in this order, because in addition to transformations in individual memory over time, I assume there is such a phenomenon as transformations of family memory over time, though again, as I stressed at the conclusion of chapter 1, all these people are telling me things in the manner in which they recall them in the present (2004–6). I have no means now, of course, to trace the actual diachronic development of my family memory. But I am gesturing toward the evolution of family memory by presenting this largest set of stories about the same events in this order.

8a

As I recounted under the heading of "Mountain Stories/Message Runner" (4d), I had the opportunity to question my oldest sister, Maria, in December 2005 when she came for a quick visit from her home in London to the United States without her family. Of the many things she shared with me, one of the most surprising was this story, surprising to me both because of how young she remembered being when she heard it and because of the improbabilities of the events it recounts. It didn't escape either of us that the two elements might be connected. She recognized—as I have often with regard to myself—that she never tried to resolve any inconsistencies in the stories herself.

IRENE: So I asked you [before we turned the recorder on], what do you know about what happened to Dad between 1937 and 1945 and how do you think you learned it?

MARIA: I have never imposed any kind of date on the memories, so I have to intellectually work out what the time frame was. What I understand is that Dad was involved in the resistance, probably as a young boy carrying messages from one place to another. And at some point he got caught and put in the camp in Mesopotamia; and after the camp was liberated, he didn't know where the rest of his family was. It's unclear to me whether the rest of the family was imprisoned too or it was only Dad. But in any event, he was not with other members of his family. After he was liberated, he came to New Jersey, and through the church was reunited with other family members. And a lot of that memory comes from an article that hung on the wall in Pappou's study.

IRENE: So, you don't remember when you first read that article or when you might have first heard those things?

MARIA: Probably, I would say somewhere around first grade, when I could read; and every time there was a new baby, we got packed off to Yiayia's. There was a huge dearth of stuff to read, so in sheer desperation, looking for things to read, you sort of found the few bits of English language material that there were and that was one of them. We spent at lot of time in that study 'cause Yiayia used to sit there and do her rug crocheting [during our childhood our grandmother crocheted rugs from scrap cloth].

IRENE: So, do you remember at all how you felt about that idea that Daddy was arrested, or separated from his family or anything like that?

MARIA: You know, I don't know I have any feeling about it; it's just the way it was.

You know, Daddy did a lot of storytelling, but for me Daddy's storytelling was never believable; it always reminded me of, uh, "And to think that I saw it on Mulberry Street" [title of the first Dr. Seuss book, which we read and adored as children].

IRENE: Uh-huh? [laughs]

MARIA: That's immediately what comes to mind whenever Daddy is conveying information.

IRENE: Even as a kid?

MARIA: Even as a kid. I can't—

IRENE: That book—that reference is a good dating. Because that book is a book from our childhood.

MARIA: That's right. I can't remember ever believing what Dad said at face value. For me it was always discounted because there were so many demonstrated disconnects between the truth and what Daddy was describing.

IRENE: Uh-huh. So, can you remember any stories where you thought that? Or does this one fall into that category? Did you assume that this idea that he was running messages for the resistance was false or—that he was in a camp was false or that he was separated from his family?

MARIA: I don't have any doubts that—and I never disbelieved that he was in a camp; now, what kind of camp that was I think became progressively more elaborate over time. And I'm—I know I was told in Mesopotamia and in Italy—and you know me and geography: I can make the wrong choice between left and right 100 percent of the time—I had no idea if Mesopotamia is in Italy and I've never bothered to look it up. But I probably have doubt whether it was a Buchenwald type concentration camp. I don't doubt that he was separated from at least part of his family. I uh—

IRENE: You don't remember ever—Like you can't even—not even—You can't construct a situation other than you know you looked at that article? You can't construct a situation in your head when you heard Dad talking about this?

MARIA: I heard Dad talking about it so many times to other people, and there were so many contradictions in what he said, that I never accepted as truth anything that he said.

IRENE: Uh-huh.

MARIA: And that may sound terrible but—

IRENE: No, no. That's—It's very helpful to me that you remember hearing him tell different people different things—

MARIA: Yes.

IRENE: Because one of the things about my project that's been very interesting is all of us have very—not just very different stories about what happened to him, how it's gotten encrusted for us, so to speak, but people have different ways of learning whatever they think they know. Very different. And I, just as an example, do not remember hearing those kinds of stories. I have a general image about Dad as a storyteller like you do, but I don't remember ever hearing those stories about the war; I cannot construct any conscious recital that I was witness to.

MARIA: Right. How much—how many times do you remember being sat in the back of the classroom while Daddy was teaching or, you know, being parked while Daddy was doing something else; so, he's talking to a group of people and you are being babysat by being parked in the back of the room with your book or whatever? I remember a lot of instances like that. So Dad was waxing lyrical and telling a group of people this very dramatic story that was completely different to the dramatic story that he told a few days earlier.

IRENE: Uh-huh. Yeah. See now, this is the other thing. Like even the idea of being parked, I definitely have that, but mainly in different contexts: like, um, at track meets; one really overwhelming one for me is being dragged to who knows how many track meets. So there it wasn't quite the same in terms of recitals, because Dad wasn't necessarily physically close to where I might have been.

8b

As I said to Maria, each of us siblings has a very different way in which we remember hearing our father's stories in general, but in particular in hearing the story of his arrest and deportation. My brother Tom told me in an e-mail about his precise memory of where he was when school friends related to him what they in turn had heard our father say the night before at the Jewish Community Center. I solicited memories from Tom and received his answers in late March 2004. From my questions it's obvious that I didn't have any doubts in my own head at the time that our father had been deported as a Jew. I also note that Tom passes on the story to me by reconstructing as a quotation what he had heard from his friends.

[Irene's e-mailed question:] At what point in your own life exactly did you find out that he had a relationship to Nazi persecution of the Jews in WWII?

[Tom's e-mailed response:] Very early on, but I'm not clear when it was. Sometime between age 8 [1971] and 12 [1975].

[Irene's question:] From whom and how did you find this out?

[Tom's response:] Multiple sources: Uncle Harry & Aunt Stella. I definitely asked him about it during this period and got some small amount of information. As fuzzy as my memory of this early period is, I have a blazingly clear recollection of the day I got the most vivid information, albeit secondhand from some Jewish classmates. When I see this conversation in my mind, I remember the lighting, I remember the position I was standing in turning away from my locker and looking up hearing my name called in the third floor hallway of Eastview Junior High School. I was in 7th grade in the fall of 1973 (or '74?) [1975], and the Holocaust had become a mainstream topic. Two kids I knew ran up to me and began talking excitedly about the "cool" story my father had told at the JCC the day before as a Holocaust "survivor."

[Tom then wrote the section about our father running messages for the underground that I have already quoted in 4c and do not reprint here.]

The gist of the conversation was along these lines: "Tommy,

you never told us your dad fought with grenades and guns when he was younger than us! You should have been there (the JCC) yesterday, all the cool kids were completely shut up from the story—it was completely silent when he was telling about how the Germans came into town and rounded up the kids from playing and made all the little boys drop their shorts to find the Jews that were circumcised. And then the parents would come in from the fields and the SS grab all the Jews to take them to the concentration camp in Yugoslavia, but he was from the U.S. so they grabbed him too." Days of driving to the camp and then waiting to find out what would happen to them. "Then the guy tries to get a favor by telling the guards your dad is part of the resistance and the SS torture him for three days burning cigarettes into his forearm to make a swastika, but he doesn't say anything and they beat him. Then his uncles radio the British secret service that drop them supplies and tell them they have to get the kid before he talks, so they get Tito and the communists to go knock over the concentration camp just to get him out and Tito shoots the SS guy right in front of your father, grabs him and busts out. Then they smuggle him back to Greece, dodging German patrols the whole way!"

I felt confused by the fact that these kids knew more about my father than I did regarding this amazing story. These kids were obviously imagining a war movie in their heads and were excited by the identification with a boy their age blowing up German convoys with grenades in the middle of the night and the torture and escape from the camp at the hand of resistance guerrillas. I don't know that they embellished the story or reported it accurately, but I've never had any reason to totally disbelieve it either. I remember seeing some kind of scar on the inside of his forearm and wondering what it was prior to that, and I thought at the time they were telling me this, "Oh, so that's what that thing is."

The youngest of the six of us, Peter, seems to have learned about our father's past at about the same time (not age) as Tom (mid-1970s); he is three years younger. It would make sense if my brothers had talked to each other about it, but neither indicated that they had. While "the story" came out in Tom's e-mail in response to my question about when and from whom he had heard the stories, in reaction to the same questionnaire (reproduced in chapter 1) Peter recounted his version of my father's arrest in response to my question about his attempts to elicit further information.

[Irene's e-mailed question:] Did you make attempts directly yourself to elicit further information from him? from others? Why or why not? What information did you hope most to find out?

[Peter's e-mailed response:] Yes, I have fairly frequently sought to elicit more information both directly from the parents and from others if they indicated that they had been told something that perhaps I had not.

Because I would like to know more about their history. I feel like I have only fragmentary information like little vignettes here and there, but no complete chronology. I'm not even necessarily sure of some of the basic facts. For example, I have a vague notion that at one point they were betrayed by fellow visitors as "Americans" and that to explain why they had been circumcised, they said they were Jews and were then sent on a train in the direction of a concentration camp, but that somewhere along the way, somebody figured out that they weren't and sent them back. I'm really curious to know if that is the real story and what were the details of how that happened, especially that they were sent back. Where did that happen? How?

8d

As I mentioned in chapter 1, the sisters directly older and younger than I, Tina and Georgia, attended one of the talks my father appears to have given over the years at White Plains Jewish Community Center. I recall that Georgia phoned me the next day and reported what they had heard. Based on my own recollection of receiving that call, I believe they would have heard this talk in February or March 1989. When, however, I sent Georgia the same questionnaire from which I've just quoted my brothers' responses, she didn't mention anything about the JCC talk or the phone call to me. She did have a version of the mistaken identity story, though. Interestingly, it is given in reaction to a yet different question I posed. I am quoting below her written response to my e-mail of 2004.

[Irene's e-mailed question:] How would you describe (now) your father's relationship to the Holocaust? As a survivor? a refugee? someone who was persecuted? some other way? none of the above?

[Georgia's e-mailed response:] None of the above, except that I always understood that when the Germans found out that Dad and his brothers were circumcised, that they were suspect and in danger, but I have an image of a frantic Yiya quickly proving this wrong and setting things right.

[Irene's question:] At what point in your own life exactly did you find out that he had a relationship to Nazi persecution of the Jews in WWII?

[Georgia's response:] must have been in my teen years because I don't even remember understanding prejudice against Jews until Jr. High when I was shocked to hear about it, from my Jewish friends I might add.

8e

My conversations with my sister Tina to get her version of things occurred the most recently of any interactions with my siblings on this topic; that is to say, in summer 2006. She knew by then, of course, that I was in the process of writing a book on this subject. In an e-mail and then in a phone conversation that I was transcribing as we spoke, she tried to reconstruct for me as much as she could about the talk she had heard our father give at the White Plains JCC in 1989. It came as a relief to me that she definitely remembered Georgia being with her. I note that, even though I had mentioned to her in a preparatory e-mail my estimate that the talk occurred in 1989, when she tried to place the date herself during our conversation, she put the talk about ten years earlier.

These first numbered snippets came out in her e-mailed response to me when I told her I was hoping we could find a time to talk about how and when she had learned about Dad's time in Greece and how she felt about what she learned.

[Tina's e-mailed response:]

1. I heard Dad's story mostly when he spoke at the JCC in White Plains. As I recall Georgia was there but you were not. Is that correct? At that time I felt a bit strange that Dad was telling all these strangers all these things I knew nothing about. Like there was no relationship between us other than audience and presenter. I felt closer to the other members of the audience than to him.

2. Then when Uncle Nick died [1992] Dad and I drove around looking at real estate in New Jersey and he told me some more. [. . .]

3. Then for some reason, years later, I started hanging out with Uncle Harry and he told me a lot too. He wanted me to write it up so he could get the backing to make a movie about his experiences. [. . .]

4. When I arrived at the hospital after Dad crashed the car [January 2, 2005] he was talking to the chaplain about being held in a concentration camp in . . . ? Yugoslavia? Tom and I

walked into the room and he paused as if he was hoping we would leave. It was the shtick about how he was rescued by the royalist general of the guerrillas who somehow Dad was his only living heir. The emotions associated with this recollection are terribly negative, rejection mostly. Sensing how Dad was so intimate with this stranger and wanted to keep interacting with him and have nothing to do with me and Tom.

On July 31, 2006, Tina shared with me in a phone call what she remembered from the JCC talk. I note with interest the parts she puts into our father's voice even all these years later.

TINA: This is the arc that I remember: Going back to Greece and then, um, fighting with the guerrillas. The story about: people were in the village. Men and women were separated, and the men had to pull down their pants. We were taken for Jewish. We were marched to border and beyond to this camp. I don't remember him saying much about the march. In camp—he went into description about not having anything to eat. They ate the garbage of the Germans and their leftovers. They fed the dogs better than us. He went into that at some length as I recall.

And then there was this miraculous liberation by the head of the royalist guerrillas, who was named, I can't remember the name, but I know he named them. Then he went into the distinction between royalist and communist guerrillas.

I had read the Stratis Haviaras book [1984]. I questioned it [Dad's explanation] later. This might be a question I asked Dad in episode after Uncle Nick's death.

People who were loyal to king were the ones who liberated them, and they came to do this liberation because Dad was there, and Dad's family, and they were looking specifically for them. That seemed to me hard to believe. They were liberated from the camp and then they went to fight.

I'm going to throw it in here: I remember there was no need for them to be taken, because they had these American passports. Had they shown them, they would have been okay. Dad's so good with bureaucracies—in some ways, anyway. I know compared to me, he's good at getting things from the system. So he was annoyed about this situation, but it wasn't up to him. Yiayia was the one to have done this. If they had shown these American passports, they could have avoided the whole thing; they wouldn't have been taken.

[Tina recounts other things she thinks Dad talked about on that occasion, including for example, going to Athens from Itéa in what I have reconstructed was probably April 1941 and having to turn back because the fighting was so fierce.]

I remember sitting there and looking over at Georgia, coming out of being in Dad's daydream, and being very reassured about her presence. It—It felt strange of course to be at the JCC, which was not our place. Maybe that's why the memory was triggered of the Presbyterian church when I wrote to you the other day. [When we were young, our father used to take us to the local Presbyterian church, among other places of worship.] Well, I wasn't as young in this situation. But, you know, normally, people go to their own church. We were always in these odd places in which we didn't really belong.

People have always thought I was Jewish. What I'm trying to say is that I had this strange unfolding: People thinking I was Jewish, finding out about Jewish culture. And having this identification with being Jewish. And then hearing this story from Dad of them having been taken for Jews. I really felt like the next thing to find out would be that we were actually Jewish. I mean at the same time, I was learning from my friends about so many families that had denied they were Jewish. It was a very strange position to be in. All this questioning about our name that never fit in. That was always very strange. It haunts me still.

So, um, there was this thing and I remember sitting there. There was food; tables; dressing up; it was really a nice occasion—Georgia doesn't remember being there at all?

IRENE: No. When I asked her about it directly in 2004, anyway, she said she didn't remember calling me to tell me about the talk or even the talk itself.

TINA: I remember her being there. There were a lot of people. It was crowded. Nobody was shouting him down or questioning him. I remember being home from college at that time [Tina was in college from 1974 to 1978]; I don't know if it could have been when I was at college; I remember Georgia being at THINK [IBM's in house magazine] or something. No, she did that after I got out of college.

IRENE: Do you remember the age of the other people in the audience?

TINA: It was definitely mainly older people; not younger people; I remember we were the exception as family, as being a young adult and the other people being middle aged.

IRENE: It was an evening event, right?

TINA: Well, actually, I would have said it was afternoon; but I might be mixing it up with Mr. Uhlman's funeral. I would have said it was 3 o'clock on a Sunday, or 2 o'clock, or 1 o'clock. Wow, when you start realizing—what do you remember, really . . .

8f

Well, actually, Tina remembered quite a lot, especially from my perspective today after working on this project about family memory. I have no recollection of how much Georgia remembered and then relayed to me in the immediate aftermath of that talk when she phoned me in 1989. But here is the kernel of what I thought I remembered in 2004 (based on what Georgia had told me in 1989). I was trying to answer the same questions I had posed to Tom, Pete, and Georgia (and quoted in parts in 8b, c, d above). I have not edited my own answer to bring it up to date with what I know now. For that reason, I am particularly struck by my "mistakes" (e.g., the discrepancies in giving the age when I "found out" and writing "Greek" instead of "American" passports toward the end); and by the echoes of themes also communicated by my siblings. It's only a partial explanation of my "mistakes," that I put myself under time pressure in answering my own questions (I gave myself one hour for the whole questionnaire, the answers to less than half of which I reprint below).

Q. At what point in your own life exactly did you find out that he had a relationship to Nazi persecution of the Jews in WWII?

A. I remember quite distinctly, though not the exact date. It was in late winter 1989. I was thirty years old. It was toward the end of my graduate career. I had just moved out of the house from my (first) husband. I was trying to support myself by teaching an enormous amount. I was teaching four discussion sections: two with Erich Goldhagen for a General Education class called "The Holocaust and Comparative Genocide" and two for Rick Hunt, a Lit and Arts core curriculum class called "From Weimar to Nazi Germany." My younger sister, Georgia, called me on the phone and she said: Irene, you wouldn't believe what just happened. Dad asked if Tina and I wanted to come hear him give a talk at the Jewish Community Center. We went, and he talked about his experiences in a concentration camp! I now don't remember all the details or how many details my sister actually related to me, but the gist of it was that our father had been identified as a Jew because he was circumcised, and that he and his family (two brothers, a sister and his mother) were taken off to a camp where they were gathering Greek Jews for deportation. The conditions were awful. But at some point, the Greek resistance fighters came through and liberated all those who were in the camp.

Q. From whom and how did you find this out?

A. see above: my sister; on the phone

Q. Any recollections of how knowing about his experiences made you feel toward him? toward his family? toward yourself?

A. Yes, as I hinted above, it immediately clicked for me. Therefore, there was a certain sense of relief. It seemed to explain much about his anger, his impatience, his brooding silence, most especially about the taboos that seemed such a part of our upbringing. As if we knew there were secrets and we weren't supposed to ask about them (a little like our relationship to the Greek language: despite how much we were criticized for not being fluent in Greek, it was also clear that our parents liked having a language we didn't understand, and so somehow we complied and agreed to try not to understand it).

I remember too a sense of dread, dread that the worst was true. And that somehow the circumstances under which I found out (most especially that I was teaching FOUR classes related to the Holocaust) made it feel not only overdetermined, but also as if this were somehow my destiny. I had always felt close to Jewish people, and my very best friend, David Bush, is Jewish. I remember telling my therapist, maybe a year or two later: I feel that I am a Jew, and her asking me what that meant. I don't remember what I answered.

I also felt a lot of fearful compassion, not quite as much for my father as for my grandmother, who though very clever, was not well educated, and was stranded in wartime Greece without her husband and with four little kids to care for. There was supposedly some confusion over whether she should reveal that the children were all born in the United States and had Greek passports. I could feel her dilemma over whether this would help or hurt.

8g

In the majority of the versions we kids had, our father and his siblings had been identified/misidentified on the basis of the physical "proof" of the boys' (note the plural) circumcision. Maria's version does not make any reference to circumcision; its role in the story Tom got is confusing.

It is some kind of factor in the versions of Peter, Georgia, and Tina. In my own head it was the primary motivation for the arrest of the whole family. In December 2004 I still wasn't sure in which direction my research would take me, but when I finally had the chance to visit with my aunt Stella for the first time since the loss of her husband, my father's brother Harry, the year before, my explanation went something like this (I was not yet working with a cassette recorder constantly at my side, so this is a reconstruction of the conversation made shortly after):

IRENE: Well, I'm very interested in what and how children learn about catastrophes that have befallen their parents. I've been working on published memoirs of offspring of Holocaust survivors. But I'm also trying to figure out more about what happened to my dad, Uncle Harry, and the family when they were in Greece during the war.

STELLA: Like what?

IRENE: Like where they were taken exactly when they were identified as Jews because the boys were circumcised.

STELLA: Your uncle was not circumcised!

IRENE: [silence; then starts laughing] What?!?

STELLA: Your uncle was not circumcised.

IRENE: Wow! That comes as a real shock to me. I've always heard all the boys were circumcised because they were born in U.S. hospitals. My dad is circumcised.

STELLA: Well, Harry wasn't! [short pause] I'm not sure why Harry wasn't.

IRENE: Maybe it had to do with that baby who died?

STELLA: Yeah, maybe. Maybe Yiayia didn't trust the doctors anymore and she wouldn't let them touch him.

IRENE: And then by the time Uncle Nick was born she had reestablished her trust?

STELLA: Could be.

By spring 2005, when I finally got my father to talk to me about his childhood in Greece, I had reimmersed myself in Holocaust studies and had read quite a lot by and about children of Holocaust survivors. I also had in my head what my aunt Stella had told me a few months prior and the accounts of my father's experiences given by my three younger siblings, Georgia, Tom, and Pete; I was aware of the contradictions in the stories I'd heard by then, but I mainly didn't make explicit reference to them in talking to my father. I had not yet tried to educate myself further on the unfolding of the war in Greece. What I knew about the Nazi persecution of Greek Jews was mainly restricted to the deportation of the community in Thessaloníki, a city in which, incidentally, I myself had studied twenty-five years earlier. In sharing here how my father spoke to me of his arrest, I remind my readers that the entire conversation had been launched by my announcing that I was planning a trip to Greece to visit the places he had been. I did not myself initiate questions about his being identified as a Jew, being arrested or deported. My mother was in and out of the dining room where I was interviewing my father, but my recollection is that she was not in the room for most of the parts I quote below.

IRENE: Do you have any recollection at all, Dad, of approximately how much time that was that you were selling the cigarettes? I mean was that months and months or was that more than a year? or—

JOHN: Well, I'm trying to think of the events, uh . . .

[Very long pause of approximately eighteen seconds.]

I know I put that stint in when, uh [pause; exhalation], when the Germans identified me as a Jew, I remember I was in Athens at that time—

IRENE: That—that's where you got identified?

JOHN: Yeah, they used to round up, strip down the males, and I was circumcised and—

IRENE: Right.

JOHN: —and that was good enough proof and ended up in the camp in Yugoslavia.

IRENE: How—What can you tell me about that, Dad? You were by yourself completely?

JOHN: All I know is that, yeah, I was all by myself and couldn't even notify Captain Pétros, who knew I was in Athens . . .

[Then comes the sequence about my father and the *Vellisários* quoted in 6b and not reprinted here.]

IRENE: So Dad, you were—you said that at some point you think you ended up in Yugoslavia, what do you remember about that?

JOHN: That, that, trying to put that in perspective.

IRENE: Right, um-hum. 'Cause I wanted to ask you about one other thing that Aunt Stella told me about, that, you know, her memory could be as off as anybody else's, but, um, she thinks that in the village too you guys were rounded up once for a check. That all—

JOHN: Yeah, we were.

IRENE: Was it a pretty common occurrence?

JOHN: Yeah, sure.

IRENE: So every time that happened, it was a problem for you. You had to explain yourself.

JOHN: Yeah, for us [big emphasis on "us"] I, uh, umm, because we were the only people in the village that were circumcised. [pause] Anyway, I don't remember. What do you want me to—

IRENE: Well, I was just—because I'm trying to sort of go to the different locations of places that you might have been, I was just wondering what you remember in your own mind. You associate it with Yugoslavia, but I'm just trying to figure out where you actually went and what kinds of signs you might have about that. I mean here's a—you know it's a very, very small map, but, um, you know it gives you a bigger area.

JOHN: I know we were in Thessalónika [he enunciates the syllables very distinctly and places emphasis on the o] and then they moved us into Yugoslavia. I know that—

IRENE: You remember specifically? You remember like some buildings in Thessaloníki [accents the penultimate syllable] or people telling you: we're in Thessaloníki now?

JOHN: Yeah, we were in a—sto stratopethon [στρατόπεδον? Greek for "camp," but see below; I am unsure even after listening to the tape multiple times whether this is the word he used] . . .

IRENE: [interrupts] You were in a train?

JOHN: . . . with a lot of Jews from Kérkyra that had been assembled there . . .

IRENE: Uh-huh.

JOHN: . . . that had been assembled there . . .

IRENE: What was the word you used just now, Daddy, you were in a what? You used a word. I didn't understand it.

JOHN: In a group.

IRENE: In a group.

JOHN: We were assembled there. And then went into some part of Yugoslavia and my uncle, uhh, somehow got the word, I don't know how. Uhh, Psarrós, John Psarrós, was one of two Greek generals that never surrendered during the war.

IRENE: Uh-humm . . .

JOHN: Zérvas, who was in Épirus, and my uncle who was further south.

IRENE: He was related to you on your mom's side or your dad's side?

JOHN: Psarrós, he was a cousin of my mother's. In fact umm for some—I don't remember the reasons, but, I was heir to his property because there was no family of them or whatever, στο Χρυσσό [in Chryssó] . . .

IRENE: Oh, okay.

JOHN: Well, anyway, so, he was the Greek underground guerrilla for the βασιλικούς, the royalists.

IRENE: Uh-huh.

JOHN: And the royalists had airplanes coming in and out of Gióna, that's the mountains behind Kolopetinítsa and, uhh, uhh [pause], let's see what the hell—Anyway, all what I—my recollection is that they took us someplace besides Thessaloníki and to Yugoslavia and uh . . .

IRENE: Uh-huh—

JOHN: . . . All of a sudden I—while in camp and this guy was putting the swastika on my arm with cigarette butts to [get me to] tell where my father was. Well, of course, I didn't, so—

IRENE: Uh-huh—

JOHN: —so, uhh, in the meantime, my uncle was apparently good friends with, uh, Tito. They were both the leading generals that never surrendered to the Germans. And the story goes that as a favor, he asked Tito to see if they could liberate part of the camp because I was there—the only heir to the family and this and that and, sure enough th—I was almost like kidnapped, covered up, and taken back into Greece.

IRENE: So they didn't liberate the whole camp, they just came to get you?

JOHN: Well, uh, I, and a number of other people.

IRENE: Uh-huh . . .

JOHN: I don't remember how many or anything like that and we came in through Albania—

IRENE: Back into Greece?

JOHN: —Back into Greece, until I was delivered to my uncle through the mountains of northern Greece all the way down to [I think he's saying στην πλάτη της Γκιώνας που λένε, which would mean "to the 'back' of Gióna, as they say"] Gióna. The mountains where Kolopetinítsa is είναι η Γκιώνα [is Gióna], and that's all sort of mountain ranges. That goes—it even shows it here [points to map in front of us] all the way into central Greece, okay? And up there στη Λάρισσα [in Lárissa] was my uncle's . . .

IRENE: Hideaway?

JOHN: Hideaway, right. So uh—Thýmios, my—if anybody remembers anything of that period, he would be the one; because he was a young guy, a shepherd, and he was the one that they trusted in Kolopetinítsa to be in contact with my uncle. My uncle was a royalist and, uh, at the train, at the bus station in Patrás, there's a big bus station, and right behind it there's a hotel, a very decrepit hotel, and in it they have a whole room dedicated to my uncle the underground leader, το βασιλικό [the royalist]. You see, Greece had already—το EAM ήτανε [the EAM was] communists. And the πέμπτο σαρανταδύο [5/42; Greek name of Psarrós's resisters] and my uncle were royalists [pause] . . .

IRENE: So did you see that room in the hotel at some point after the war?

JOHN: Yeah, they have it very well decorated with all kinds of pictures of my uncle and my, uh—

Well, anyway, pictures of him, because they were royalists. Part of the group in—στο χωριό [in the village] Dimitrópoulo, they were royalists. [Dimitrópoulo is a small farming village in the Pelopónnisos where my parents owned a home for a few years in the 1990s.]

IRENE: Oh yeah? Huh.

JOHN: This one guy that used to sell us things, always wanted me to go with him on a trip across to the mainland to show me the άγαλμα, the statue they built honoring my uncle, who wasn't well thought of because he was a royalist. [In fact it's a statue of Dedoúsis, a different member of the 5/42 who was a royalist.]

IRENE: Uh-huh. [pause] So, Dad, umm, to get even to Thessaloníki from Athens is a big trip; do you remember how you did it?

JOHN: All by train.

IRENE: Oh, it was all by train?

JOHN: All by train.

IRENE: So, you have a recollection of being—do you remember anything about being gathered up and put on the train?

JOHN: Oh, it was so dark you couldn't see anything.

IRENE: So, it happened at night?

JOHN: Until they let us out in the camp.

IRENE: You mean both the trip from Athens to Thessaloníki and the trip from Thessaloníki to the camp were in the dark?

JOHN: Yeah.

IRENE: Uh-huh.

JOHN: Thessaloníki is where the trains went. From Thessaloníki to Yugoslavia is—that's a separate trip, that's—

IRENE: That's what I mean, yeah. Was that also by train?

JOHN: Yeah.

IRENE: Uh-huh. [pause] So but you don't have any recollection where you were in Yugoslavia if I try to find it?

JOHN: No idea, no, except that, uhh, all through those northern mountains I was delivered to my uncle.

IRENE: For—On the way home. And what was that transportation? Were you on a donkey?

JOHN: Donkey, walking, all kinds, hiding. [pause]

IRENE: So there was also a period when you worked for the British?

JOHN: That's after the liberation.

IRENE: Oh, that's after liberation.

As my time with my aunt Pearl was running out, I decided to ask her directly about something she had not brought up on her own. Our conversation took a turn toward much more recent family history after this exchange, and then she had to leave for her radiation therapy. Her husband, my uncle Allen, Archpriest Veronis, had returned from church and was present for this part of our conversation. It's hard to know where to place the origins of this story, since my aunt is reacting to a question of mine and presents it in the hypothetical: "if he was." I include it, nonetheless, because it communicates so well her view of my father and how he handled the ultimate challenges of the war.

IRENE: Did you ever have any information that my dad was arrested by the Germans?

PEARL: Um, you know if he was, and I think I remember hearing about it, it was when he was in Athens, because you know he stole from them. You know he—Oh, my goodness.

ALLEN: For survival.

PEARL: For survival. Of course, for survival. But uh, I think he was. And I think because of the relationships he made when he was arrested with them, they just dismissed him. You know, it wasn't a long arrest, they let him go because of who he was.

IRENE: Of what he convinced them of. They should let him go.

PEARL: Right.

9

saved *or* return to america

When we got back Uncle Nick didn't know what a fork was.

They put me in second grade even though I was fifteen because I couldn't speak English.

This is supposed to be the happy end, because my father, his siblings, and my grandmother did make it out of Greece alive and together, and they were reunited with my grandfather in the United States. A lucky thing it was, too, that they got out when they did, because otherwise they might have been swept up in the third, most vicious round of the Greek Civil War and experienced even worse tragedies than those they had already gone through. However, considering all the family stories I now know about the postwar period, I cannot miss the fact that the reality of **return to america** after eight years in Greece was more fraught than my childhood notions of **saved**, learning about silverware, and acquiring competence in English imply.

9a

This is the first version I got of the conclusion of my father's years in Greece. It is part of the original interview I did with him in April 2005, and it directly follows the segment reprinted in section 8h. I note how powerfully several events are enchained for him. It was hard for him—and me—to pull them apart. My father seems to collapse the pullout of the Germans (October 1944) with the fight for control of Athens between the communists and the British and those loyal to the newly installed Greek government supported by the British (December 1944–January 1945).

JOHN: During the Liberation I was in Athens.

IRENE: During the actual liberation—which you probably remember—

JOHN: At that police station kitchen.

IRENE: Oh, okay.

JOHN: Now the—the two brothers, Leonídas and his other brother, they had a diner, made a lot of money in Hackensack [after the war]. They were older than I am so—

IRENE: [checks in her notes and blurts out:] Pantelís.

JOHN: Pantelís. Their father was from Ándros. They were much older than I, so they can tell you all kinds of details what our life was like down there.

IRENE: But do you remember, umm, being told something, that Greece was liberated, or did you see something?

JOHN: No, I actually experienced it, because we were in that room which was the kitchen I told you, the third police precinct, and one night the guerrillas broke in—cause that's how much the communists had invaded Athens—Athens, only because of the Sherman tanks that the Americans gave to the British were able to hold the road between Omónoia and Sýntagma [large squares in central Athens]—the rest of Athens was occupied by the communist guerrillas, the αρνίτες [rebels].

IRENE: So one night they broke into this kitchen—you were sleeping there . . .

JOHN: . . . and they liberated us.

IRENE: And they told you—

JOHN: Yeah, they didn't bother us, they just wanted to know where the nationalists and the communists were. There was a theater across the street from us, and they had a lot of storage in that theater. That's Plateía Káningos, that's where the police station and kitchen was.

IRENE: Uh-huh. And in that theater, Dad, when you said they had storage there, who had storage, who had stuff there, the communists?

JOHN: Where?

IRENE: You just said that across from the kitchen there was a theater they used for storage. The communists? Who stored things there?

JOHN: The communists, the communists, 'cause they almost took Athens, they almost took Athens.

IRENE: Did you see that as a bad thing at the time?

JOHN: Huh?

IRENE: Did you experience that as a bad thing at the time? Were you scared about that?

JOHN: Well, I was adventurous and I was trying to help the umm, the British, you know, gain control of that area.

IRENE: So from your perspective, the Brits were from the start the good guys.

JOHN: Yeah, they were good guys because they were the only guys that you would talk to. Don't forget that the—I don't know which conference Roosevelt gave away Greece to England and England was to be the sphere of influence there—

IRENE: But you experienced it on the ground, I mean you didn't know that at the time, you experienced it.

JOHN: Yeah I didn't—and that's how from having helped them, by helping them recapture part of Greece [Athens] street by street I ended up in the British army—cause the guy, the officer, I think I showed you those discharge papers.

IRENE: Uh, no, I've never seen those. [I searched for and found them two months later.] I know that you had an official relationship to the British.

JOHN: I have them downstairs. Well, anyway, [sigh] from there, from that kitchen I ended up as a [pause] lift boy at British headquarters in Athens στο Ταμείο [at the treasury building], the big block. And I stayed at that job because we were already in contact with my father through the Swiss embassy. And it was a matter of getting some money from them [in Greece] that my father was paying here [in the United States]. So we were being helped and waiting, and we made it with the second trip of the Gripsholm [name of ship]. So, when I left for—even my passport picture has—I was wearing my British uniform, the tank corps that was all in Athens.

20. The Kacandes children's passport photo of April 1945. Left to right: Pearl, Nicholas, John, Harry; the passport itself has disappeared.

IRENE: But that contact starts at the moment of liberation forward, it hadn't been, uh, d-during—

JOHN: Yeah, well, the embassy came back and that's when the, I met this guy, the, uh, the Πρόξενος [Consul] in Athens, he turned out many years later to be a Cornell graduate.

IRENE: Uh-huh, the American próxenos.

JOHN: Yeah.

9b

My sister Maria is the only one of us siblings who offered a story about Dad getting out of Greece. She had a different set of events linked in her head. I repeat the relevant part of what is printed in 8a. It's possible to read two liberations here: from the camp and from Greece.

MARIA: And at some point he got caught and put in the camp in Mesopotamia; and after the camp was liberated, he didn't know where the rest of his family was. It's unclear to me whether the rest of the family was imprisoned too or it was only Dad. But in any event, he was not with other members of his family. After he was liberated, he came to New Jersey, and through the church was united with other family members.

9c

I first learned the fact of the family's return to the United States on the *Gripsholm*, as all my siblings did, from reading the article about our father published in the local Asbury Park newspaper in October 1945, which my grandparents framed and had hanging in their home. When my grandfather died, my father hung it in our house, which is where my brother Peter remembers reading it (8c). It wasn't until July 7, 2005, the day I was trying to distract my father from my mother's departure for London, that I found out a little more about the actual journey back to the United States. Since my intention really was just to engage him, I didn't have the cassette recorder on. My journal was close by, and when I realized he was in a talkative mood, I started taking notes; the following is reconstructed from those scribblings. I later found Eve's name and address in my father's postwar correspondence log and her picture in his photo album; however, I had never heard about her before that day.

JOHN: We made it back on the second journey of the *Gripsholm*. We went all over the eastern Mediterranean: Cyprus, Ha-ha—

IRENE: Haifa?

JOHN: Haifa, Alexandria. There was this girl on the boat who was trying to get to Israel. Eve Bloodgood. She wanted to buy some of the Greek occupation money I had. She thought it would be a good souvenir. For me it was worthless. When we got back [to the States] there was this woman in Ocean Grove [New Jersey]. She told my father, if he really wants to learn English, I'll send him to a good school. That's how I got to Pennington.

IRENE: Dad, I thought your English must have been pretty good if you were working for the British in Greece.

JOHN: Are you kidding me? That reminds me, when I was working the elevator for high-ranking officers at HQ. I was told to only let men in uniform on to the elevator. One day this civilian tries to force himself on me. He says, I'm the British ambassador. And I said to him: Well, if you're British ambassador, I'm John Kacandes. You can't use this elevator. He got annoyed and pushed me out of the way. See, I didn't know what "ambassador" meant. I was friendly with this Australian general. When he heard about it, he laughed his head off. Luckily I didn't get fired.

IRENE: That's a great story, Dad. I never heard it before.

My father started skipping around. He told me about chasing the communist guerrillas from Athens to Patrás with the 50th Royal Tank Regiment. Then he recounted a visit of his own father in the late 1960s to Greece to see if he wanted to retire there. He recounted my grandfather's coming upon an unusual celebration in Aráhova, a beautiful mountain town to the east of Delphi, in which former German soldiers and local Greeks were commemorating how the town did not get burned down during the war. Then I asked him about the relative he hated so much (see 5e), and he talked about his mother's near death and the loss of his maternal grandparents in Chryssó (probably 1943 and 1942 respectively), which led to remembrances of selling a lot of fish in Chryssó (1940–41). What I don't recall is how we got from that recollection immediately back to the first weeks in New Jersey (October 1945). But we did. And I then got a version of a story that was very familiar to me (see chapter 1), along with a few details that weren't—like what kind of sacks they used and where he got them, or that he had sheep on his mind, whereas I had goats imprinted in my memory.

JOHN: So, we saw all these people cutting their lawns, and we noticed right away that there were no sheep to eat the grass. So, I got these potato sacks from the Neptune Diner and we filled them up with grass and put them in the garage. They started to stink and my mother was worried my father would find out. So we took them to the post office. And when the postmaster figured out what we were trying to do, he called his friend at the newspaper. And they came to interview me.

IRENE: And that's how the lady from Ocean Grove heard about you.

JOHN: Right.

9d

In the difficult interview my cousin Nick and I conducted with my father ten months after the one just quoted (April 2, 2006), Nick posed a direct question about the trip back. I had never heard my aunt Pearl's impressions about their return, while Nick obviously had, nor had I heard this anecdote from my father about his gun.

NICK: What was the boat ride like coming back? Aunt Pearl says that every family lost at least one member of their family.

JOHN: What are you talking about?

NICK: That people were weakened. They didn't have enough food, so they died on the boat.

JOHN: How could they not be well fed? There was all the food in the world on the boat. The boat had good cuisine. What I remember is that I had some kind of Luger gun that I had from the underground. And when we got into New York, word came on board that they were confiscating guns and everything. I remember going forward to the bow and dropping my gun in the water.

IRENE: Do you remember anything about first seeing your dad when you arrived?

JOHN: I know he took us from there to that hotel in Asbury Park. [turns to Nick] Is that still there?

NICK: Not sure.

JOHN: It's a white building. Lucie, are we going to eat tonight?
[It's two in the afternoon.]

9e

Of all the topics I covered with my aunt Pearl, the actual boat ride was not one of them. She recalls, correctly as I was able to confirm, that they were on the ship twenty-seven days, and she gave an enormously detailed account of what happened once they got to New York (the ship actually arrived in Jersey City). Unfortunately for me, at that point I had run out of tape, and I was taking notes. Here I offer the closest reconstruction of what my aunt had said to me by quoting from the transcription of what I said to my sister Maria three days later. Parts of this story my aunt obviously could not have witnessed herself. So she in turn must have had versions from my grandmother, my father, and my grandfather, whose confidant she often was. The length of the family's stay in the hotel, I realized later, can't be factually correct, since they arrived in New York harbor on October 9 and the article that was published about my dad on October 28 already lists the family as residing in their home on Eighth Avenue in Neptune. In the wake of my recounting to my sister what our aunt Pearl had told me a few days prior, Maria realized that the version she has had all her life (9b) cannot have been accurate.

IRENE: Aunt Pearl said—I'll give you the whole story, 'cause it's a pretty great story.

She said, they got off the ship in New York and the Red Cross was there. And they were serving hot chocolate and doughnuts. And she remembers very well that they were allowed to have as many doughnuts as they wanted. And so—you had to—they had to do it by pictures; you gave them a picture and then they went looking for whoever is supposed to be picking you up. So Yiayia had a picture of Pappou, and she had given it up. But she didn't trust them of course to find him. So she said to the three younger kids: she said: you stay right here. They were parked on some kind of uh, you know, bench or stool or something, eating these doughnuts with the hot chocolate. And Yiayia took Dad and went where she saw the crowd of people, because, you know, they were physically separated by some kind of barrier. And she was calling in Greek, Giórgio, Giórgio! So Daddy and Yiayia were both calling Pappou's name. And Aunt Pearl reports that Pappou told her: When he heard his name and looked towards the people who were calling him, he was so horrified he just wanted to get back in his Pontiac and leave. [long pause] But he didn't leave; he collected them. And then he took them and he put them—he drove them straight to a hotel in Asbury Park that faced the water, because he figured they were used to being near the water. And then he kept them locked up there for two months. They weren't allowed to leave, while he fed them, 'cause he didn't want anyone to see how awful they looked. And then she describes our father as being outraged that Pappou wasn't bringing them more food. [pause]

And you know, this is where my work in Holocaust studies really helps me, because these are not unique stories; people were horrified when they saw what these survivors looked like coming out of the experiences that they did. And the food was never enough, you know? They— I mean, you'd like to really believe that after so many decades you could distinguish food that helps you from food that hurts you, but I think for Dad it's—I'm not making any excuses whatsoever for his overweight, but it is understandable to me. That that feeling of having been hungry for so long was so profound that every time he gets hungry it's this trauma; it's this complete panic. And he just has to stuff something in his mouth. [pause]

MARIA: So that doesn't sound like—That sounds like Dad came back with everybody. It doesn't sound like the story that was told where he came separately and—

IRENE: That's not right. They all came together. [pause] I was very interested when you said that, but I didn't want to interrupt you because, uh . . .

MARIA: I mean, I, I—don't know a lot, but that was one of the things I would have bet the ranch on, because I'd heard that so many times.

IRENE: Right.

9f

There were two short quotations in Greek that my aunt had shared with me and that I had written into my notes, but didn't remember to tell my sister. One gives the inverse of the perspective recounted above, that is, when the family saw the father for the first time. Evidently, my uncle Harry, who was just a month and a half shy of his thirteenth birthday, got a look at this father they'd been waiting to reunite with for so long and said:

PEARL: [reporting Harry's words:] Τι κοντός που είναι! [How short he is!]

The second remark comes from my father when they were in the hotel being "fattened up." I was particularly interested in my aunt's quotation because it confirmed what I'd been told when I was a child after my grandfather died: that my father expressed his anger at his father partly by refusing to call him "Dad"; my father is addressing his own father with the word "uncle" below (I also mentioned this in chapter 1). The remark reflects, too, the insatiability of those who have been near starvation. My aunt remembers my father complaining:

PEARL: [reporting John's words:] Μπάρμπα, δε θα φέρουν άλλο ψωμί; [Uncle, aren't they going to bring more bread?]

9g

This is another snippet from the difficult conversation with my father in which he was so reticent about saying anything at all (April 2, 2006). I note that my cousin has better success as an interlocutor. It was only afterward that I realized that my father might not have been suffering a memory loss on the issue I was asking him about. Rather, he may not have been privy to such "sibling suffering competitions," because within about a month of their return to the United States, he was sent to a private boarding school and thus was separated from his family once again.

IRENE: So Aunt Pearl said that when you got back, Pappou told you not to talk about it.

JOHN: What are you talking about now?

IRENE: I don't have this on my own authority. I'm repeating what Aunt Pearl said. Let me try again. She said that when you guys got back from Greece, Pappou didn't want you to talk about the war.
     [John shakes his head.]

IRENE: Okay, so you don't have any recollections about this. She said that when Pappou wasn't around, you would share stories with each other and sort of compete about who had the worst time of it in Greece.

NICK: What was that like when you came back?

JOHN: I had been the head of the family. I was jealous of my father. It wasn't good. I remember one incident that blew his mind. He looked in my wallet and I had rubbers in there. He didn't expect it.

IRENE: Did he hit you?

JOHN: I don't remember.

9h

I end this collection of family stories with another section from my conversation with my aunt Pearl, because it summarizes quite a lot of the history I have covered here and because her analysis of my father's postwar frame of mind seems so perceptive to me. Without knowing my private term, Daddy's War, Pearl confirms indirectly, that she, too, thought of it on some levels as her brother's—my father's war. Furthermore, my aunt's comments here are as happy an ending as I can locate. This is an actual transcription from before my tape ran out that day.

PEARL: See your dad's bitterness was: How could you leave us in Greece for eight years and not know whether we were alive and dead? And my father would not talk about it.

He took us to Asbury Park; put us in a hotel by the sea. Kept us there for three months. And your father would look at the bread. Μόνο αυτό θα φέρουνε; [They're only going to bring that much?] You're in America now. I don't want to hear about anything about what you went through. This is a new life. Nothing. How could he deprive—So, your dad turned him off immediately. And then your poor dad goes to elementary school at Bradley Park. And within weeks they're calling him every name imaginable. A young man that fought with the British army. I mean a grown, mature sixteen year old. They put him in elementary. They put me, eleven years old, in first grade, and they considered me mentally retarded. All of us in Bradley Park. They had never seen immigrant children. So we were put in these special classes, separated from each other. So, the first person that called your dad a dirty Greek and what are you doing here? He went home and he got a butcher knife and he came to school. Well, the principal goes home and says to my father: I cannot have this boy in school; he doesn't belong here. So here he is, deprived of his dad for eight years. Then he goes to Pennington Prep School—one of the best prep schools in the area.

So, he's away from the family again. I mean your dad has his own unique story, completely separate from the rest of us. And I love John. To this day, Allen says to me, up until a few years ago: "Pearl, every time you talk to John, you're so afraid of him. You talk with such respect." I mean I—I—your dad was always a father to me. He was never a brother. Because he provided for us. If it wasn't for your dad we would never have survived the war. He went to Athens and worked in the streets. He begged from everyone. And sent us packages back in Itéa. And that's how we survived the war. And my mother considered John a husband. I mean that's the relationship my mother had with your dad. That's why he was her favorite son. But it was a strange relationship.

So honey, the years we came—we never bonded again as a family. My mother and father, I remember them fighting all the time. My mother accused him of having other women. Because he left Newark, and he went

21. John leaves for Pennington Prep, November 1945, pictured on the steps of the new family home on Eighth Avenue in Neptune, New Jersey. Left to right: Harry, Pearl, Chrysoúla, Nicholas, John.

to Quantico, Virginia. He worked on a marine base. And that's where he made all his money. When we came back, my father was a wealthy, wealthy man. And he wanted to provide everything for us. But he never realized, how we gonna bond as a family? There was no counseling. We struggled through every day of our lives. I mean we—I—if it wasn't for your dad, I would never have gotten married and I would never have gone to college. Your brother—your dad saw immediately that I was a slave to my mom and dad. My mother had convinced me that if I would have left home, they would divorce the next day, that's how bad it was. So they used me. I was a pawn between them. I loved my dad, but I couldn't express it to my mother because she resented him so much.

22. Photograph found with Chrysoúla's last will and testament, picturing Chrysoúla and George on a terrace in Delphi in May 1969.

They made a go of it, I don't know how they survived it. But it was years. At the end of their lives, they were getting along beautifully.

Coda

As if in fitting confirmation of what my aunt had reported about my grandparents' relationship at the end of their lives, in the last stage of my research I found some papers belonging to them. In an envelope labeled in Greek "my will, Chrysoúla Kakánde [her preferred spelling of

23. Back of photograph found with Chrysoúla's last will and testament.

our last name]," I found not a legal document, my grandmother's last will and testament, but rather her emotional last will: a small inscribed color snapshot of my grandparents sitting together on a sundrenched terrace in Greece from their only and final trip there together. My grandmother had labeled the white border of the front side with their names, Giórgios Chrysoúla Kakánde, the location, Delphoí, and the date the photo was taken, May 2, 1969. My grandfather died in July 1970; my grandmother in October 1983. Inscribed on the back side of the photo, also in my grandmother's handwriting in Greek is the following benediction, which I translated with the help of my mother since my grandmother used a few expressions I had never heard before:

1972

Our dear children,

May you always have our blessing; may all you siblings have love; may the one help the others, so that your children may see all this. Whatever you find, may you share it with love and understanding. May you be happy. May Christ and the Panagia enlighten you to the good. May everything you touch turn to white gold.

With love,

Your parents

[3]

Analyzing Daddy's War

Insights from Established Theories

O nce I had assembled the stories presented here in chapters 1 and 2, what did I make of them? To be sure, my first reactions were emotional. These anecdotes are poignant, sometimes heartbreaking, occasionally even tragic—and only very rarely funny. They recount hardship, determination, generosity, and courage, but also confusion, exploitation, meanness, and fear. They describe some events, relationships, and emotions that are highly familiar in the context of immigration, remigration, and war, and some that seem strange, improbable, a few even fantastical. Every section contains elements the tellers experienced themselves and elements the tellers must have heard from others; mostly, the tellers do not remark on the difference. To consider together these stories from my different family members is to notice how much they overlap and contradict and in some cases don't even intersect. Often the reasons for such differences seem obvious due to the identity of the teller, his or her age, gender, birth order—aspects of identity that have an impact on one's experiences but also one's ability to hear and process things one has been told; other differences between versions confound. I observe how brief and bare any one account seems. No one sat down with me and said: this is how the family's years in Greece unfolded. Although sometimes speakers went on at great length without pausing, what they were saying almost never involved multiple, sequential events.

While the emotional burden of these stories has continually and anew made its impact on me, once I had processed some of my initial sadness about what befell my family, I quickly moved into interrogatory mode. Why, I found myself asking, is our family memory of the war so fragmentary? Why are most anecdotes so barren of detail and particularly of affect? Why do some few episodes seem to have been narrated over and over again? Why did only certain people hear certain stories? Could I ever make sense of the disparities in stories about my father's arrest and deportation? Such questions multiplied rapidly. Luckily, once formulated, I discovered that I could tackle at least some of my questions with the analytical tools and knowledge I had acquired over the years as a student and teacher of comparative literature and cultural studies, specializing in narrative theory and Holocaust studies.

Clearly some characteristics of the way my interlocutors remember Daddy's War can be identified as cultural; we are a Greek American family, and certain aspects of what and how its members narrate are due to the particular ratio of their Greekness and their Americanness. Issues of bilingualism and translation underlie, in a sense, everything I have recounted here. I hypothesize that some words come out in Greek because the speaker simply does not readily know the word in English, because there is no true equivalent, and/or because it is not a word the speaker has occasion to use in English, like my father with *lóngos*, *roúcha*, or *enéseis* (approx. "grove," "cloth/clothing," or "injections," respectively) or my mother with *madrí* (sheepfold). I also observe that certain quotations came out in Greek, in several cases because my interlocutor always spoke in Greek with the person being quoted, for instance, my aunt with her mother (see chapter 2, section 7b); other examples might be more attributable to the emotional imprinting of the exchange, as with my father's quotation of his uncle John's refusals to help.

I also want to raise the issue of (imperfect) biculturality/bilinguality with regard to some other types of possible misinterpretations. I note that the proclamations of someone being a κλέφτης (thief) or of throwing or being thrown into the street—με έριξε στο δρόμο (he threw me in the street)—could be considered literally and/or metaphorically; they are Greek social tropes. My father most probably did occasionally steal to survive; his uncle may well have forced him into the street; however, there is also a metaphorical dimension to such turns of phrase and the anecdotes that make use of them. The Greek reality may not have been as extreme as the English rendition or audition of the narrating of such incidents. Calling someone a κλέφτης might be an accusation, for instance, but it can also be a form of praise for someone's cleverness, an interpretation that did not occur to me as I stood in the village square of my paternal ancestors that day in 1984, yet one that I entertain now. As for the manner of narrating, when I spoke to my father's first cousins who never left Greece, I saw certain behaviors magnified from the way I noticed them in my father, mother, and aunts who had spent a long time in the United States—like narrating achronologically, involving the listener, and situating every event, person, and location relationally rather than abstractly. This signaled to me again, that the significance I was giving some characteristics in our family stories might need to be modified or that those characteristics might be more attributable to cultural style than to individual personality.

To my mind, other features of these stories, like their fragmentariness, barrenness, and paucity of affect are more fruitfully understood by considering the traumatic nature of the events the tellers are trying to remember. As I originally gathered these stories and as I tried to make sense of them, I had to keep reminding myself of the facts that all my eyewitnesses were children or very young adults during the war and occupation, and as I suggested through the opening of this book, that the next generation came into consciousness of these stories essentially from birth, therefore also shaping how the stories could be incorporated into consciousness and eventually be retold.

I have named chapter 3 "Analyzing Daddy's War" because I'd like to share here the insights I have gained by considering these family stories in light of established theories of oral storytelling, memory, trauma, and witnessing, topics I have been teaching and writing about for years, but am now applying to material I have hitherto refused to consider in a professional context. As a researcher, one is also obliged to try to probe established theories and discover if one's data lead one to believe that those theories might need to be modified or extended. To make this mode of my professional reflexes more apparent, I place ruminations on Daddy's War that might invite extensions or reconsiderations of our current theoretical understanding in a separate section, chapter 4: "Grappling with Daddy's War: Speculations for Extending Theories."

THE ADDRESSEE MATTERS

Working on this project only convinced me more thoroughly of principles many sociolinguists and anthropologists count as foundational: oral storytelling is a basic form of human interaction, and storytelling is an interpersonal activity (Nofsinger 1991, 162; Ong 1982, 34; Kacandes 2001, 33; see also Sacks, Schegloff, Jefferson 1974; Mandelbaum 1989; Kacandes 1994). I believe that the idea of storytelling as a joint activity is rather self-evident and in any case amply illustrated in chapter 2, but let me cite just one obvious example: when my father is recounting his rescue from deportation, it is I who offers the clarifications that he went from Albania "back into Greece" and that he was taken to his uncle's "hideaway" (chapter 2, section 8h). While the destination of "Greece" followed rather logically from what my father was saying, it was not originally clear to me why I might have piped in with the word "hideaway"—it's not a typical part of my idiolect, and the word had not yet come up—except that at that point, my father and I were "in" the story and the storytelling together. Some conversation analysts even refer to the listener/audience as "coauthor" of the story (e.g., Duranti and Brenneis, 1986; Mandelbaum 1989).

I was particularly reminded of the importance of the identity of the addressee when questions posed by my cousin Nick elicited story segments from my father at times that a question from me did not. For instance, when I queried my father about his childhood, he didn't respond with stories, but rather only a few spare facts: the date of his younger brother's birth, the name of the town they had lived in. When Nick asked my father about who his friends were and what he liked to do, my father responded with a memory that he liked to walk along the train tracks and that once he had stolen money from his father (chapter 2, section 1b). I have also indicated how, as willing as my father's first cousin Zoé was to share many things with me, she would not divulge any information about her aunt Loukía (chapter 2, section 7f). As my mother put it to me when I told her this: "She knows; she just doesn't want to tell you those kinds of things about the family." In other words, as a younger family member, I was not considered by her to be an appropriate auditor for such a story. My mother's theory is supported by the fact that several individuals in Chryssó who are not related to my family did not hesitate to tell me that my great-aunt had had an affair that resulted in an illegitimate child; it was not to or about a member of their own family they were divulging negative things. I further observed that most of my father's first cousins, as his more distant cousins the Gerentéses, were quite unwilling to say anything negative to me about members of our family, unless they were sure they had witnessed it themselves. To cite just one of many examples, Chémo did not want to speculate about the real nature of my grandparents' relationship to each other (chapter 2, section 1c). (I will recount an important exception in the epilogue.)

The role of the addressee is also poignantly reflected in the fact that many of the anecdotes in chapter 2 related to me by my siblings actually came to them second or third hand. That is to say, they, as I myself, were for many years, not told these war stories directly. Without having been exposed to sociolinguistics or narratology, my sister Maria reports in chapter 2, section 4d, "I was there, but not as part of the audience, as parked in the back of the room, as being babysat for." Tom relates in chapter 2, section 8b, "Two kids I knew ran up to me and began talking excitedly about the 'cool' story my father had told at the JCC the day before as a Holocaust 'survivor.'" And Tina recounts a distance between herself and John the storyteller even though she was in the audience at a different JCC talk years later. She reports feeling that our father wished she and Tom would leave when they walked in on him recounting his war stories to the hospital chaplain after the car accident, sensing "how Dad was so intimate with this stranger and wanted to keep interacting with him and have nothing to do with me and Tom" (chapter 2, section 8e). While co-construction of stories is a feature, at least some sociolinguistics would argue, of all conversational storytelling, the refusal to address his children on these topics is more particular to our family. Or rather, it is one of the features our family shares with some families of survivors of the Holocaust and of other tragedies (see, for example, chapter 6 in Bergman and Jucovy 1990; and Fresco 1984, passim).

However, it is also important to notice that our father's silence with his children was not global. Both our brothers reported (separately) that they had heard some stories directly from our father at a point when he was not talking to his daughters on these matters at all, neither as addressees nor as overhearers. Peter, for instance had been told as a child the story of the bombing of the *Vellisários* (chapter 2, section 6a). I don't think this gender split is coincidental and hypothesize, rather, that the general "adventure story" aspect of what our father told our brothers, as well as the fact that their gender, age, and activities matched his of the period recounted enabled his recital. Tom mentioned the detail of "running": when he began to run competitively, my father recounted stories about his own running (chapter 2, section 4c).

Even though the specific story of mistaken identity due to discovery of the circumcised male body was not recounted to any of us directly until recently, when my father addressed a young audience at the JCC in the 1970s, he knew these stories would get back to my brothers, who had many classmates who attended the JCC, and such an outcome must have been acceptable to him, if not intended. I count the answers my brothers gave me in a follow-up question to our initial e-mail interview (2004) as at least a partial confirmation of my theory that my father was more comfortable with them as male addressees of this particular story. I asked Tom and Pete, "Because the one central story has to do with circumcision, I was wondering if that affected you in some kind of specific way? I don't know much about what circumcision means or doesn't mean to non-Jewish men, so any thoughts you can share on this would help." Tom responded,

> Apparently circumcision became a "health" practice (less careful cleaning required) in the US before Dad was born, but wasn't in Europe during the 30s & 40s. I never attached any meaning to that feature of the story except that it was an unanticipated identification method that triggered a case of mistaken identity. (In this case it was something no human being should have to deal with, so I felt natural empathy for the people who were so identified on that level.) I did not have any classmates who were not circumcised at that time and have not met more than several men who have not been circumcised; in my view, it is a non-issue in most American men's consciousness.

Peter, separately, gave me a similar description of feeling: "Probably not very strongly one way or another." Dad sensed, I suspect, that that aspect of the story would be a "non-issue" for my brothers. Nothing related to sex or the human body, however, could have been a comfortable topic of discussion for our father with his daughters, as I have recounted in chapter 1. And thus, the fact that none of us sisters remembers hearing this story until recently no longer surprises me.

I'm not sure there are any "objective" ways to test exactly how the identity of the addressee affects the story told, but the examples of my father in the presence of two interlocutors responding to my cousin

Nick's questions more fully than to my own, of my great-aunt not wanting to talk to a niece about a sexual transgression in the family, and of my brothers hearing the story of mistaken identity because of circumcision at a much younger age than any of their sisters certainly provide evidence that the addressee's identity generally and gender in particular are significant factors in who gets told what.

ORAL STORYTELLING, "ORAL" STORYTELLERS

As I remarked in introducing chapter 2, I tried there to transcribe exactly what I heard. This includes, as readers will have immediately noticed, hesitations, pauses, unfinished sentences, and to a lesser extent exact pronunciation of some words. When first exposed to these kinds of transcripts, one could conclude that the speakers are not well educated, rather than that most casual speech includes more false starts, stumbles, and incomplete thoughts than we realize—or than we really "hear" and remember. However, even taking the recording of "normal" speech into consideration, these transcripts reveal certain features that we could associate not just with the recording of any informal oral interaction, but more specifically with a cultural way of relating information, in this case of the hybrid oral-literate style of my Greek American family.

Greek civilization has, of course, known writing for millennia. Nevertheless, because of historical circumstances, like the centuries-long Ottoman occupation (with its repression of Greek schools), oral strategies have played a large role in shaping and preserving the culture of modern Greece. Walter Ong, one of the most important exegetes of the differences between oral and literate mentalities counts modern Greece as a culture, among others, with high "residual orality" (1982, 68–69). Ong's point has been important to me and my understanding of modern Greek literature (Kacandes 1990, 1992, 2001). I suggest that some additional evidence for Greece as a culture with high residual orality is available to us through the story snippets I have gathered in chapter 2.

Of the nine characteristics Ong discusses in a chapter called "Some Psychodynamics of Orality," many jump out when one considers my family stories. Perhaps the two most obvious ones concern these stories as mainly "additive, rather than subordinate" (1982, 37)—you have probably already noticed how many times the word "And" begins sentences—and as including much redundancy and repetition (39–40). I'd like to use a few of Ong's other categories to explain features of the stories that perhaps are not only less obvious, but also might be valued negatively by cultures less tinged with orality than the Greek and therefore Greek American. I attribute some of my own irritation at certain dimensions of the interactions to the domination of the "American" element in the particular ratio of my own hybrid mix. A productive offshoot of this frustration, though, was that it helped me identify some features as linked to the Greek-oral side of my parents' generation that might have been less apparent to me otherwise. In turn I could revalue them as belonging to a cultural rather than personal communication style. These features include an "agonistic" (Ong 1982, 43) tone to many interchanges; multiply narrating the same story; and situating story information in interpersonal networks, this last being the most ubiquitously displayed.

"Agonistically Toned"
If there was one type of interchange that would trip my ire switch, it was a certain kind of retort of my father's like the one included in chapter 2, section 4a, when I was trying to ask him about grazing his sheep and which I reprint here:

IRENE: Did you come home every night or would you go for several days and then come back?

JOHN: Did you ever see my father's house? How was it?

IRENE: It was small, but there were two parts. And one part was for the animals. The sheep stayed on the ground floor.

I remember that at the time of this particular interview—one in which my father appeared to be a very reluctant participant despite the fact that his nephew Nick had driven several hours to see him—I felt under attack. And when my father asked me this particular question he sounded especially annoyed—for no good reason, I remember thinking to myself. It was only after the passage of much time and a rereading of Ong that I could count this as a good example of a common strategy of orally steeped storytellers to interpret a request for information "interactively" and instead of answering the request, to "parry it" (Ong 1982, 68). Ong illustrates this interactive principle with a humorous anecdote about a stranger asking an Irishman if the building he's leaning in front of is the post office, and the Irishman in turn questioning the stranger about whether he is looking for a stamp. Ong comments that the Irishman "treated the enquiry not as a request for information but as something the enquirer was doing to him. So he did something in turn to the enquirer to see what would happen" (69).

Looking back on my annoyance with my father's reply when I asked him about grazing his sheep, I realize that Ong's interpretation of the encounter of the Irishman and the stranger fits my interaction with my father like a glove. Dad parries my question with one of his own. As if to confirm for me the correctness of this interpretation for the family interaction, I was able to notice that in the original interview, my mother then does exactly the same thing to my father, only intriguingly, and as if to underscore where this behavior comes from, my mother parries my father's question in Greek:

LUCIE: There was a μαντρί [madrí].

JOHN: Τι λες; [What are you saying?]

LUCIE: Ξέρεις τι θα πει μαντρί; [Do you know what madrí means?]

JOHN: Of course.

For a "literate," in the sense of someone who comes from a culture that does not carry as much residue of oral psychodynamics as my family's, these exchanges can appear aggressive. Indeed, being that much more steeped in American culture than my parents, I myself first interpreted them that way, becoming frustrated by—among other things—the fact that in these kinds of interchanges with my father the question first posed is never subsequently answered. I wanted information, and I did not get it. I still do not know whether my father would graze his sheep daily or go out for several days at a time. However, if I am reading Ong correctly, the issue of my need never being met would not register with the orally steeped participant, because for the oral creature, the privileged goal of interaction has been fully accomplished (Ong 1982, 69). This brings me to an additional category of Ong's that I believe my siblings and I have had similar trouble tracing to a cultural style rather than to a character defect or personal intention to frustrate or humiliate us.

Multiple Versions of the Same Story
For Ong, the phenomenon of story variation can be traced to the need to preserve information, that is to say, to what Ong labels the "conservative or traditionalist" psychodynamic. Ong explains that oral societies "must invest great energy in saying over and over again what has been learned arduously over the ages" (1982, 41). My father wanted us to learn certain lessons too, and my sister Maria's report that she "cannot eat bitter green vegetables without being flooded with memories of Dad telling those stories" (chapter 2, section 4d) provides one illustration of the efficacy of the transfer of knowledge through repeated versions of the same story. Indeed, the day we talked in 2005 my sister was able to quote to me the information she had learned through these stories almost forty-five years prior: "'All we had to eat was hórta for weeks and weeks and weeks.' And 'you need to appreciate what grows in the ground and can keep you alive'" (chapter 2, section 4d). Though he did not express himself in these terms, my father wanted to pass on knowledge to us that could save our lives if we ever got into the same predicament he had been in.

Under the same rubric of "conservative or traditionalist," Ong makes the related point that in oral cultures, "narrative originality lodges not in making up new stories but in managing a particular interaction with this audience at this time—at every telling the story has to be introduced uniquely into a unique situation, for in oral cultures an audience must be brought to respond, often vigorously" (1982, 41–42). I think Ong's interpretation here can be *added* to my sister Maria's analysis, also in chapter 2, section 4d, where she reports having heard certain stories "hundreds of times," and that our father would seem to launch into them "when he needed pumping up." I would rephrase Maria's evaluation slightly by borrowing from Ong: our father got pumped up when he succeeded in making the audience "respond, often vigorously." I think my sister Tina was making a similar point when she suggested to me that our father's exaggerations, embellishments, and sometimes untruths, were part of "how you get people to remember." Chapter 2 of this book contains numerous traces of evidence that our father's stories certainly did have an impact on his audiences. Consider, for instance, how difficult it is to get teenagers to listen to anything adults say: Tom's friends report to him that even "all the cool kids were completely shut up from the story" (chapter 2, section 8b). I myself received uncanny proof of the efficacy of my father's storytelling when I reconnected with a high school math teacher of mine recently, and he launched into an account of my father's arrest by the Nazis, mistaken identification as a Jew, and subsequent deportation and liberation, completely unsolicited; he had no idea I was working on family stories. This math teacher and my father had taught in the same high school, but the day the math teacher narrated my father's story to me was approximately twenty-five years since the last time he could have seen my father or possibly have heard the story. For him, I have to conclude, when the name or thought of "John Kacandes" arose, this story came with it. These points about the interactions of the storytelling itself bring me to a characteristic that has always been easier for me both to identify in our family storytelling style and to value more positively than the "parrying" I illustrated above or the seemingly endless recital of inconsistent stories that irked my sister Maria as a child. I would identify it as an obsession of family members with situating any story segment in a social network. (I have worked on this problem once before in a context that had nothing to do with the War Experiences; see Kacandes 2001, xviii–xx.)

Situating Stories in Interpersonal Relationships

This feature of our family stories overlaps with two of Ong's categories: "close to human lifeworld" (1982, 42) and "situational rather than ab-stract" (49). In explaining the former, Ong references the famous cat-alog of ships and generals in Homer's *Iliad*, commenting that it is not "a neutral list but an account describing personal relations" (43). Ong adds that "oral cultures know few statistics or facts divorced from hu-man or quasi-human activity." In explaining what he means by "situa-tional rather than abstract" thinking, Ong reviews the research of the Russian A. R. Luria, who did extensive questioning of illiterate Rus-sian peasants, administering, for example, a test in which the infor-mants were shown four images (a hammer, a saw, a piece of wood, and a hatchet) and were asked which one doesn't belong. The question did not make sense to the peasants because, Ong explains, all the items were connected to each other through the activity of gathering and cut-ting wood. The peasants did not have available an abstract category of "tool" that would eliminate the image of "log," even when offered that explanation by the researchers. "'Yes,'" one replied, "'but even if we have tools, we still need wood—otherwise we can't build anything'" (as re-counted in Ong 1982, 51–52).

Although all the people I interviewed are educated to highly educated, I would suggest that something of this situational thinking remains with them because of its role in Greek and Greek American culture. At least in the context of these family stories, for the Greeks I interviewed, dates and chronology resembled the concept of "tool" for Luria's illiterate

Russian peasants; as just illustrated in the previous section, my interlocutors could and did explain to me interpersonal connections, but when I asked about dates, the request did not compute. Of course, it is relevant to mention again here that most of my interlocutors were children at the time of the events I am asking them to recount; dates generally do not register with children either.

Some early research of linguist Deborah Tannen lends support to my observation. In a comparative study of young adult Greek and American women (two groups), who have watched and then are asked to report on the same silent film, Tannen observes that the Americans discuss the film as film, recounting details and reconstructing the temporal sequence. The Greeks, in contrast, tended to offer explanations of the events and characters in the film, omitting the movie frame and details that didn't contribute to their philosophizing. Tannen's conclusion that the Americans seemed to pride themselves on being able recallers and the Greeks on interpreting the motivations behind the film's story and managing the interaction with the researcher (1980, 55) interests me the most with regard to our family stories. In the particular mix of cultures that marks my own family, I would say that signs of both American and Greek reporting styles are present, but that the "oral" Greek behaviors stand out more strongly in my father's generation, and the resort to abstraction, need for chronology, and attention to detail that Ong and Tannen assert characterize more purely literate cultures, in this example the American, are more prominent in my own cohort.

In the majority of interviews with my family conducted for this book, members do not remember very many dates per se, nor do they adhere to chronological narrating very often. To put it differently, no one but me seemed to be particularly concerned about when something happened, and my interviewees were, rather, more concerned with the who, what, and why. On the one hand, I suspect this is a fairly common feature of private memories. We're not necessarily that interested in when a certain event occurred in relation to an "abstract" date, except perhaps when that event happened in relation to another memorable event that might be attached to a particular date. Even though I was only twelve years old, I know my paternal grandfather died on July Fourth, because we were celebrating that holiday with my mother's family when we got the sad news. On the other hand, my family raconteurs were quite strikingly consistent in embedding "events" in interpersonal connections; I place the word "events" in quotation marks because often explaining the interpersonal connections dwarfs the action. I attribute this in great part to their Greekness. No Greek encounters another Greek for the first time without asking: Από που είσαι; (Where are you from?) While many strangers from many cultures will ask one another where they are from, the prominence of this question among Greeks, I submit, is remarkable since the whole purpose of the exercise is to figure out how the two individuals speaking together are not in fact strangers but rather are actually intimately connected.

In relation to the family stories I gathered for this book, sometimes articulating connections then led to discovering a date by either the teller or the listener. For instance, when I was trying to find out whether she might have an explanation for why my father expressed more hatred toward the Italian occupiers than toward the Germans, my father's cousin Zoé immediately responded not with facts, an opinion, or an analysis, but rather with a story about the Italians executing the mayor (πρόεδρος) and burning the village in which her family had taken refuge. I was surprised to hear this story, especially since I had not (yet) heard or read of a single instance of the Italian occupiers burning villages. (I subsequently learned of several such atrocities committed by the Italians.) In response to my hesitation, Zoé restated that it was the Italians who had marched into the village. She then explained in vivid terms how she had grabbed her baby brother Harálambos (named after his maternal grandfather, my great-grandfather Tsíngas) and had fled with him in her arms to the furthest corner of the house, which the Italians ended up leaving untouched, as Zoé told me, because the owner had drawn a swastika on the exterior door. The Italians departed the house Zoé was hiding in and set the house next door on fire. I asked her when this frightening event had occurred, but she couldn't answer that question. She knew it was summer, but she had no idea about the year. At another point in our conversation I asked Zoé to clarify for me the names and dates of birth of her siblings. In that listing she told me that her brother Harálambos had been born in June 1941. It fit. I knew that the Italians had occupied Roúmeli in summer 1941, in the wake of the successful German military campaign of April and Greece's division among the Axis powers. I want to emphasize that Zoé did not and perhaps could not say to me: the Italians tried to burn down the village in summer 1941. The shaping of memory through relationships was underscored by two other things Zoé told me in that short sequence: She went to grab the baby because she was the oldest sister; that was her relation to the baby, to be its protector in the absence of her parents, who presumably were out working when this attack began. Also, when, having established why Zoé hated the Italians, I asked for her opinion of the Germans; she told me: Δεν είχα επαφή μαζί τους. (I didn't have any contact with them.) If one did not have contact, if there was no relation between the two individuals or an individual and a group, one should not have an opinion about that individual or group. Again, I heard this sentiment expressed explicitly numerous times over the course of conducting my research in Greece and with Greeks in the United States, especially when it came to making value judgments about someone's character.

The focus of the family stories related in chapter 2 is rarely just on what happened and much more often on who was involved and how the speaker is connected to that person or those persons. Zoé did not offer an opinion of the Germans because she did not interact with them. My father could not tell me the date they closed down his school in Athens, but the thought of school triggered a series of anecdotes about a few people he had known there, and in turn memory of those relationships took my father's narrating to other places and times. In one sequence mentioned earlier but not included in the family stories section—in part because it had so little narrative content—the thought of his schoolmate Giórgios Papandréou, the son, leads to an explanation of Andréas Papandréou, the politician half-brother, then of Giórgios Papandréou the politician father and Zoé Kavéli the actress mother, which leads to the thought of seeing Giórgios the son in a limousine at the end of the war, which leads back to playing hooky with Giórgios the son before the war. In another sequence my query (yet again) about when they closed school leads my father directly to Sakellaríou, the head of the police precinct, which leads to the explanation that his niece was in the school but returned to the States before the war started. My father's narration then springs forward to the fact that the schoolmate's uncle looked after my father when he realized he was still in Athens during the war, which leads to the cooks my father met in the police precinct kitchen, which leads to their identification as from the island of Ándros (which is understood as important because my mother, whom my father meets well after the war in the United States, is also from Ándros), memory of the brothers leads to the moment of liberation, and so forth (partly reproduced in chapter 2, section 3a).

Even these few examples illustrate how my family members' compulsion to explain interpersonal relationships often leads to much jumping around chronologically. This jumping around had direct consequences for the structure of this book. For the sake of comprehensibility, I often began or cut off what I decided retrospectively constituted a story segment from the longer interview to minimize some of that achronology. Despite these efforts, as I was working on the family stories section, I stopped what I was doing and created a chronology of events, which eventually served me as the outline for the most complete telling of what happened to my father, appearing in the final version of the book as chapter 5, "Cowitnessing to Daddy's War: An (Im)Possible Recital of What Might Have Happened." In other words, regardless of my intention not to write a history, I simply could not proceed to present these stories without providing some kind of chronological framework that would structure them for myself and eventually for readers. I think this point is worth rephrasing: The stories told by my relatives *are* structured; however, they are structured by situations recounted or by networks of personal relationships, not by chronology. I tried to respect this characteristic by organizing chapter 2 by "topic": "The House in Chryssó," "School Closing," and so on. On the other hand, my own proclivities led to a different kind of organization, one based on chronology. In sum, I tried to accommodate the flavor of our family memories and my own need and my perceived need of readers for chronological organization. In the context of this book as a whole, when recounting my own memories, I did so chronologically (chapter 1); with regard to chapter 2, I grouped stories by themes, but also subsumed those thematic groupings into an overarching chronology, commencing with a section on how my grandparents met and what led my grandmother to return to Greece in 1937 and concluding with versions of stories related to the family's departure from Greece in 1945 and their return to the United States—though no one narrated them to me this way. In contrast also to the achronological way I had these stories from my childhood (see chapter 1), in this book I placed anecdotes about my great-grandparents' house in Chryssó before accounts of the closing of my father's school because I had figured out during the course of my research that my grandmother must have gone to Chryssó and been confronted by the changed status of her parents' house relatively immediately upon arrival in 1937. "School Closing" comes afterward because the likelihood is that my father stayed in private school at least until the outbreak of the war in Greece in autumn 1940. I repeat here something that I mentioned in chapter 1: I did not as a child think of anecdotes related to Daddy's War in chronological series. And I have to this date never really heard more than a few segments at a time narrated chronologically by someone in the family.

Although I would say in comparison to my father, my aunt Pearl narrated mainly more chronologically—at least within a specific story sequence—her tendency to privilege personal relationships by including them in the narration is at least as pronounced as my father's. My aunt Pearl approaches the whole complicated history of her aunt Loukía's rape during the war and the consequences of it through her own relationship to that aunt and the aunt's children in the late 1950s when Pearl and her husband, my uncle Allen, lived in Greece for two years (chapter 2, sections 7c and 7d). To illustrate from just the conclusion of this long sequence, I respond to my aunt's report that Loukía's daughter, Asymoúla, "died to cancer," by mentioning that I had heard she was hit by a bus. My aunt then hypothesizes that perhaps Asymoúla ended her life as she believes her younger brother Elefthéris had, by throwing himself in front of a bus. That thought then leads to one I'm positing she must have had—but that was not said out loud—about where such an event would have happened, and that unexpressed thought leads my aunt to tell me about Asymoúla's place of employment in a hotel in Delphi and how two close friends of hers from her parish in the United States had met Asymoúla in Delphi:

PEARL: As a matter of fact, Venus and Vicki, our two good friends, our dearest friends, every year they went to Delphi and stayed a month. And they stayed at the Hotel Amalia, and one time Asymoúla heard they were American women, and she said, I have a cousin and an uncle and an aunt, cousins that live in America. We think he's a priest. And Vicki said, well, that's my priest [meaning Allen Veronis, Pearl's husband]. And they fell in love with Asymoúla. So, she could have been hit in Delphi by a bus, but Elefthéri was definitely hit by a bus.

While these connections can add to the confusion in following any given story segment, I would also suggest that they are part of what make the stories so interesting for the narrators and their auditors. One is being exposed not just to a lively plot, but to a large cast of characters who are connected to one another across time and space and who mean a great deal to the person recounting. However, I'd like to point out again that my ability to consider this a positive feature rather than a negative one is not "objective," but rather is attributable to the facts that my family members and I share the approximately same hybrid Greek American oral-literate culture and that I had already satisfied my own need for chronological order. (I eventually received confirmation that Asymoúla did die accidentally in Chryssó by being run over by a bus she had just gotten off, and that Elefthéri committed suicide by jumping from the roof of the Tsíngas home in Chryssó—tragic events that occurred in close proximity to one another and which devastated their mother Loukía in Greece so completely that it does not surprise me that my great-aunt did not try to make sure the relatives in America had the story straight.)

I would like to give one more example of competing forms of story organization, because I now realize that my instinctively chronological thinking sometimes interfered during interviews with my ability to pick up on what was important to my interlocutors. I experienced most strongly my father's and my talking past each other during a half hour of my initial interview with him (April 30, 2005), a sequence I was able to place under the topic of the *Vellisários* in hindsight only (chapter 2, section 6b). As it was unfolding, I mainly believed I was hearing about an adventure my father had trying to send money he had earned to his mother, the recital of which kept getting interrupted. Whatever "story" my father might have thought he was telling me jumps around chronologically from the midwar period when my father was selling cigarettes and was seen by Pétros Tsardákas one of the times when he was trying to send money to his mother, to the prewar period when Tsardákas would come with his caïque to Itéa, to the post-*Vellisários*-explosion period when my father was working for the Tsardákas family, to my own mother's attempt to find the family in 1967, back to the reunion with Tsardákas in midwar and then stays with that period back to the post-explosion period. Of course, any sociolinguist or narratologist can tell you that stories—oral or written—are rarely told in a strictly chronological fashion. (One of the foundational essays in my field opens with the idea of beginning in the middle, in medias res, presenting it as a basic feature of Western literature; see, beginning of Gérard Genette's *Discours du récit*, translated as *Narrative Discourse: An Essay in Method*.) However, I'd like to suggest that the achronology in this recital about the *Vellisários?* about my dad and Tsardákas? anyway, can mainly be understood from the need of the teller to foreground the relationships of the people involved, relationships that probably saved my father's life at many different points during his odyssey and at least once, if not twice, during this particular period.

It was only through consideration of relationship as a foundational principle of Greek/Greek American storytelling and not during the interview itself that I noticed that this entire sequence I have just been reviewing (my father sending money to his mother and being discovered by Tsardárkas) is triggered by a follow-up question I posed about a later event that my father had introduced (his arrest as a Jew in Athens). Because his version is different from the one I have in my head (that the family was arrested together), I ask, "You were by yourself completely?" To which my father replies, "All I know is that, yeah, I was all by myself and couldn't even notify Captain Pétros, who knew I was in Athens." My father misinterprets my back-channel response of "uh-huh" [got it] and then explains to me who Captain Pétros was in terms of our (current) connection to him: "That's Pétros's [meaning my brother's] godfather"—a fact I knew perfectly well. Then begins the whole, to me at the time, confused unrolling of connections between sending money to my grandmother, being seen by Tsardákas, working on his boat, my father being injured in an explosion, and then working for the Tsardákas family—occurrences that had nothing to do, from my perspective at the time of the interview, with the question posed about arrest as a Jew. It was only after repeatedly reading the transcript that I realized my query about being arrested by the Germans provoked first and perhaps most strongly for my father the memory that he was unable to notify anyone he knew that he had been arrested, and that memory in turn led to an explanation I could not recognize during the interview as such, of why Pete Tsardákas knew he was in Athens (and therefore would have been the person he would have contacted if only he could have): "I was all by myself and couldn't even notify Captain Pétros, *who knew I was in Athens.*" Neither Dad nor I can pick up the thread to his arrest by the Germans when this sequence I (post-interview) dubbed "The *Vellisários*" is over. As with my great-aunt Zoé's inability to say to me, "The Italians tried to burn down our village in summer 1941," my father did not—and I suspect could not—say to me, "I worked on Tsardákas's boat before I was arrested by the Germans," or, "I worked on Tsardákas's boat and then I was arrested by the Germans." As impinged as his memory might already have been then due to his increasing dementia, he, like Zoé, could recall perfectly well the crucial relational issue at the heart of the tragedy: she is the oldest sister who grabs the baby who cannot save itself; my father's arrest cuts him off from those he knows who could have explained that he was not Jewish.

Theories of differences between oral and literate mentalities and recognition that my family members, including myself, straddle a sometimes entertaining, sometimes disconcerting position between the two gave me a framework that helped me understand much about what I was hearing. However, I would not have understood enough about these family stories to be writing this book were it not for the insights of memory studies broadly speaking and trauma theory specifically.

MEMORY, ITS STRENGTHS AND FRAGILITIES

There are so many ways in which insights from memory studies have helped me understand and appreciate our family war stories that it is hard to select a few to present here. I will begin, however, with the issue that captured my attention first: some story elements seem indissolubly linked together. Not all the examples were as complicated as the connection in my father's mind between sending money to his mother, Tsardákas, and the explosion of the *Vellisários* explored above, yet still, many of my father's anecdotes, I quickly realized, contained a linking of certain elements and were never narrated without those elements being mentioned. For example, anytime the topic of his maternal uncle John Tsíngas comes up, my father mentions that this man had hanging in his store a calendar with photos of the luxury liner *Morro Castle* (built 1930) that my father's family had sent him, presumably shortly after the ship was launched—that is, at the time when my grandparents were starting their married life together in New Jersey (chapter 2, sections 5e and 5f). The *Morro Castle* itself seems to occupy a special place in my father's memory because it burned in a spectacular way off the coast of New Jersey during his early childhood (in September 1934, a few months before my father's fifth birthday); it may well be the first "extrafamilial" event he remembers. I can imagine that each time my father saw that calendar in his uncle's store, he felt a certain interest if not pride seeing that this gift was treasured by his uncle enough that he kept it for years. My father must have felt a sharp contrast between this symbol of gift giving (another important dimension of Greek culture since archaic times) and the miserliness to which he and his nuclear family were subjected during the war. There is a similarly powerfully linked connection in my father's mind between the sheep he raised in Greece and an absurd story he was told about them after his return to the United States (chapter 2, section 4a). My father was so attached to his ram, Kítsos, and his two sheep, that when they were getting ready to leave for the United States, he decided not to slaughter them, but rather to give them to his paternal uncle John Tsakíris, his aunt Argyrí's husband, and the father of his cousin Thýmios. In exchange for the sheep, the uncle was supposed to send feta cheese to his relatives in the United States. To explain the lack of cheese arriving, at some point the uncle communicated that the ram had jumped off a cliff and taken not only my father's two sheep but some of my uncle's as well—yet another example of some type of gift giving being reciprocated with penury. Although my father's ability to remember things has declined dramatically since I began this project, these two stories with their particular details still come popping out frequently and with amazing similarity to the first recitals I ever heard in 2005; I have now heard each of these stories more than a dozen times. Such enchainments of story elements seem to point to a strength of memory that seems astounding to me, especially since, as I've just pointed out, some linkings seem to survive even dementia. However, it was actually this same phenomenon and specifically the example of the connection in my father's head of trying to leave Greece, passing through Thebes, and seeing German parachutists (chapter 2, section 3a) that schooled me in the fragility of memory.

In her foundational study *Eyewitness Testimony*, which first appeared in 1979 and was reissued in 1996, psychologist and adjunct professor of law Elizabeth F. Loftus comments that "people's memories are fragile things. It is important to realize how easily information can be introduced into memory, to understand why this happens, and to avoid it when it is undesirable" (1996, 87). Loftus's concern in summarizing more than a century of research on memory, including her own, is mainly directed toward clarifying the limitations of eyewitness testimony in legal proceedings; she devotes considerable attention, for instance, to the timing, manner, and content of questions asked of witnesses by police investigators or lawyers and how those interactions affect what the witnesses believe they remember. Her explanations about how easily information (accurate or inaccurate) can be introduced into an individual's memory of an event personally witnessed or experienced should serve as sober warnings to any would-be memoirist or biographer: "In real life, as well as in experiments, people can come to believe things that never really happened" (62). We each probably have our favorite example; Loftus recounts the great psychologist Piaget's report of an attempted kidnapping of himself as a two-year-old child, the unfolding of which he says he can see "most clearly," even though he and his parents learned about a dozen years after it had supposedly occurred that the nanny had made up the attempted crime (as quoted in Loftus 1996, 62–63). My reading of Loftus reinforced my sense that reconstructing an accurate history of my family's wartime experiences in Greece from our family stories was an unattainable goal. More importantly, it helped me identify some aspects of those stories that might be traceable not to duplicity or ill will or "bad" memory, but rather to introduced information. Additionally, I realized that even hypothesizing about this process could provide me with further insight into my family's experiences.

For example, I have no reason to doubt that at some point in 1940–41, my grandmother tried to leave Roúmeli with her children and get to Athens for the purpose of leaving Greece altogether. It seems logical to assume that the event that pushed her to take this step would have been the invasion by the Italians at the Greek-Albanian border (late October 1940), since Greece had basically been unaffected by the war in the rest of Europe until that moment. I similarly assume that the circumstance that prevented her/them from succeeding would have been the invasion of Greece by the Germans (commenced April 6, 1941), since the German army overwhelmed the Greek and British forces and arranged for an Axis occupation of the entire country (May 1941). Did my grandfather tell my grandmother when to try to make the escape? When did the two lose contact with each other? I can't be sure about what transpired between the spouses, but a letter my grandfather sent to the U.S. State Department on October 1, 1941 (which I discovered only after the period of my interviewing), reports that my grandfather's last contact with his family had been on March 11 of that same year, in other words, well after the commencement of the Albanian campaign but before the actual German invasion. Did the American embassy in Greece contact my grandmother and advise her to evacuate? That's what my father and my aunt "remember." But for an official communiqué I can find no confirmation. Even if advice had come from the embassy, I don't know how much time might have elapsed between when my grandmother would have received such a warning and when she would have physically tried to make it to Athens. By spring 1941 my grandmother had been in Greece for more than three years, and what to do with her possessions, including her precious loom and articles woven on it, must have made the idea of flight even more difficult than it would have been otherwise. In short, I cannot accurately date when the family tried to flee.

The failed attempt to leave Greece, like so many anecdotes, came up more than once during the first interview I had with my father (April 30, 2005): the first time when I was trying to figure out when and under what circumstances he left private school, and the second time when I posed a question about what he had told me the first time, following a long segment on his family in Roúmeli. Here is the first mention (part of chapter 2, section 3a):

IRENE: So what do you remember about the day they actually dissolved the school? Were you just kind of going along—

JOHN: The school? No . . .

IRENE: How did that happen that?

JOHN: I think probably that probably Italy had started the war in Albania and um when we got to—When my mother got notice to report to the American Embassy, whatever date they invaded Greece, I don't know—

IRENE: October 29, 1940, yup?

JOHN: And then we. We were already on our way to Athens to leave with the last of the Americans before the German occupation. But we got as far as Θήβα—Thebes is a big city before Athens—

IRENE: Yup . . .

JOHN:—and from those plains we watched the Germans parachute into Athens.

IRENE: Uh-hum; you actually saw that yourself?

JOHN: Oh yeah.

My father can't tell me a date, but he associates the message from the embassy with the "date they invaded Greece." This is ambiguous, since he could have meant when the Italians invaded, as I obviously was assuming at the time by offering the date of late October 1940—I note now that the actual invasion began on October 28th, not the 29th; I had assumed the 29th because I knew the ultimatum from Mussolini was delivered to Metaxás on the 28th—or he could have meant when the Germans invaded six months later. But in either case, my father tells me something I had never heard before: that from Thebes he had seen Germans parachuting into Athens. A few moments later (after speaking of the family's retreat to Roúmeli, moving back and forth between the villages of Itéa and Kolopetinítsa, and explanations of family connections in the latter that I didn't know about), I try to return to this topic. Note that even though dates had come up just minutes prior, the issue of when the attempt to leave Greece occurred is contested again (this part of interview not previously quoted):

IRENE: So, um, you lived there [in Kolopetinítsa] for a while, and then you referred to going to Thebes and trying to get out of the country; that was after that period.

JOHN: [raised voice] Oh no, I never mentioned going to Thebes! No— when we were called by the American Embassy to get ready to leave, Greece, in 1930—

LUCIE: —it must have been 1939 . . .

JOHN: —1939, we got as far as Thebes and the Germans had invaded.

IRENE: No, the Germans—that's why I'm asking you, Dad—the Germans didn't get there until early in '41. In '39 they had invaded Poland. And so the Americans might have been wanting to get you guys home.

JOHN: Let me try to get this str— [sounds very annoyed] From Thebes I watched the Germans parachuting into Athens.

IRENE: Okay, good. So I can figure out when that was. [switches subject to diffuse tension] Uh, so, while we have the map here, where did you sell the cigarettes? Where were you living?

To recuperate a previous part of my analysis, my parents both offer the date of 1939, I suggest, not because they remember their own war starting then, but because they learned later that the Second World War began in 1939, so "beginning of the war" and "1939" are linked together in their memories. The new point of interest here is that I actually could *not* figure out when my father might have seen parachutists, because not a single historical source I consulted, including specialized histories of Greece and of the German Luftwaffe, and some of the world's leading historians on these subjects, mentioned anything about parachutists being part of the invasion of Attica, the area including and surrounding Athens. To be sure, German bombers were involved in the attacks all over Greece. They took out some Greek and British installations, including a dramatic bombing in the port of Piraeus of the Scottish warship *Clan Frazier*, which was carrying 250 tons of explosives. The Luftwaffe hit resulted not only in the destruction of the *Clan Frazier* but of twelve other warships as well and rendered the port nonfunctional for several weeks (Time-Life Editors 1982, 110). I have myself seen the monument Greeks erected near a tree hundreds of yards away that still contains a piece of an exploded ship. My family would not have been able to leave the country at that point, even if they had gotten to the port. Why is it that my father insisted to me not once, but twice that he had seen parachutists? Why did he insist they were parachuting into Athens, when one can't see Athens from Thebes? Was he trying to aggrandize the situation they were in?

I now don't think so. Rather, I believe he was remembering just how serious the threat to them was. If my grandmother were trying to get her children out of the country because she thought they were in danger, she would not have abandoned the effort unless a more immediate danger imperiled them. That is to say: I'm sure my family saw with their own

24. Memorial to explosion of *Clan Frazier* battleship by the Germans
on April 7, 1941, in port of Piraeus, Greece, at site of a fragment
of the ship that lodged in a tree hundreds of yards away.

eyes some aspect of the German advance toward the capital that made them fear for their lives and frightened them into turning around. That my father has that "something" entrenched in his memory as "parachutists" is due, I hypothesize following Loftus, to introduced information about events that occurred in the following weeks: the unsuccessful use of German parachutists to secure the strategic Corinth canal on April 26 and/or the German invasion of Crete on May 18—a Pyrrhic victory. Given the proximity of Itéa and Corinth, it is at least hypothetically possible that my father might have been traveling east and seen something of what occurred at Corinth, though he never told me he did, and when I asked him about it directly he said he had not seen the maneuver. He could not have personally witnessed any aspect of the Cretan invasion. My point here is that both were reported widely in Greece. And the Cretan invasion was discussed all over Europe and the world for its scale, its loss of life on both sides—and its ten thousand parachutists. It would have been virtually impossible for my father not to have heard something about the German-Greek-British debacle in Crete; he may even have seen images diffused in newspapers, magazines, or broadsheets—although these were hard to come by in rural Greece. (I have myself seen such images in the French magazine L'Illustration of June 1941.) The fact that any information about German parachutists would have come to him closely following his own eyewitnessing of some aspect of the German invasion would have facilitated the addition of parachutists to his own memory. As Loftus puts it, "Postevent information can not only enhance existing memories but also change a witness's memory and even cause nonexistent details to become incorporated into a previously acquired memory" (1996, 55).

Once the idea of parachutists as part of the German invasion had been introduced to my father, it never left. In 2005 he tells me, "From those plains we watched the Germans parachute into Athens." The language in which my father related his memory to me might reveal the enhancement of it, how the additional element was added: from the "plains"

of Thebes, he may well have seen or heard a lot of "planes." Four The-
ban eyewitnesses to the German invasion whom my cousin George Kacandes (Harry's son) and I consulted in December 2006 insisted there
had been no parachutists. However, they all recalled vividly seeing the
destruction caused by the bombs the German Stukas did drop in that
area, describing the earth as "jumping into the air." Whether or not my
father had also seen this, I hypothesize that once he had heard about
and possibly seen pictures of German parachutists, he saw them in his
mind's eye too, jumping from the planes that he really had seen and
heard. This remains my own theory, of course. And I see no way to confirm or disprove it. If you ask my father, as I have, he will certainly insist to you that he saw parachutists no matter how many history books
you show him that assert otherwise. In fact, in my most recent query to
him on the subject, he even specified that he had seen the parachutists
from the window of the bus his family was traveling in to Athens. Luckily, this is not a court of law, and no one is at risk from my father's testifying to "parachutists."

TESTIMONIAL "TRUTH" VS. HISTORICAL "TRUTH"

The idea of something that may not in fact have occurred empirically
becoming part of a personal story has also been an important concept
for psychoanalysis for many decades. To my knowledge, Donald Spence
first introduced the concept of "narrative truth" in relation to "historical truth" in a pathbreaking study by that title in 1982. Spence defines
narrative truth in the psychoanalytical encounter as "the criterion we
use to decide when a certain experience has been captured to our sat-
isfaction. . . . Once a given construction has acquired narrative truth,
it becomes just as real as any other kind of truth" (1982, 31). Historical
truth, on the other hand "is time-bound and is dedicated to the strict
observance of correspondence rules" (32). Spence uses the distinction
between narrative truth and historical truth to draw his colleagues' attention to the *construction* of narrative truth in psychoanalytic sessions,

despite a longstanding belief that analyst and analysand are reconstructing something that corresponds to the past as it really happened (35).

Psychoanalyst and cofounder of the Holocaust Video Testimony archives at Yale University, Dori Laub, relies on Spence's insights (without quoting them) for a different purpose when he recounts a debate among historians, psychoanalysts and artists who had viewed together the video testimony of a woman who had experienced the crematorium explosion at Auschwitz. "'All of a sudden,' she said, 'we saw four chimneys going up in flames, exploding'" (as quoted in Felman and Laub 1992, 59). The historians, Laub reports, could not give credence to any aspect of this woman's account, because it was inaccurate and incomplete: not four, but rather one chimney was blown up, inmates were executed, and the attempted escape foiled, the revolt put down, unsuccessful in great part because of the betrayal of the Jewish underground by the Polish resistance (60–61). Laub, who through his work with the Holocaust video archive at Yale had been the original interviewer of the witness, evaluated what the woman had to say differently: "She had come, indeed, to testify," Laub writes, "not to the empirical number of the chimneys, but to resistance, to the affirmation of survival, to the breakage of the frame of death" (62). In this respect, Laub concludes, she actually *could* be thought of as adding to the historical record (63). She does not remember or know the correct number of chimneys blown up, but she knows that that act of resistance broke the frame of annihilation of the human spirit that was the core principle of the Nazi extermination camps.

I am of course neither a psychoanalyst nor a professional interviewer, nor do I believe my father had any conscious sense of contributing to the historical record during his talks with me. Still, Laub's account of the *meaning* of the witness's testimony to the Auschwitz explosion helps me reevaluate what my father says he saw from Thebes. "His" parachutists can now serve as a confirmation for me and I hope anyone else who is interested, not of exactly what the family saw from Thebes, but rather *of the quality of the fear engendered by what they had seen:* the sight of whatever transpired in Thebes that day must have been as terrifying to them as that of thousands of German parachutists to the Greeks or their British allies on the ground in Crete. It cut off my family's advance toward "Athens," too far away to actually be seen from Thebes, but the place that meant: escape, America, their spouse and father, and safety. This obstacle between the family and Athens meant that they were now **trapped**, a word my father has used over and over again, a word I "knew" from my earliest childhood (see chapter 1; this topic will also be discussed in chapter 4). I want to use the distinctions from Loftus, Spence, and Laub about the historical record and the personal inscribing of the historical record in individual memory to explain what in a number of different frameworks is the most painful, the most difficult part of what my father told me: his account of misidentification, arrest, and deportation. I mention again that whatever vague stories I had carried inside me since childhood, it was the report of these events that made me go in search of Daddy's War. To make this part of my search comprehensible, though, I needed to backtrack to some basic ideas about trauma.

TRAUMA

Τραύμα. A word of Greek origin meaning "wound" and used also for the last hundred years or so to refer to the state of being psychically wounded or to the agent, force, or mechanism that causes such a state (*Merriam-Webster's Collegiate Dictionary*, 11th ed.). Since 1980 the American medical establishment has officially recognized a certain set of symptoms by the designation "posttraumatic stress disorder" (PTSD): numbness, isolation, withdrawal, disruption in intimate relationships, persistent dysphoria, self-injury, suicidal preoccupation, depersonalization, hallucinations, amnesia, and reliving experiences or flashbacks (APA 1994, 424–29). My purpose here is not to conjecture if my father has suffered at some point in his life from PTSD. To be sure, my father experienced the kinds of atrocities that have been known to produce trauma. From my own lay observations, he has most obviously displayed persistent dysphoria and sleep disturbances from nightmares. Still, that's not my point here. Rather, some things I have learned about trauma over the years help me appreciate certain aspects of my father's recounting of his war experiences—whether or not his state in the aftermath of those experiences would have been counted by medical experts as posttraumatic.

For one thing, it is hard to predict what will cause trauma. It is well documented—and has been incorporated into the medical definition—that trauma can be caused not only by direct threats to one's own existence, but also by witnessing or even hearing of the violation or death of another person (APA 1994, 424: Criterion A1). Furthermore, as I reviewed in chapter 1 in relation to my experience of my friends' murders, experts and amateur observers point out that not every individual will react the same way to the same stressors. Thus, the very same events that lead to traumatization in one person, might not in another (Caruth 1995, 4; Wigren 1994, 417). Previously traumatized individuals and victims of racism, poverty, and sexism are more susceptible to traumatization than the general population (Galea et al. 2002; Root 1996).

After living with Daddy's War my whole life and now concentrating on it for more than three years, it seems likely to me that the, to paraphrase my sister Maria, something not nice (chapter 2, section 4d) that happened to our father was not a single "thing," not a single violation that caused a specific trauma. And yet which of the so many events recounted in chapter 2—or events of which he has perhaps never been able to speak—might have been more difficult for him to process or have produced more harmful consequences? I doubt I will ever know exactly. According to the research just cited, it is not irrelevant that my father experienced years, not months or weeks, of being undernourished. I think it is also possible that due to his exact age, gender, birth order, and familial role accordingly assigned to him, he experienced the war and its dangers more fully than his siblings. To be sure, my grandmother and all four of her children suffered terribly. But I suspect there may have been a lack of awareness of some of the real dangers on the part of the younger siblings; I'm not sure my uncle Harry could have stolen a German soldier's boots off the dock in Itéa or a German shepherd puppy from a dog that belonged to one of the billeted soldiers, if he had fully grasped what the consequences would be if he were caught. Additionally, because my father's siblings were younger than he, they generally received greater portions of food, and they also bore less of the responsibility for providing that food. As my aunt Pearl put it to me, "I mean your dad has his own unique story, completely separate from the rest of us. [. . .] I mean I—I—your dad was always a father to me. He was never a brother. Because he provided for us. If it wasn't for your dad, we would never have survived the war. He went to Athens and worked in the streets. He begged from everyone. And sent us packages back in Itéa. And that's how we survived the war" (chapter 2, section 9h). And yet, because my father was still a child—after all, only thirteen years old when he worked on the *Vellisários*, for example—he was not always able to live up to the role assigned to him or effect his own fate the way an adult—indeed his own mother—could. (In deepening my understanding of my father's experiences I have found Susan Suleiman's (2004) work on the "1.5 generation," of Holocaust survivors, that is to say, individuals who were children during the war, to be very helpful.)

In terms of discrete, potentially traumatizing situations, it seems relevant to me that my father himself did experience combat. The attempts to treat "shell shock" during and in the aftermath of the Great War and to deal with the flashbacks of veterans of the Vietnam War were two sequelae of combat that pushed doctors to try to understand mental trauma better (see Herman 1997, chapter 1). From documents and photographs in his possession, as well as from a comparison of his own reports to those in a history book about the 50th Royal Tank Regiment of the British army (Hamilton 1996), it is clear that my father fought with the British, after the liberation of Greece from the German occupiers, against communist forces for control of Athens and then Patrás. His

25. John (center) with tanks of the 50th Royal Tank Regiment of the
British Army in Patrás, February 2, 1945; soldiers unidentified.

26. John (right) with unidentified members of
the 50th RTR, Patrás, February 13, 1945.

commendation from his British captain states that "he risked his life on several occasions in the forward positions." I have never heard details; my father's report to me was vague and calm, almost sheepish: "I was adventurous and I was trying to help the umm, the British, you know, gain control of that area." History books report that the street fighting in Athens was ferocious, but again, I do not know what harm my father might have inflicted himself, had inflicted on him or seen inflicted on others. I do know that even though he was obviously older when he was fighting with the British than when he experienced some other horrific events, he was still only fifteen.

In terms of those other events, I recall here that during the occupation my father witnessed terrible things happening to people he loved: the deaths of his grandparents and the near death of his mother, my speculations about rape aside. Furthermore, it seems that my father was incarcerated at least once by local Greek collaborationist authorities, probably in 1941 or '42 when he was only eleven or twelve years old (chapter 2, section 4a). Something took off part of his toe (chapter 2, sections 6b and 6d), and he has a scar on the tender side of his arm that he says was inflicted by a German interrogator (chapter 2, sections 8b and 8h). Surely he could have been traumatized by any and all of these events.

WITNESSING TO TRAUMA

Trauma theory also provides a possible explanation for my father's manner, frequency, and chosen audiences and venues for telling his story. As psychiatrist Judith Herman explains in her widely read book *Trauma and Recovery*, "The conflict between the will to deny horrible events and the will to proclaim them aloud is the central dialectic of psychological trauma. People who have survived atrocities often tell their stories in a highly emotional, contradictory, and fragmented manner which undermines their credibility and thereby serves the twin imperatives of truth-telling and secrecy" (1997, 1). Herman summarizes helpfully that "the fundamental stages of recovery are establishing safety, reconstructing the trauma story, and restoring the connection between survivors and their community" (3). Researchers Bessel van der Kolk and Otto van der Hart, following pioneer Pierre Janet, propose slightly different terms but along the same lines, speaking of "traumatic memory" that is inflexible and has no social component and "narrative or ordinary memory" that integrates experience into other memories and can be narrated in different versions to different addressees (1995, 160, 163, 164). Since the infliction of trauma involves some inability to act, the taking of action by turning the unassimilated experience into a story seems to promote healing, the transformation of the traumatic memory into narrative memory. Exactly how this is accomplished remains a mystery, but it appears that "the traumatized person has to return to the memory often in order to complete it" (176). Because most victims have phobias of the traumatic memory, this revisiting can usually be accomplished only in the presence of a sympathetic, committed listener or other "appropriate social supports" (Wigren 1994, 417).

To my knowledge, my father has never availed himself of professional expertise in working through what he had experienced as a boy. The only time I ever heard "experiences in the war" and "visiting a mental health professional" put into the same sentence, my father was rebuffing the notions that his present behaviors or moods had anything to do with the war and that he was in need of help. He certainly never succeeded in reestablishing connections between himself and the Greek community in which he experienced the atrocities. As I recounted in chapter 1, he refused to return to Greece for more than forty years after leaving; to my knowledge he never reconciled with his uncle John—though he did choose to visit him when he went to Greece in 1986. His attempt to settle in another part of Greece after his retirement—an experiment that only lasted a few years—failed to bring him peace. I think my sister Maria's assessment that our father was trying to exorcise the ghost of his experiences by repeatedly telling stories, though, is essentially correct (chapter 2, section 4d). I would add that my father handled his past in a way that made cultural sense to him: by seeking out listeners he thought would be sympathetic to what he had to say, starting with the criteria of display of basic interest and lack of their own knowledge and opinions of the Greek tragedies; his audience was most decidedly American. (In fact, the three times that my father was present as I interviewed other Greek eyewitnesses to the events, he remained almost completely silent.) The content of what he told his selected auditors may also point toward a self-treatment characteristic.

I now want to consider my father's story of mistaken identity, arrest, and deportation. My thoughts about it are necessarily more speculative than the thoughts I have shared above. Therefore, I am breaking this section on "witnessing to trauma" into two installments. Since I am switching from a cooler, more objective mode of analysis to one higher in conjecture and affect, I am placing the second installment under the metaphor of "grappling."

[4]

Grappling with Daddy's War

Speculations for Extending Theories

WITNESSING TO TRAUMA, CONTINUED

I attempt here to make sense of the family stories gathered in the earlier sections of this book in a more speculative register. I will use Laub's account of his witness's testimony to the explosion of four crematoria chimneys in Auschwitz that was considered in chapter 3 as a roadmap for returning to my father's story of arrest and deportation.

Laub devotes more than four pages of his text to his experiences with this witness to the crematoria explosion. She remains anonymous, as do his colleagues who view her testimony. This discussion is embedded in a chapter called "Bearing Witness or the Vicissitudes of Listening," in which Laub makes two main points about giving testimony to "massive psychic trauma": one, that the testifying itself can become the place, the occasion, by which the witness him- or herself comes to know the event for the very first time; and two, that the listener enables that event of cognition to take place and in doing so becomes a participant and coowner of the event (Felman and Laub 1992, 57). For Laub, then, what the historians missed by focusing on the factual inaccuracy of what the woman had to say is that she *is* witnessing to history—to the "breaking of the frame" of Auschwitz through any degree of resistance—and also that she is experiencing that breaking of the frame itself through, in, and at the moment of her testifying.

Perhaps this discovery stands out for Laub because of another discovery: that she had worked in the "Canada" commando; Laub deduces this from her account of leaving each morning separately from the others and returning in the evening with shoes and clothing she could give to her fellow inmates. When Laub asked the witness if she knows the name of the commando, she replied she does not, and when he followed up by using the term he knows, "Canada commando," she also replied "no" that she has never heard of "Canada commando." Furthermore, reports Laub, she is "taken aback, as though startled by my question" (Felman and Laub 1992, 60). In Laub's interpretation of this interaction, he had "probed the limits of her knowledge. . . . We did not talk of the sorting out of the belongings of the dead. She did not think of them as the remainings of the thousands who were gassed. She did not ask herself where they had come from. The presents she brought back to her fellow inmates, the better, newer clothes and shoes, had for her no origin" (60). This backing off on both their parts from what she does not know allows her to testify to what she does know. It permits too the listener, Laub, to take in what she knows and in part comes to know through the very act of her speaking.

Laub concludes that lack of knowledge can have some benefits in the testimonial process, offering two examples of such benefits. In the first instance, the woman does not know where the clothes come from, and when Laub realizes this, his not probing further allows her to testify that she was doing good: by giving the inmates she knew clothing and shoes, she was increasing the chances they would survive. In the second example, Laub comments on the limits of his own knowledge about the fate of the inmates who started the revolt and the extent of the Polish underground's betrayal of that attempted revolt. He hypothesizes that had he known and posed questions to his witness about these disturbing facts "such questions might have in effect suppressed her message . . . might have interfered with my ability to listen and to hear. . . . And whether my agenda would have been historical or psychoanalytical, it might unwittingly have interfered with the process of the testimony. In this respect, it might be useful sometimes, not to know too much." Knowledge is necessary, he goes on to say, for the listener "to be able to pick up the cues." "Yet," he decides, "knowledge should not hinder or obstruct the listening with foregone conclusions and preconceived dismissals should not be an obstacle or a foreclosure to new, diverging, unexpected information" (Felman and Laub 1992, 61). Tall order. It is some comfort to me that not only do the professional historians at the conference viewing the testimony miss the balance, but that Laub himself reports in the next section of the chapter on the difficulty and the effervescence of his own hearing of the "password" that allows such "illumination" to take place (63).

I have revisited this scene and analysis of listening at length because the details of the process Laub describes help me comprehend my first receptions of my father's story of misidentification, arrest, and deportation, and this process opens up another way for me to receive and evaluate my father's story. In short, I believe I have moved from trying to ascertain the historical truth of what happened to my father, to trying to hear what he was actually testifying to and what work this testifying was doing for him. As I recounted in chapter 1 of this book, I first heard a report from my sister Georgia in 1989 on the telephone that my father had been misidentified as a Jew because of his circumcision, arrested, and deported to a transit camp. The news seemed wondrous—our father in a Nazi camp?—and yet I found myself believing the story on the basis of how the dynamics in our family seemed to resemble those of Holocaust survivor families I had just read about shortly before Georgia's communication. I realize now that I made the story even more believable to myself by filling in the bare plot my sister passed on to me, grafting historical details I knew about how the Nazis treated Jews in northern Europe onto the landscape of Greece and what I thought I knew about the German occupation and the resistance there. Thus, I pictured to myself, for example, small Nazi patrols scouring the arid mountainous countryside and small villages, accosting individuals they suspected might be Jews and herding them into collection points in anticipation of deportation to death camps in Poland. It seemed completely plausible to me that Greek resistance fighters who knew those hills so well might come across such a "transit camp," overwhelm the Nazi guards, and liberate the prisoners, and that this was in fact what had happened to my father and his family and that that was how they avoided deportation out of the country. (I was able to confirm the historicity of at least one similar scenario in research I did much later; see personal account in Abatzoglou 1983, 112–15.)

I also recounted in chapter 1 the various and complicated reasons why I didn't pursue this or any other aspect of Daddy's War systematically for many years after. Still, I did make attempts to learn more about or at least have confirmed for me what had happened by suggesting my father give testimony to the Yale archive, by showing him what I'd written, by enabling the production of his memoir. I mention these details again now, because by the time my father did give me a recital of his arrest and deportation (April 30, 2005), much time had passed and much energy had been expended. I was more skeptical and hostile than Laub's historians, and I'm trying to account for what had changed in my own attitude. Partly, indeed, it was knowledge—I did know more about what had transpired in Greece during the war. Still, it wasn't that much more. No, I think it was mostly that I now had an agenda, an agenda about finding out the "historical truth." And with each rebuff from my father of my attempts to find out "what happened," the more I began to fear that this part of his story was invented. I had always been somewhat skeptical, but my skepticism began to grow when I collected versions of the story from three of my siblings in 2004 and realized how different they were, including critical details like whether the entire family was actually seized or not.

And my skepticism increased exponentially when I found out from my aunt Stella that my uncle Harry was in fact not circumcised; at the very least, I was forced to realize, the events could not have unfolded in the way I had them in my head all those years: that is, that the whole family had been deported, because all the boys were circumcised.

Due to its length, I won't requote here the full recital I got from my father in that first—and to date only—version I have ever had from him directly (chapter 2, section 8h). My first set of observations about that interchange, however, concerns my own hostility. The tone with which I asked him questions can only be heard on the tape, but my challenges to him can also be perceived in a written version of the transcript. For one thing, I set him up with my question about the Germans examining villagers' penises, and specifically with my comment, "So every time that happened, it was a problem for you. You had to explain yourself." The "you" is ambiguous, but "yourself" is not; it can only be singular. My father consciously or unconsciously picked up on these challenges and emphasized the plural in his response: "Yeah, for us, because we were the only people in the village that were circumcised." Even though I don't push him on this point by revealing what I know about Uncle Harry—that is, that one of my father's brothers was not circumcised—my challenging stance is also evident a minute later when we come to the topic of Salonika. My father uses an obscure pronunciation for the name of the city: Thessalónika. In my follow up question, I am challenging him overtly to name something he saw that allowed him to realize he was in Salonika (and to prove to me that he was). I now see clearly how my stance of thinking I know better than he does—that is, that I know he is making up what he's telling me—also comes out through my modern Greek pronunciation of the name of the city: Thessaloníki.

The second point I want to make concerns the historical "facts." An outline of the "events," as he recounted them that day will be helpful, as they are quite different from the way I had heard them previously from my sister. They are the closest, I observe, to the version my brother Tom had from his schoolmates in the mid-1970s (chapter 2, section 8b). I am extracting only my father's comments from this part of the interview; words in square brackets often summarize something I have just said or asked and to which he is responding:

When the Germans identified me as a Jew, I remember I was in Athens at that time.

They used to round up, strip down the males, and I was circumcised.

And that was good enough proof and ended up in the camp in Yugoslavia.

I was all by myself and couldn't even notify Captain Pétros, who knew I was in Athens.

We were the only people in the village that were circumcised.

I know we were in Thessalónika and then they moved us into Yugoslavia.

We were in a [camp] with a lot of Jews from Kérkyra that had been assembled there.

We were assembled there. And then went into some part of Yugoslavia.

And my uncle somehow got the word, I don't know how.

Psarrós, John Psarrós, was one of two Greek generals that never surrendered during the war. Zérvas, who was in Épirus, and my uncle who was further south.

Psarrós, he was a cousin of my mother. In fact for some—I don't remember the reasons, but I was heir to his property because there was no family of them in Chryssó.

Well, anyway, so he was the Greek underground guerrilla for the [. . .] royalists.

And the royalists had airplanes coming in and out of Gióna, that's the mountains behind Kolopetinítsa.

My recollection is that they took us someplace besides Thessaloníki and to Yugoslavia.

All of a sudden [. . .] while [in] camp and this guy was putting the swastika on my arm with cigarette butts to [get me to] tell where my father was.

Well, of course I didn't.

So, in the meantime, my uncle was apparently good friends with Tito. They were both the leading generals that never surrendered to the Germans.

And the story goes that as a favor, he asked Tito to see if they could liberate part of the camp because I was there—the only heir to the family and this and that.

And sure enough I was almost like kidnapped, covered up, and taken back into Greece.

Until I was delivered to my uncle through the mountains of northern Greece all the way down to the "back" of Gióna as they say.

And up there in Lárissa was my uncle's hideaway.

So Thýmios—if anybody remembers anything of that period, he would be the one, because he was a young guy, a shepherd, and he was the one that they trusted in Kolopetinítsa to be in contact with my uncle.

[The trip from Athens to Thessaloníki was] all by train.

It was so dark you couldn't see anything [. . .] until they let us out in the camp.

Thessaloníki is where the trains went. From Thessaloníki to Yugoslavia—that's a separate trip [also by train].

[I have no idea where I was in Yugoslavia] no idea except that all through those northern mountains I was delivered to my uncle.

[On the way home we used] donkey, walking, all kinds, hiding. (extracted from chapter 2, section 8h)

In the months that followed this interview I dedicated myself most assiduously to learning about the war, occupation, and persecution of the Jews in Greece. Without tracing all my steps, I want to share the intensity with which my albeit untrained historical instinct was operating: I latched onto anything that seemed to confirm or contradict what my father said had happened to him, particularly in relation to the sequence of events quoted above. For example, when I was transcribing the interview of April 30, 2005, and reached the section when my father said that he was in Yugoslavia and had come back into Greece through Albania with his saviors, I realized I was doubting that could even be possible without myself being able to picture the geography of the Balkans very well. So, I went to check out maps, first in a general atlas and then in Martin Gilbert's *Atlas of the Holocaust* (1988). Upon studying in the latter the photos, the maps, and the arrows Gilbert added to the maps to indicate the directions Greek Jews went and where Jews were active in the Greek Resistance (Gilbert 1988, 180–81), I started crying, realizing that my father's story, in terms of the geography at least, was plausible. I finally let myself have the thought: what if they had gotten him? I was similarly persuaded and moved when I rediscovered my own notes from an interview with a Christian Greek partisan in the Fortunoff Holocaust Video Testimony archives that I had listened to fifteen years prior—and completely forgotten—in which the witness testified to having been forced by the Germans scouring his area for Jews to pull down his pants. I sought out eyewitness testimony from Greek Jews, published or passed on orally. I became particularly interested in the fate of the great-uncle of a Greek Jewish friend of mine, because some elements of his story resembled somewhat elements in my father's account. He was a pharmacist and had been passing as a Christian. He was picked up individually in Athens after the general roundup of Jews because a rival pharmacist denounced him to the Nazis as a Jew. He was questioned, sent to Haïdári (a large prison situated between Athens and Piraeus) and subsequently deported on a train through Thessaloníki heading north for Auschwitz. At some point before leaving the Greek capital, he scribbled on a piece of paper the address of a trusted family friend who knew where his family was hiding, in the hopes that someone would find the note and deliver it to the friend and he to them (which is what happened).

When the transport reached Yugoslavia, he and two others decided to jump from the train. My friend didn't know the fate of the other jumpers, but her great-uncle landed safely, managed to find aid among the local population, worked as a doctor there, and after the withdrawal of the Germans from the Balkans made his way back into Greece. Another detail that caught my attention was that some eyewitnesses had used the phrase παρτιζάνοι του Τίτο (Tito's partisans) to refer to Slavic-speaking (Greek) partisans in northern Greece (personal communication from historian Aléxios Menexiádes).

It was thus that some aspects of my father's account began once again to seem possible, if still improbable, because I could not get historical facts to line up with several key elements of my father's story. For one thing, physical inspection was not the primary way Jews were identified as Jews in the capital: it was betrayal; they would be denounced by Greeks who knew they were passing as Christians. For another, there were major problems with chronology. Athenian Jews were rounded up in the largest numbers on March 23, 1944, sent to Haïdári, and deported in early April, arriving in Auschwitz the second week of the month; the Jews of Kérkyra, in contrast, were not deported from their island until early June 1944 (see, for instance, Kalaphátis 2001, passim, and Lanzmann 1985, 128). The two groups would not have overlapped in Haïdári or anywhere else along the way. Of course, there were discoveries and individual arrests in Athens following the main deportation, as with my friend's great-uncle, and these Jews may have been added to the transports from Kérkyra that passed through Athens in mid-June 1944. The same historian who had told me about the phrase "Tito's partisans" informed me that by surveying surviving Athenian Jews in recent decades, the Jewish Museum of Greece has come up with the estimate that between 120 and 600 Athenian Jews were arrested and deported after the major roundup in March. Still, were my father deported later, and thus indeed able to be in the presence of Jews from Kérkyra, his account would run into a different snag in chronology: my father says he was delivered to his relative the resister Colonel (not General) Psarrós, who had made my father his heir. To be sure, Psarrós was from my grandmother's village of Chryssó, he and his wife were in fact childless, and his partisan group, 5/42 Evzónon, operated mainly in the area north and northwest of Chryssó. These facts lend credence to my father's account. However, Psarrós was assassinated by his communist rivals on April 17, 1944, and the group essentially disbanded at the same time. Even if I hypothesize that my father, in his extreme anxiety, did not realize where he was at any point after his arrest and that he was liberated from within Greece, discounting the detail that he was at any point in the company of Kérkyrans, it would still be difficult to get the timing to line up between the arrest of Athenian Jews and a deliverance to Psarrós, who had his relations with his communist rivals on his mind—not the whereabouts of his purported heir—for many weeks prior to his assassination (see Kaïmáras 1988). If I take the opposite approach and discount the personalized rescue of my father by partisans sympathetic to Psarrós, it is possible that he could have been arrested individually in Athens, encountered Kérkyran Jews in Haïdári, and was somehow released from there when someone figured out that he actually was not Jewish.

What conclusions is one to come to? What conclusions have I come to?

It seems possible, indeed probable to me, that at some point during the occupation my father was arrested by German authorities in Athens. He told a journalist that this was the case in the interview he gave to the local newspaper upon his return to the United States in October 1945: "In Athens he was arrested by the Gestapo but released on the recommendation of the Swedish Red Cross" (article reprinted in appendix D). However, even this report closest to the time of the events under scrutiny raises doubts. For whereas the Swedish Red Cross did distribute much aid in the form of food and medicine in Greece, and even occasionally delivered correspondence to prisoners, there is no indication in the official records I could access, anyway, that they ever intervened for the release of incarcerated individuals. When I raised the issue of arrest with my father's sister, she mentioned nothing about the newspaper account or about my father being mistaken for a Jew, yet she immediately assumed that my father could have been arrested for stealing (chapter 2, section 8i). The boy was hungry and fending for himself. I repeat that not only theft, but also getting caught for it at some point seem completely plausible to me, too. It also seems possible, however, that, as in the case of my friend's great-uncle, someone in Athens who knew my father was circumcised tried to curry favor with the German occupiers by pointing him out as a Jew and the Nazis picked him up for that reason. Seeing that he was indeed circumcised, they retained him. Was my father then deported as a Jew? In contrast to many other places in Europe, there are no deportation lists for Athenian Jews from the time. There are lists of the Athenian arrivals in Auschwitz, and my father is not on them. Of course, he never says he arrived in Auschwitz. Still, very, very few people escaped en route as did my friend's great-uncle. There are numerous additional historical, logistical, and logical problems with my father's story as he told it to me from the point of deportation onward. The two things that seem the most improbable to me are that the group he was deported with experienced a transit camp in Yugoslavia, and that any group of partisans (much less Tito's or even Slavic-speaking Greek partisans) came to liberate said camp. Neither I nor the experts at the Jewish Museum in Athens could locate or recall any testimony about such actions by partisans to the benefit of Jews in relation to known camps—of which there were very few in the areas my father claimed to have passed through.

One sole thing is certain: my father was an anomaly as a circumcised male Christian in a country where only Jews and Muslims were circumcised. Were he to have been arrested by the Germans for whatever reason, one additional thing is certain: my father stopped being detained at some point before the Germans left the country. The assistant cooks, Leonídas and Pantelís Manoúsos, the brothers from Ándros, are witnesses to my father's presence in the police precinct kitchen in October 1944 during the liberation of Athens.

How to account for the existence and the persistence of the implausible details in my father's account? Following Loftus, and in the same vein as my explanation of my father's parachutists, I think that if my father were arrested by the Germans—and I repeat that this seems not only possible but probable—it is also probable that certain elements were added later to his memory of what must have been a frightening situation. Arrest by the Germans would have been scary for anyone, but perhaps even more so for my father, who would have been young—only fourteen years old if my estimates that this occurs in 1944 are correct. His terror, furthermore, must have been compounded by having been incarcerated once before, earlier in the war (chapter 2, section 4a), and, as I have heard tell only since conducting my family interviews, by having been threatened with jail or even actually having been jailed overnight as a young child in the United States by his father trying to teach him a lesson. If my father were in any kind of German detention situation, including the notorious camp Haïdári at any point, he might have encountered Jews there, Jews who were then deported. When he learned more about their fate, he could easily have imagined having shared it. Two details my father has recited about the camp support my theory that he may have indeed been in Haïdári and that it was there he temporarily shared the fate of some Greek Jews. We have numerous eyewitness accounts that there was an inordinate number of dogs roaming around, and that prisoners were fed by the Germans throwing the refuse from their own meals onto the ground. Why then has my father never mentioned the name "Haïdári"? Is that a traumatic black hole? What of his specific memory that he was with Jews of Kérkyra? On the one hand, they too were taken to Haïdári in the complicated, multistage course of their deportation, and it is certainly possible that their incarcerations there could have overlapped with a detention of my father were it to have occurred in June 1944. On the other, it seems just as possible to me to account for that specific detail by the fact that my father would have had some contact with the Jews of Kérkyra when he went to that island on the *Vellisários* in 1943. When my father heard about their deportation in summer 1944, he could have collapsed the two memories, of detention and of meeting some Jews in Kérkyra, with the new piece of information, that those Jews had been deported.

There are at least two additional ways to account for my father's story that have occurred to me as I have poured over the interviews. One is that he was actually captured by the Germans twice, in the period in which he runs messages for the partisans in the mountains (probably late '42 to early '43), and then a second time in Athens closer to the period of both the deportation of Athenian Jews (spring 1944) and of the liberation of Greece (fall 1944), and that with the passage of time he put the two stories together. The hint for this explanation came in my first interview with him in a moment when my "agenda" prevented me from hearing what he was saying. In an exchange from that interview that I have not yet quoted, I commented with wonder at how frequently my father appeared to have gone back and forth between Athens and Itéa, a trip that is still not easy today because of the mountains and the quality of the roads. His response to my wonderment goes in a direction I'm not expecting, that is, explaining to me why he wasn't in Itéa very much:

JOHN: I was very little there. I had to . . .

IRENE: Because of . . .

JOHN: Because of the fear of being recaptured and uh we needed uh some source of income . . .

IRENE: Right and Athens was more a source of income than the village areas. [April 30, 2005]

I simply did not register the phrase "fear of being recaptured" until I was transcribing the tape many weeks later. I didn't ask him about it at the time, and, unfortunately, it's impossible to do so now because of his dementia; he does not hold in his mind that we talked about these issues and that I am trying to probe things he said then. At the point in time when I am writing this, if asked about the war, my father recites pared-down versions of just a few episodes, like about Tsardákas finding him in the port of Piraeus when he is trying to send money to his mother or about his uncle John Tsakíris claiming that his sheep committed suicide. In conjunction with my sister Maria's memories that our father's stories about the mountains included close encounters with the Germans (chapter 2, sections 4d and 8a), I'm wondering if he wasn't actually arrested by them one time in Roúmeli. In that place and period, his claim that Psarrós sent a team to "liberate" him is much more plausible. And again, he might have collapsed that "liberation" with one from detention before (threat of) deportation as a Jew.

Another way to account for my father's claim of persecution as a Jew and specifically for the escape through the mountains occurred to me while thinking about an anecdote my aunt Pearl shared with me of a Jewish man from Thessaloníki whose family was arrested by the Germans in the massive deportations of 1943. He was absent at the time of the original forced departure from home, and when he realized the whole community was being deported, he fled south from Thessaloníki, traveling through the mountains and eventually ending up famished and near death in Itéa. According to my aunt, my grandmother hid this Salonikan and fed him until he regained his strength and wanted to go on to Athens. I got some corroboration for this story from my cousin George who, without my mentioning the story from our aunt, remembers his father, my father's brother Harry, telling him about carrying a Jewish refugee's coat from one room of the house to another and being intrigued by what objects hidden inside the coat could be making it feel so heavy. I don't believe my father was in Itéa for much of 1943. However, were my father to have been mistaken for a Jew and arrested by the Germans at any subsequent point, I wonder if he didn't recall stories his mother and siblings must have told him about this gentleman's flight through the mountains and imagine—or attempt?—a similar possible escape for himself.

THE HOLOCAUST AS A PUBLIC NARRATIVE

To return now to the version of the arrest, deportation, and rescue as I got it from my father in 2005, I note that, of course, my father might have consciously or unconsciously added any of its details at a later point in time. As far as I can reconstruct, deportation as a Jew and rescue by the partisans are not initially a part of his story—at least neither is mentioned in the 1945 article nor in the stories my sister Maria remembers from the early 1960s (chapter 2, section 8a). These elements have appeared in our father's accounts of his war experiences by the early 1970s when my brother Tom got a similar version (chapter 2, section 8b) to the one I heard from our father in 2005 (chapter 2, section 8h). My mother has listened to so many versions of my father's war experiences over their five decades together, and she has been so closely involved in my speaking with him in the last years, that she can no longer clearly distinguish among how he has told it at what times nor among the various theories I have shared with her as I have progressed in my research. Still, one day when I asked my mother directly about the possibility of my father's having been deported as a Jew, she said to me, "I do not remember him telling me that when we met [mid-1950s]."

I will be the first one to insist that, unlike seeing or not seeing parachutists, recounting that one has been deported as a Jew when one has not carries social and moral consequences: I need only mention the case of Binjamin Wilkomirski's *Fragments*, a book that the author claimed was his memoir of his childhood as a Polish Jew surviving the death camps. When investigations revealed that the author, whose legal name was Bruno Doesseker, had been born in Switzerland, put up for adoption, and raised by a Protestant couple near Zurich, he denied it and stuck to his claim that the book recounts his early life. Doesseker/Wilkomirski owned a library with thousands of books on the Holocaust. It appears he truly believed he experienced the camps as a young Jewish child (see, for instance, analyses in LaCapra 2001 and Suleiman 2006). If you ask my father today, like Doesseker/Wilkomirski, he will tell you deportation is part of his life story. Is he, too, deluded? Is he consciously lying? Have I just not uncovered the evidence to prove that he was deported? Without being a mental health professional, I cannot answer the first question, and maybe I'm not capable of answering the second, either. Having talked to him a number of times on the topic of his war experiences, I don't believe he is consciously lying—at least not now; perhaps he was conscious of adding this element at an earlier point in time. A positive answer to the third question remains a possibility; there may still be a way to confirm his arrest or deportation that I have not thought of and therefore have not pursued.

At this point in my own analytical journey, it seems important to me to return to my starting point in thinking about our family war stories: addressees matter. Even though there was some initial local interest in what happened to my father when he returned from Greece in 1945, as evidenced by the interview and article published in his local paper, for the most part immediate postwar America did not want to hear about war refugees: there were too many of them, the indigenous population felt that it too had suffered, and the mood of the country was to move on. (A confirmation for this attitude is provided by passages in many memoirs of European war refugees; see, for example, that of the Latvian Agate Nesaule 1997, 184.) Then, too, my father wanted to move on. He made an enormous effort to learn English properly, learn about American tastes in music, dance, popular culture, go to college. And yet, I doubt that he was "done" with his war. It seems probable to me that when my father, like so many Americans, learned more about the Nazi Judeocide in the late 1960s and early 1970s, certain aspects of that history seemed to resonate with and to complement his own general experiences of hardship, suffering, and injustice. Such knowledge may have resonated even louder with his perhaps specific experiences with being identified and arrested as a Jew. My father's experiences, one might say, were contiguous to the events we group under the heading "Holocaust," a word that itself began to be used more frequently in just this period to describe the complicated and varied modes of persecution and Judeocide perpetrated by the Nazis on European Jewry. That my father added in a sense a chapter about deportation to his autobiographical narrative seems even more probable to me, given that in addition to a general burgeoning interest in the United States during the 1960s and '70s in the Holocaust, my father himself began to have even more contact with Jewish Americans, by beginning graduate work in education at Yeshiva University (from 1964 to 1969), than he had already had through residing and teaching in White Plains, New York. At Yeshiva he might have been an addressee for personal stories of persecution of Jews by the Nazis or he would have had Jewish addressees for his war stories. To paraphrase Ong, in managing a particular interaction with that audience at that time, my father might have added details—indeed whole episodes—that would ensure that that audience would respond "vigorously" (see Ong 1982, 41–42). The tiny percentage of Holocaust survivors from Greece and general ignorance in the United States about how the war unfolded in southeastern Europe would have facilitated my father's ability to add such an episode, since his auditors were unlikely to have their own direct knowledge about the events and personages in his stories.

As I write this section I feel like I can sense the skepticism and perhaps even disapproval of some of my potential readers. Against these voices in my head, I continue to write in part because I believe that consciously or unconsciously borrowing from publicly known narratives to construct one's own personal history is probably a ubiquitous practice that deserves to be studied much more carefully than I can do here. I am reminded of Marianne Hirsch's perceptive analysis of Art Spiegelman's use of widely circulated images of the concentration camps. In "The

First Maus," for example, "the son can only imagine his father's experience in *Auschwitz*," writes Hirsch, "by way of [a] widely available photograph by Margaret Bourke-White of liberated prisoners in *Buchenwald*" (2008, 112; my emphasis). Spiegelman framed his own understanding through a public image that was broadly available. In my own research on children of survivors, I have come across similar attempts to understand what happened to the parents. When Helen Gerzon Goransson was exposed as a young child to Allied pictures of emaciated prisoners and piles of cadavers from the Nazi death camps in books owned by her parents' survivor friends, she assumed this is what her parents had experienced, even though, as I relayed earlier, her parents suffered the cold, hunger, and forced labor of Soviet camps, not the intentional death machinery of the Nazis (Goransson 2004).

While critical and moral faculties should be deployed for parallel analysis of borrowed narratives (as opposed to images), I believe that pure condemnation of the phenomenon, in many instances, is not merited and would prevent us from learning from those particular personal stories. Is it okay for Art Spiegelman to use public imagery because his father was in fact persecuted as a Jew and not okay for John Kacandes because we can't prove that he was? Perhaps. There are critical differences between the two situations including the generational one: Art is the son trying to imagine for himself his father's experiences; John is the purported victim propagating a perhaps false version of events. To borrow Halbwach's term, John needed a "social framework" (1992, 38–39 and 182–83) for his memories, and he seemed to have found one in the Holocaust. My father endows his adopted memories with the right affect, but not with a strong enough factual basis. Given my own interest and training in Holocaust studies, I'm not sure I could have or should have avoided trying to establish that, and (probably) when an element about being deported as a Jew was added to my father's memory of (possible) misidentification and (in all probability) arrest. For now, I have to content myself with noting the phenomenon of the (probable) borrowing, and realizing, along with Ross Chambers, that audiences' ability to accept my father's story—the White Plains JCC's numerous invitations—reflects on the society in which it was told, too, a "haunted society, in which an individual can mistake the collective consciousness of a painful past for a personal memory" (Chambers 2002, 95). This analysis obviously includes me, as I readily believed the story when I first heard it. Having established the improbability of this particular episode and raised the specter of its impropriety, I want to return to Laub's approach and speculate about what my father was doing *for himself* by telling it to me and many others the way he did.

SELF-HEALING OR RESCUE

Following Dori Laub's cue about listening for what the witness is actually able and needing to testify to, I now consider the raison d'être of this segment of my father's story to be an attempt at self-healing by creating a story of rescue, a story of rescue by the father.

I remember "receiving" my first tip toward this interpretation during the interview itself, but I didn't know what to make of it at the time. When my father reported having a German use cigarette butts to burn a swastika into his arm, he said his torturer was trying to get him to "tell where my father was." He was the faithful and courageous son: "Well of course I didn't [tell]." I remember thinking to myself while he was speaking these words: why would the Germans care where his father was? And if my father were being tortured, why wouldn't he have told his torturers that his father was in the United States? What would the harm have been? It was only after I had satisfied much of my determination to pin down the historical improbability of this whole segment, that I realized this story was not so much about arrest and deportation as it was about rescue by "the" father, the father in this instance being necessarily a substitute father, and more specifically, the local hero Psarrós. It is this father, of course, who would be of much more interest to the Germans, and who, in my father's version of events, arranges in quite elaborate ways for young John's rescue—and his future prosperity, by making him his heir.

Even as a layperson, it makes perfect psychological sense to me that a boy who felt he had been abandoned by his biological father would be searching—and finding—substitute fathers. John Kacandes's stories are filled with them: his uncle Vasílis Paphílis (Zoé's father), from whom he wants to learn carpentry; Sakellaríou (his schoolmate's uncle, the head of the fourth, not third police precinct, as it turns out), who lets him sleep in the kitchen; Tsardákas, the captain of the *Vellisários*, who invites him on board his ship; Tsardákas's surgeon brother, who operates on his toe; Thýmios, the older cousin who takes him to the resisters. The partisan Psarrós (aided by Tito!) seemed quite a stretch, and based on historical facts one that was impossible for me to make, having found no references to connections between Tito and Psarrós, and having learned that Psarrós was assassinated in the earliest period in which it is plausible that my father would have been arrested and deported as a Jew from Athens.

However, another curiosity about my father's account helped me develop a theory about how he added this element to his memories. In speaking with me, my father kept referring to the partisan as John Psarrós. He spoke with such authority that when I first looked up the man in history books, I assumed the historians had his name wrong since he was always listed as Demétrios Psarrós. It was only after I had listened to many more of my father's stories that I heard of another Psarrós, someone who had a bakery in Itéa. In fact, almost every time my father tried to describe something about Itéa or someone from Itéa, it was in relation to του Ψαρρού το φούρνο (Psarrós's bakery). One of these stories involved Κόζαρης (Kózaris), a cousin of my grandmother's who took his nephew, a local boy named Γιάννης (John), and made him his adopted son, the manager and the heir to his taverna/grocery store, which inevitably turned out to be near Psarrós's bakery. Here, then, is another plot my father may have borrowed: an older man of some means makes a livelihood possible for an impoverished adopted son. It appears that the baker's first name was Chrístos, but given how common a first name Giánnis, John, is in the area, and how many families from the area, I have since learned, carry the surname Psarrós, I wonder if my father didn't in fact know a John Psarrós and/or in any case just transfer the name onto the local leader, thus creating even more of a reason for him to want to make my father, a young person bearing the name John, his heir.

The facts that my father 1) always refers to the resister as "John Psarrós"; 2) has never indicated that he is aware that the historical actor partisan Demétrios Psarrós was assassinated by communist rivals; and 3) never mentions the fact that he did not inherit anything from this person, indicate to me that the sequence of events my father tells of is a conglomeration and that he had a tremendous internal necessity to believe that such a rescue of him could have occurred. I am reminded of Laub's observation that his witness does not know the name "Canada commando" and never mentions the origin of the clothes and shoes she gives to her fellow inmates. Indeed, she needs to remain completely ignorant of their origin, according to Laub, so that she can bear witness to her role as helper in a world that functioned by a hyper-strict interpretation of survival of the fittest (Felman and Laub 1992). In the chaotic and dangerous world that was occupied Athens, my father needed to believe that someone would not only have noticed that this one beggar-thief-child had disappeared, but would also move heaven and earth—even call on his friend Tito—to get him back to safety. My father could make up and believe this story because if my father was arrested, he must in truth also have been "rescued," rescued by someone somehow, and that rescue must have felt wondrous to him. Perhaps his fear during incarceration was so great that that rescue felt as wondrous to him as the explosion of four crematoria chimneys to Laub's witness in Auschwitz. To be sure, whatever the "real" circumstance of my father's life in mid-1944, it seems wondrous to me that my father was alive and relatively well in that police precinct kitchen when the Germans retreated from Greece in October 1944.

After more than fifteen years of unconsciously and consciously mulling over the possible deportation of my father, what most deeply impresses me is this: to be a circumcised male anywhere in Europe in the period of Nazi hegemony was to be a target. Whether or not my father was actually arrested by the Germans as a Jew, he had to live with the fear of this possibility from the moment he first became conscious of the facts that he was circumcised, most of the other males around him were not, and this circumcision, through no fault of his own, made him the object of a deadly hunt by the Nazi occupiers of all those who carried this mark in their flesh. In many ways, my father's situation can serve as yet another illustration of Reverend Niemoeller's point: once anybody is allowed to be chased, arrested, and exterminated on the basis of a group identity rather than individual action, no one is safe.

"COLLATERAL DAMAGE" AND "CONCOMITANT LOSS"

As different as my father's set of experiences during the Second World War and occupation in Greece may have been from a discrete violent act like the Zantops' murders, my family's stay in Greece also engendered a whole series of concomitant losses. Let me explain what I mean.

When feelings and thoughts first started trickling into the numbness that possessed me after learning that my friends Susanne and Half Zantop had been murdered, one of my earliest concerns was about the children: foremost their two (adult) daughters whom I knew and loved, but also the young children of the Zantops' many friends. How could the shock, horror, fear, and deep sadness of their parents not affect them profoundly too? "My kids heard me scream when I found out the news," one mother told me. I could immediately understand her worry, since I could only too well imagine to myself what that scream sounded like. In the weeks and months that followed, the "losses" just kept mounting. While the police investigation was still open, we were asked to think about possible suspects. For me, to think about each person I knew who had known my friends and to consider whether that person could have killed them was a transformative act, a destructive transformative act. I experienced that transformation particularly negatively with regard to my students. Because both Zantops had been professors, students were among the first suspects. I remember walking into my classroom and finding myself, against my conscious will, thinking, could one of these lovely young people be a killer? Could one of them have killed my friends? Could one of them kill me? In the first week following the murders I even developed a suspicion about a particular student and reported it to the police. He was briefly questioned and found to have had nothing to do with it. I have never forgiven myself for that accusation. It didn't ameliorate the situation much to find out that the actual perpetrators were not Dartmouth students, but rather area high schoolers. A dimension of trust had disappeared from my life in general, but especially from my pedagogical activities, and I mourned its disappearance. When I decided to try writing about the experience of losing my friends, I felt I needed to describe these types of losses as well. I did not find any term in the technical trauma literature to name the phenomenon, though there were mentions in case studies of similar "side effects." I proposed two terms myself: "collateral damage" and "concomitant loss" (Kacandes 2003, 175). In the context in which I initially proposed them, the first term seemed to suit the infliction of fear onto the children of my friends, for example, whereas the second reflected better what I felt about the change in my relationship to my students. Given the brutality of the murders and the suddenness of the loss, the military echo of the phrase "collateral damage" seemed mostly more appropriate to me at the time, but with the passage of the years, I have come to prefer the more pacific phrase "concomitant loss."

In relation to my paternal family in occupied Greece, it seems to me that the separation from father and husband for eight years could not but produce profound challenges. In addition to the disturbances to one-on-one relationships like that between my father and his father or between my grandmother and her husband that have been referred to a number of times in earlier parts of this book, my aunt Pearl points out a collective loss: "We never bonded again as a family" (chapter 2, section 9h). There was also the complementary loss of sense of family between my grandmother and her children and all the extended family members who continued to reside in Greece. My grandmother herself did not go back for many years. When she did visit with her husband in 1969 (shortly before my grandfather died), she refused to even consider staying with her brother John, who was still alive then. To this day his children talk about how that slight pained him. My aunt Pearl returned to Greece and to Chryssó as a young wife and mother when her husband was training to become a priest (1959–61). She described her mother's sister coming to where she was staying (at her mother's cousin's house) and "cussing me out." As Pearl explained to me, "She wanted me to go to her house. And I never even thought of going to Theia Loukía's!" (chapter 2, section 7e). I have mentioned several times that my father did not return to Greece for forty-one years. I remember that after I myself had started to travel to Greece regularly, he occasionally offered this explanation for his own lack of interest in visiting: "I'm waiting for a few people to die first." How sad. Much to his credit, I believe, once my father did actually make a commitment to trying to live in Greece, he also tried to include his first cousins in "family events." I recall, for instance, that when I was asked to be the godmother for my cousin George's second daughter (named after our shared paternal grandmother Chrysoúla) in Greece in 2000, my father called all his first cousins whose telephone numbers he had; granted, it was short notice, but still, none attended. I believe my uncle Harry probably had the most contact with his Greek relatives, yet that contact remained one on one and did not lead to development of a general sense of extended family. To my knowledge, the youngest participant in the fateful events described in this book, my uncle Nick, made no effort to maintain contact with any of the relatives who stayed in Greece, and he himself never returned to visit.

To be sure, there were some attempts at extending contact to the next generation: Harry's only daughter, my cousin Dina, reported how our common paternal grandmother had exacted a promise from Dina's maternal grandmother to take Dina to Itéa as part of her first trip to Greece (see chapter 2, section 4b); and I have also mentioned how my own mother took her children to Roúmeli to meet some of her husband's relatives (in 1967 with the two oldest and two youngest of us siblings, and in 1974 with the middle two of us). It doesn't go unnoticed by me that making these introductions was a task assigned to individuals who had married into the Kacandes family and not to original members of it. While one could cite the inherent difficulties in keeping any extended family that is stretched over two continents together, most Greeks in America succeeded better than we did. In fact, with regard to my own nuclear family, we had more contact with our paternal than maternal relatives in the United States, but a much closer relationship to and sense of our mother's family than our father's in Greece. I mentioned in chapter 1 that when I first interviewed my father in 2005, I did not know the names and birth order of his aunts and uncles, much less his cousins, many of whom were still alive. When I finally went to Greece for the specific purpose of researching my father's past, I began with a few days vacation, noting in my journal, "Going to Ándros, to my mother's home, to my mother's people is so much more familiar to me. This is like going to *my* home. Whereas the thought of going to Chryssó or Itéa is very different. Not quite scary—well, not at all scary—but certainly not familiar" (August 14, 2005). My research helped me transform that feeling, but here I want to underscore once again, that I, for one, count not knowing my father's family as a concomitant loss of the traumatic experiences of the war and occupation of the previous generations. Does this concomitant loss, as I want to call it, actually constitute an additional trauma? I would say not. Yet, perhaps my even considering it worth mentioning points toward an important, if controversial, issue I also need to raise here: the possibility of inherited trauma.

Almost as soon as reports of Concentration Camp Survivor Syndrome were published in the 1950s and '60s, mental health experts began to speculate about whether the children of survivors would display specific psychopathologies: "will there be an intergenerational transmission of maladaptive behavior?" (Solkoff 1981, 30). The psychotherapeutic community today is still quite divided with regard to the answer to this question, as they are divided on the extent to which research on Holocaust survivors and their children can be extended to other "multigenerational legacies of trauma." Despite such doubts, this last phrase, for instance, serves as the title of a huge international handbook covering situations as diverse as combat related trauma, the Armenian and the Cambodian genocides, the fates of indigenous peoples, domestic abuse, and AIDS (see Danieli 1998). Two things are certain: research into inherited trauma has been prolific over the last decades, and the controversies surrounding it do not seem to be diminishing.

Simultaneous to research in the psychotherapeutic community, there has been a increasing number of persons who, themselves the children of Holocaust survivors, have written about their own lives and the lives of their families in both memoir and fictional forms. Likely spurred by, among other things, the publication of journalist Helen Epstein's 1979 interviews with "children of the Holocaust"—the title of her book—these writings discuss the fates of families in the Nazi Judeocide, and often concentrate on the effects of those fates on the next generation. In other words, the authors presume a personal inheritance of some legacy from the negative experiences of their parents, though not all would use the framework of trauma. Interestingly, there has been a parallel writing boom in German-speaking countries by the children of Nazi perpetrators.

These developments in the psychotherapeutic and survivor communities have been accompanied by a virtual explosion in the broader field of

Holocaust studies, especially since the late 1970s. More recently within that general expansion has developed a lively subfield that in part explores the memorial literature I have just mentioned, but has mainly been concerned with "second generation literature," fictional texts about the Holocaust and its legacies, in numerous genres (novel, short story, poetry, drama) written by the generations born after the Second World War, some of whom were connected to the Holocaust through their families and some not (see Berger and Berger 2001, and McGlothlin 2006; Sicher 1998).

It was in this complicated and dynamic context that Marianne Hirsch proposed the term "postmemory" in an argument about the role of photographs in Art Spiegelman's original graphic novel treatment of the Holocaust, *Maus* (Spiegelman 1991), to identify "an intersubjective transgenerational space of remembrance, linked to cultural or collective trauma which is not strictly based on identity or on familial connection" (Hirsch and Kacandes 2004; see also Hirsch 1997). In Hirsch's conception "postmemory is distinguished from memory by generational distance and from history by deep personal connection. Postmemory is a powerful and very particular form of memory precisely because its connection to its object or source is mediated not through recollection but through an imaginative investment and creation" (Hirsch 1997, 22). Though first developed in relation to children of Holocaust survivors to describe their experience of growing up "dominated by narratives that preceded their birth," and their "own belated stories" as "evacuated by the stories of the previous generation," Hirsch has since stressed the relevance of postmemory for "other second-generation memories of cultural or collective traumatic events and experiences" and for other types of emotional investments besides those of children in their parents' stories (2008, 107, 108).

In my own work studying both the psychotherapeutic research and the memoir-like texts of children of survivors mentioned above, I have found numerous parallel definitions and echoes of what Hirsch has termed postmemory. In *The Cry of Mute Children*, for example, Israeli psychoanalyst

Ilany Kogan describes the case of her patient "Isaac," who felt "that he shared his father's secret without having really known it, as if he had always been with his father, even before his own birth" (1995, 101). Kogan further explains about her second generation patients that "because their minds were permeated with traces of their parents' experiences, they lived in a double reality—their own and that of their parents" (149). Kogan's analysis is confirmed by self-reports of at least some children of survivors. Scholar and fiction writer Lisa Appignanesi labels her experiences as those of "transgenerational haunting" (1999, 8). Echoing another part of Hirsch's analysis, Appignanesi observes that "children can experience the tragic weight of their parents' past lives as something which is so much greater than their ordinary, everyday plaints, that these can never be voiced or shared. As a result, their own feelings are nullified" (220). Author and cultural critic Eva Hoffman describes experiencing her "memories—not memories" of what happened to her parents as an "enigmatic but real fairy tale" and as "emanations of wartime experiences" that "kept erupting in flashes of imagery, in abrupt but broken refrains" (2004, 6, 9). Michael Skakun, another offspring of a survivor, describes his father's past as becoming "the substance of my life, until it achieved an immediacy as palpable as my own skin" (1999, 3). These general and metaphorical explanations resonated deeply within me. However, I kept scouring for more details: so what were someone's postmemories exactly?

In chapter 1 I described how precisely I remember the moment when Marianne Hirsch first shared with me her concept of postmemory and how it not only "clicked" for me, but how her words took me back to a feeling, to a state of being that I had not experienced in decades. When I set out to write this book, I knew that one part of what I wanted and indeed felt I needed to do was to try to describe as precisely as I could what I thought were my own postmemories. That is how the opening lines of this book came into being. Though the language I use there is of course not the language of a toddler, I did my best to convey the manner in which I experienced as an extremely young child my father's memories, to communicate the quality of the existence that his memories had in my own consciousness. More concrete than "emanations" or "images," to the best of my ability to recollect my infantile experience, my father's War Experiences existed as incarnated feelings lodging in our home, contact with which I tried to avoid. What I cannot reconstruct are the activities that resulted in me developing that sense of cohabitation. Nor can I describe the process by which those ugly beings turned into (more manageable) narratives. However, I have tried—again to the best of my ability—to share how, once those kernels of narratives entered my consciousness, they expanded and changed.

It is obvious from my remarks here and from the very shape and content of this book that I accept the idea that trauma can be passed on in some sense. Much of the controversy about this contention, in the Holocaust studies community anyway, derives from the component of "memory" in the term postmemory. Gary Weissman, for example, has argued that "no degree of power or monumentality can transform one person's lived memories into another's" (2004, 17). I would say that Weissman's proposition is true on its surface. But what I regret about the academic controversy over postmemory is the way a need to be intellectually "careful" with one's definitions and analyses has led precisely to an obfuscation of lived experience. What do I mean? Children of Holocaust survivors who were born after the war do not "remember" being in Auschwitz or in hiding or living under an assumed identity or watching their relatives and friends being raped, tortured, or murdered, though they may have fantasies or nightmares about such experiences. Remembrance of that fantasizing or dreaming, in contrast, is as "real" as any other memory we might conserve. So, too, some of those offspring have memories of listening to their parents moaning in the night (Goransson 2004; Hoffman 2004) or of their parents quivering at the sight of uniformed authorities (Appignanesi 1999) or of watching their parents stuff themselves with food (Epstein 1979). They may also have memories of their own experiences of the sensation of themselves being stuffed with food or of near suffocation from being dressed too warmly (Karpf 1997). Because some of these individuals are talented with words, they have been able to describe for us their memories of those experiences and other memories perhaps more inchoate and less traceable to specific events. Memory scholar Aleida Assmann speaks of acquiring memories not just through lived experience "but also via interacting, communicating, identifying, learning, and participating" (forthcoming). Some other individuals, though our parents did not live through the same events, may find resonances with what those offspring of Holocaust survivors have written.

After much reflection and research, I do not think it would be appropriate to label my father a Holocaust survivor nor me and my siblings children of a survivor, in the sense of "Holocaust survivor." I do believe, however, that our father experienced some overwhelming situations that he in fact "survived," but was not able to fully process at the time or subsequently. Some vestiges of those experiences affected us, his children. Trying to describe those effects has been one of my aims in this book.

PROUST'S MADELEINE, THE NEWSPAPER ARTICLE, AND COMPLICITY

It has often amazed me how many people know about the "madeleine" even without having read the magisterial *In Search of Lost Time* of Marcel Proust (2003). I'm fairly certain this must be because even if only told about the phenomenon, it makes sense. I suspect most human beings have had the experience at one time or another of a taste, a smell, a sound, a particular word jogging our memories: something surfaces that we had forgotten completely or that we had not thought of for a long while or that we certainly were not trying to think about at that moment. We are immediately transported to another time and place.

Such a moment happened for my father when he heard me lecture at Harvard in 1992 on the power of the spoken word and the intertwining of orality and textuality in Greek culture. In the context of trying to untangle the Kacandes family stories, I have been struck over and over again by the fragility *and* the resiliency of memory. Ultimately, I suppose, it's the vagaries of memory that interest me the most. On the one hand, something I said triggered this memory so vividly for my father that when he started to narrate what I call for myself "the death flier anecdote," I could practically see what I think he was seeing before him at that moment: that godforsaken, barren village of our grandfather where the goats had to eat in the cemetery to survive. I did not then and still do not doubt that my father was recounting something that he had actually experienced (in contrast to the very first time I myself heard the story of arrest and deportation). On the other hand, when, more than a dozen years later, I began to ask him and he finally began to narrate to me his wartime memories, this story about German pamphlets never resurfaced; it seems to have gone back to some inaccessible location in his brain. The only "trace" of it I could find was Dad's insistence that he had raised some sheep, including the ram, Kítsos, animals he appears to have still possessed at the end of his family's ordeal in Greece, since he decides to leave them to his uncle in exchange for shipments of feta cheese instead of slaughtering them (chapter 2, section 4a). What happened to the "goats"? I was sure my father had said "goats" when he told the story in Cambridge. I even published the anecdote that way in my first book. There are so rarely ways to verify memories of private events; was it Dad's memory or mine that proved faulty about what kind of animals he was tending? Of course, my father might also have tended goats, but now that I have seen pictures of him with his sheep and heard his cousins speak of them as well, my stronger suspicion is that I registered "goats" for sheep when I first heard the story because I had been so impressed by the goats on my mother's island when I made my first trip to Greece as a teenager.

The goats—or, rather, sheep—that make their appearance in the death flier anecdote make me think about another aspect of that story and the way it foregrounds a slightly different point about memory: when I could actually figure out a way to check them, numbers and quantities often proved inaccurate, usually exaggerated upward. It reminds me a little of the Lake Wobegon syndrome in the world created by Garrison Keillor, where all the people are above average in some respect. Loved ones discussed are perhaps always very beautiful in the mind of the rememberer; for Greeks, they are often light in color. As for numbers per se, Aunt Pearl reports that her brother had "three toes hanging" after the explosion of the *Vellisários*. Dad reports that one was dangling and subsequently removed by a surgeon. As painful as this injury must have been, the reality is that my father is missing the top portion of one toe. I had read about German reprisals in Greek history books. These numbers go in the opposite direction, an underestimation. Of course, since I don't know exactly which fliers my father saw, I can't be sure. Still, as awful as the retribution ratio he mentioned sounds—"For every German found dead, ten Greeks will be shot"—the reality was even worse. Historian Mark Mazower reports that when the Germans reoccupied the country in 1943, the Wehrmacht high command "issued precise quotas for reprisals: 50–100 hostages were to be shot for any attack on, or death of a German soldier; 10 if a German was wounded, and so on." In fact, the numbers were so high that the practice often proved "unworkable because it was impossible to arrest enough hostages" (2001, 177). In the case of the death flier anecdote, the number in my father's head was much too low, something that is understandable to me since it is nearly impossible to comprehend the true magnitude of the Nazi insanity. Whether over- or underestimated, once a number gets into people's heads, it seems hard to dislodge it, and this same number can pop into a situation where one has no knowledge. The number eleven appeared in many of my aunt Pearl's stories. I'm not sure if this is because she herself returned to the United States at this age. But in any case, she reports my grandfather as being eleven when he comes to the

United States, my grandmother as being eleven when she learns how to weave, and so on. She repeated this number to me several times on the phone even after she had read a draft of this book.

Having worked rather extensively with Holocaust testimony, I was familiar with the frequent experience of witnesses remembering things during the interview that they had not recalled previously. This "madeleine" or other type of remembering has occasionally occurred in interviews I have conducted for this project, as with my father and the death fliers, or with my mother remembering after all these years my father telling her about brothers pimping their sisters in Kérkyra because they were so hungry (chapter 2, section 6e). However, what I had had no experience with previously was the complementary phenomenon: interviewees forgetting things that they had previously known, like again, my father with the death fliers . . . Is there an opposite of a "madeleine"? I couldn't find a term for it. I don't think this case, anyway, is Freudian repression. My father forgetting an anecdote he had already told me (especially a dozen years later) didn't surprise me as much as what happened with my sister Georgia, even though that "forgetting," too, may have happened over many years. Perhaps I have not communicated adequately how flummoxed I was when I e-mailed questions to my younger sister in 2004 and she didn't reply a word about hearing our father's talk at the JCC. I am reminded of a phrase in a family memoir by Lisa Appignanesi, a daughter of Holocaust survivors I've quoted before: "the whole complex tangle of remembering and forgetting" (1999, 6). To underscore the "and" in Appignanesi's formulation, I share that my sister Georgia did eventually remember going to hear our father speak at the JCC. Her memory was "jogged," as the idiomatic expression goes, when I read some sections of this book out loud to her, Tina, and our mother at Christmas in 2006. I was watching her face as she said, "Oh, now I remember. I remember exactly what he said."

I bring up Appignanesi's "tangle of remembering and forgetting," too, because of the role The Newspaper Article has played in mediating my and my siblings' knowledge of what happened to our father, the one headlined "'Never Leave the United States'" and reproduced in appendix D. Unlike oral stories, a written text can be consulted over and over again. The article was framed and hung in our grandfather's study until his death, after which our father brought it to our house. My siblings each mentioned reading it when I asked them how they learned what they think they know about our father's past. I chuckled at my sister Maria's explanation that given how little English language reading material was available in our grandparents' house, "in sheer desperation, looking for things to read, you found a few bits and that was one of them. We spent a lot of time in that study!" I, too, had read the article many times as a child, yet, curiously, I was at work on this project for many months before it occurred to me that I could consult The Newspaper Article.

Once I did reread it, I laughed at myself for how many things I thought I knew because of that article that are in fact not in it and for how many things that are in the article that I had forgotten about. To mention just a few knots in my own tangle of remembering and forgetting: I definitely had the date wrong in my memory. I was sure the family had returned to the United States in December 1945, whereas the article was published October 28, 1945, and reports that the family had returned almost three weeks earlier, on October 9. I'm not sure if a December return was in my head because our father's birthday is in December or because at some point it was communicated to me that they could not get out of the country right away at war's end, and I "knew" that the war ended in Europe in May 1945 and in the Pacific in late summer, and therefore translated "not right away" as meaning the end of 1945. It was only in doing this research that I got it straight that Greece was liberated from the Axis in October 1944, and so my family's departure was indeed many months after war's end, indeed almost a full year later. Having talked to both my father and his sister about their return, I now suspect that my having the idea of December or end of the year 1945 in my head may also be some kind of reflection of their own emphasis (and disappointment) that they didn't make it out on the "first" boat of returning Americans, but rather on the "second." Aunt Pearl explained this specifically to me: "We would have been on the first ship if Yiayia was an American citizen. Because the first ship was only American citizens." The glitch of mother and children having different nationalities seems to have played a decisive role at several critical points in their sojourn, such as at the commencement of hostilities in Greece when they appeared to have tried to leave, and, according to some versions anyway, in the matter of being arrested by the Germans. Or to reflect another aspect of the analysis offered in this book, this issue of passports may have been used retrospectively to explain why many things happened or did not happen to them. I felt a real tug at my heart when I finally found my grandfather's letters to Immigration and Naturalization and to the State Department and realized how desperate he was to resolve his wife's citizenship in her absence.

Another item I thought I knew from this article was that even though my father was fifteen when he returned to the United States, he was placed into second grade because his English was so bad. The article unambiguously reports that "John is now in the seventh grade" at the Bradley Park School, which is where he had "recently told of his experiences abroad in assembly and showed many snapshots taken in Greece." Hmmm, how did I skip over that clear statement of what grade he was in? Or rather, why did I not notice earlier the discrepancy between what was stored in my brain and what was printed in the article? Speaking of discrepancies, why did I not figure out that if my father had spoken in assembly about his experiences, maybe his English wasn't so bad after all? I can still hear ringing in my head the "words" of the rich woman who is said to have contacted our grandfather to tell him that "if your son is so interested in improving his English, I will send him to a good school where he can learn it properly." Though my father is quoted several times in the article praising America, nowhere does it state that he specifically wants or needs to improve his English (though it does mention that "the younger ones must first learn to speak, read, and write in English"). How did the lady who read the article and became his benefactress know he wanted to improve his English? Was this her assumption in reading the article? My point now is not at all about the real status of our father's English language abilities in 1945—though I now have much evidence that it wasn't that competent. Nor is it about contradictions between what I know now and what I thought I knew then. Rather, I'm wondering about that child I once was, who was particularly proud of how well she could read and how smart she was, never noticing the logical problems in what she was reading—the article itself contains outright mistakes, as well as dates and claims that can't be reconciled—nor the contradictions between it and "the stories" she had in her head.

Thinking now about why I didn't use The Newspaper Article to pose a few questions to my father earlier, brings me to another item about which I have speculated. I could not find any one term for it in the psychotherapeutic literature dealing with inherited trauma, but I have seen it referred to there as "complicity," "conspiracy," or "co-conspiracy" of silence. In my notes to myself for this project I have described it as "collusion," "tacit agreement," and "willed ignorance." This phenomenon is surely related and perhaps a necessary outcome of the "dialectic of trauma," about which Judith Herman speaks: the will on the part of trauma victims "to deny horrible events and the will to proclaim them aloud" (1997, 1). Herman gestures toward the connection I'm raising when she briefly comments, "It is difficult for an observer to remain clearheaded and calm, to see more than a few fragments of the picture at one time, to retain all the pieces, and to fit them together" (2). Nadine Fresco, who was one of the earliest cultural analysts in Europe to talk to children of Holocaust survivors, describes a silence that was "all the more implacable in that it was often concealed behind a screen of words, again, always the same words, an unchanging story, a tale repeated over and over again, made up of selections from the war" (1984, 419). What does the child do with these stories? As Fresco explains about one of her inter-locutors, "The child let his thoughts play only within the narrow limits laid down by a complicity from which there was no escape" (420). This reconciled for me, in a sense, my own recollection of never having heard any war stories from our father directly, while nevertheless having nar-rative fragments in my head, with, say, Maria's insistence that she had heard the same story "hundreds of times," including on occasions when I must have been present. It seemed to explain too why I have no recol-lection of my siblings and I ever talking to each other about Dad's war stories—until I started this project. It wouldn't surprise me if, at least with regard to my preschool years, I not only understood less of what our father was actually saying than my older sisters, but also if as a mid-dle child, I complied more fully with the pact of silence emanating from our parents, indeed so fully that I banished Dad's acts of narrating from my consciousness almost altogether. (The snippets that come out in my father's voice indicate some residue of my experience of taking in his stories; see chapter 1.) Evidently there was another reason why we did not talk about the War Experiences amongst ourselves. As a child my sister Maria had tried passing on our father's stories to an adult once. When she told me this in 2005, she couldn't remember exactly when it was or to whom she had started to tell the anecdotes, but she remem-bered clearly the consequences: our father overheard her and beat her. She didn't repeat any of his war stories for many, many years. Though I do not claim to remember this beating in particular—alas, I remem-ber witnessing others—I am sure its lessons for all of us then and for a long time to come were apparent to me: Daddy's War was still danger-ous, and it was best to avoid it as fully as possible.

I had always been one to emphasize how close my siblings and I are in age and emotionally. However, this project has shown me not only that we remember different things and sometimes the same things dif-ferently, but also that we did not necessarily react to or comply with the exigencies of our home life in the same way. Speaking only for myself, then, I wonder if ceasing to understand Greek, though it was our mother tongue, wasn't also part of my compliance with the taboo on Daddy's War and a reason why learning Greek later was difficult and awkward for me, though I have acquired fluency in other languages easily.

THE CURSE OF THE GREEK MYTHS OR REENACTMENTS

I remember one time, I believe during graduate school, when I was trying to read up on Greek mythology, I was struck by the ubiquitous pattern of an ancestor committing a violation against the gods for which he does not adequately atone, and the gods simply revisiting horrible circumstances on the subsequent generations until some descendant finally pays a price that satisfies the gods. The thought I had upon noticing this pattern at the time was in relation to our family, though not specifically in relation to my task here of tracking Daddy's War. It wasn't unrelated either, of course, as nothing in our family is completely free from the tug of the War Experiences. My thought then was more generally about emotional health, and how important it would be for me to obtain it so that I would not pass problems onto my offspring—so my logic went in my early adulthood, anyway. Though I ended up not being able to have children, I hope I am not fooling myself about having acquired a modicum of mental health. In the course of my research into our family for this book, the thought of unconscious perpetration of behavior that infuriates the gods came back to me, because I found traces of uncanny repetitions of disastrous situations in more than one generation of our family. My observation resembles one Appignanesi relates, though she deploys the metaphor of a waterfall: "Memory," she writes, "cascades through the generations in a series of misplaced fears, mysterious wounds, odd habits" that the child "inhabits" (1999, 8). Our family memory cascades strike me as analogous to finding out that our paternal great-grandfather John Kacandes died of a heart attack at age thirty-two. Bad hearts run in our family, as do bad marriages. By studying our family history, I have discovered some even more specific parallels between generations.

The most salient, to my mind anyway, is that our mother and father, essentially, though I believe unconsciously, succeeded in restaging our grandmother's flight to Greece exactly thirty years later. The reasons for our mother going back to Greece in 1967 were couched in some of the same terms: Mom visiting her family, whom she missed so much and hadn't seen in fifteen years; the children's more thorough familiarization with Greece, the Greek language, and Greek culture. Our grandmother and our mother both headed off to Greece despite dictatorships, Metaxas and the colonels, respectively. Of course, on the surface of things, our mother's visit was never supposed to last longer than the summer—and in the end, thank God, it didn't. Yet, even at the time, the way our parents bargained over us siblings struck me as odd: "Maria should go, it will be a good cultural experience"; "Well, if Maria comes, there won't be anyone to take care of the baby, so Peter has to come too"; "Tina doesn't have any plans for the summer. It would be a good cultural experience for her also"; "So Tom comes too." I was scheduled for a summer music program, and Georgia seems to have stayed home by default, only to get enrolled at the last minute in day camp. The logic seemed so arbitrary. I once worked out in therapy during my twenties that Georgia and I were being held hostage by our father so that our mother would return. I was bitter about that discovery for a long time. However, I hasten to add that when I realized in the context of this project that our parents' bargaining resulted in our mother going to Greece with exactly the same number of children as our grandmother had in 1937, I literally laughed out loud—not without a clutch in my throat, of course.

The uncanny counterpart to the exodus of the majority of the family members is that at nine years old, I became, well, surely not a breadwinner, but a surrogate housewife for the summer. My father drove me to the grocery store, where I did the food shopping; I cooked the meals and did the dishes; I washed the clothes and ironed them; I vacuumed and dusted. I remember one stormy afternoon being dropped off after my music program and finding my sister Georgia sitting on the front steps sobbing. I asked her what was wrong and she told me she was scared of the thunder. I tried to comfort her, but it didn't seem to help much. She told me later she was missing Mom. I remember her words resounding with an ache in my heart and a pervasive sense of inadequacy I was trying to ignore; I was all too aware that I couldn't replace our mother for either of us. I tried nonetheless. I would stay awake at night until I was sure my sister was asleep and our father had returned from teaching night school. I would wake up often in the middle of the night to check that my sister was breathing. Terrified when I couldn't hear her one time, I slipped out of bed, descended to the living room, and told our father. He took the stairs three at a time, rushed into our bedroom and shook my sister awake. Poor Georgia had no idea what the commotion was about. I was so relieved to see her animated, that I wasn't even scared Dad would get mad at me. I think he was that relieved too, because I don't remember being scolded.

When I have told people over the course of the years that I cooked and cleaned for an entire summer when I was a child, I always encounter their disbelief and reexperience my own. More than once I have recalculated my age. By today's childrearing standards, I couldn't have done those things at age nine. But I did. I turned nine on May 18, 1967, and our mother and four of us siblings departed for Greece in late June. My vivid memories of a burned meatloaf, scorches on more than one handkerchief, and our father's weight loss (though intended) provide some kind of evidence of my role. To be sure, there was no official war being waged around us. No matter how bad my juvenile cooking was, life and death were not at issue. Still, at 22 Hawthorne Street in summer 1967 there was some type of reenactment going on. In their perpetually ironic manner, the Greek gods had assigned my father his own father's role and I one of substantially helping to keep the family afloat at much too young an age, the way my father had in Greece from 1941 to 1945.

Georgia once criticized me for never acting like a child. That charge stung with truth. I realize now, it wasn't in this script. I'm not sure what twist of fate allowed our mother to change her part and return after eight weeks instead of eight years, but I was grateful then, as I am grateful today. A few months ago I was cleaning out my filing cabinets and came across a construction-paper folder decorated with crayons called "My Stories." The object wasn't familiar, though I did recognize my childish handwriting. I opened it up and read a piece called "Happiness," dated January 29, 1968. The penultimate paragraph reads, "One experience I had was a full summer with just my sister and father. When the rest of the family came back, I was so happy I cried." My gratitude today stems from a different source. Though I have been blessed with never living in a war zone and with never going without food for long, I count those experiences of being called on to "provide" while feeling inadequate to the task, of being deprived of a parent during one's childhood and later of losing my friends the Zantops to violent death as ones that caused me to develop a surely limited and yet personal sense of some of what my father went through in Greece.

Another bizarre repetition of hurtful behavior in the family came to my attention unsolicited. Upon arriving at our paternal grandparents' house in New Jersey as children, we girls would be barely out of the car before we would go racing next door to Mrs. Perkins, the neighbor. I remember why I liked to go there. In contrast to our grandmother, she spoke English; she had lots of puzzles, toys, and books; and she always seemed happy to see us. That outweighed any fear I might have felt at her half-paralyzed post-stroke body, her purple complexion, and her chain smoking. I remember too, though, that Yiayia would be hurt by our obvious preference for spending time with Mrs. Perkins and that I felt a little guilty while I was there as a result.

When I was transcribing the long interview I did with our aunt Pearl for this project, the terms in which she was describing her own behavior with her mother's sister, Theia Loukía of Chryssó, shook loose for me

memories of ours with our grandmother vis-à-vis Mrs. Perkins. Theia
Eléni, as you might remember, was a first cousin of my maternal grandmother and her sister Loukía, who lived next door to the Tsíngas house
in Chryssó. She was better off, partly, I suppose, because she didn't have
children of her own to support. In any case, my aunt Pearl went to stay
with her when she returned to Chryssó as a young bride and mother,
and her theia Loukía resented that, citing particularly that by doing so,
Pearl was continuing a "tradition" of ignoring her (chapter 2, section
7e). Of course, as I tried to elucidate in the family stories section in the
"House in Chryssó" (chapter 2, section 2), our grandmother had had
her reasons for sending her kids to her cousin and not her sister when
they visited Chryssó.

Aunt Pearl's estrangement from and then rediscovery of her theia
Loukía, can serve as a good illustration of the phenomenon of "concomitant loss." What I want to call here the uncanniness of the repetition or the "Greek gods" aspect is that without explicitly having been
told about the relations between our grandmother, her sister, and her
cousin, it's as if through my siblings' and my visits to and our enjoy-
ment of Mrs. Perkins, our grandmother's neighbor, we were reproduc-
ing a situation from another era and place. Our behavior in a sense made
our grandmother feel what she had used her children to make her sister Loukía feel: ignored and unloved. To follow through with my metaphor: the Greek gods used us—without our realizing it—to enact Theia
Loukía's revenge on our grandmother for what our grandmother had
done to her so many years earlier: keeping her own children away from
Theia Loukía and passing on to them "those awful feelings about her."
I was fortunate to interact with my grandmother until I was in my twenties, by which point I had learned Greek well and could talk and corre-
spond with her on a number of subjects. I loved her deeply, and she gave
me her blessing before she died: Υγεία και αγάπη, Ειρήνη μου, υγεία και
αγάπη. (Health and love, my Irene, health and love.) And yet, that memory of even briefly having harbored "awful feelings" toward her disturbs

me, even though I know more fully than I ever could have before studying the War Stories where those feelings came from.

One of the riskiest, if briefest reenactments I came across concerns the car trip I took from the Athens airport to Delphi to conduct my research in summer 2005. I realize that I had very few days in Greece at my disposal; nevertheless, my decision to drive strange roads in a foreign country at night was stupid, even wildly dangerous. Not the usual Irene-type execution of plans. In my head, I was trying to maximize the time I had, but I know that even then, I felt like something not fully of my own volition was pushing me. I had taken a few days rest on our mother's island of Ándros with my sister Georgia, her son Johnny, and our aunt Stella, Harry's widow. I left on the afternoon boat from the island to the mainland, took the bus from Rafína to the airport, rented a car, and, departing around eight in the evening, proceeded to drive all the way from the airport to Delphi. My heart was in my throat most of the trip, as Greeks drive much too fast for the road conditions, tend to pass any car they encounter, and move back into the right lane immediately without having put adequate distance between themselves and the car they have just passed. As if all that isn't frightening enough, the stretch between Thebes and Delphi is desolate. My temporary relief at encountering fewer vehicles there was wiped out by the fact that on the small roads, I had to deal not only with those drivers that were passing from behind, but also with those that were passing in the other direction, heading straight at me. To move further to the right was to risk falling into a ditch or off a cliff. If something had happened to me that didn't kill me, I might have died waiting for someone to find me. It was only when I checked into a hotel room in Delphi around midnight that I came out of this obstinate trancelike mode. I remember feeling triumphant that I had arrived in the right place alive. However, I also felt more than a little sheepish. I wrote in my journal, "Was I trying to manufacture some kind of danger for myself the way Dad had experienced danger during the war making this trip?" (Tuesday August 16, 2005).

My behavior fit all too well psychiatrist Ilany Kogan's observation that her second generation patients "in their endless efforts to understand and help their traumatized parents, try to experience what the parents went through by re-creating their parents' experience and accompanying affects in their own life" (1995, 87). While I seem to have had no choice about my mother's trip to Greece in 1967, and I ran with my sisters to our grandmother's neighbor, I concocted this misadventure and its fear all by myself.

In this and the previous part of this book, I have used ideas and theories learned in the course of my research on storytelling, memory, trauma, and the Holocaust in particular to explore aspects of the family stories that engaged and puzzled me. In turn, dimensions of those stories pushed me to reexamine certain concepts like "witnessing," "postmemory," and "complicity." I claimed at the beginning of this more analytical section of this book that my formal education had prepared me better than I suspected to face Daddy's War. What I didn't realize when I began my writing was that in addition to exploring "concomitant loss," it would be one of my own concepts that would help me take the step I intuitively knew would be the most difficult, the one I had tried to take before gathering and studying the War Stories in the aftermath of the Zantops' murders, and could not: to "cowitness," to stand next to my father and to try to see what he had seen. Now I felt ready.

[5]

Cowitnessing to Daddy's War

An (Im)Possible Recital of What Might Have Happened

Dear Dad,

I write this to you aware of your failing memory. These last months sometimes you seem to register what I am telling you and many times you do not. Nonetheless, I feel the need to try to share certain things with you before you perhaps can follow even less of what I am telling you. I know you know that for a couple of years now I have been asking you, Mom, and many others about the years you spent with your mother and siblings in Greece separated from your father, who had stayed in the United States to earn money. I've gathered those stories together, and compared and studied them alongside history books and the few personal documents I could locate in your files, like your passport from 1937, your mother's passport from 1945, your "discharge papers," as you like to call them, your correspondence log from 1945 to 1948, the photo album you put together while you were recuperating from knee surgery in 1948, and papers I finally found from your parents, papers you had told me about, like the letters your father had sent to the State Department during the war trying to locate you, and papers no one seems to have known existed, related to your parents' financial interactions with your mother's parents in the 1930s. Even though these sources seem so random, I have a pretty good idea now of what happened to you, Dad, and with regard to some events I even think I know why they transpired. I couldn't make sense of or track everything I have been told, of course. Too many of the crucial actors and witnesses are dead. Too much of the documentation is missing. Too many of the events that people, including you, swear to have happened contradict other recitals or established historical facts.

And yet, what follows is what I wish you could have known for yourself, what I wish you could have told me. Why? Well, the specialists tell us that since the infliction of trauma involves some inability to act, the taking of action by turning the unassimilated experience into a story seems to promote healing. "What?" you would say to me, if we could really be having this conversation. "I've been telling stories all my life." And I would respond, "But which stories, Dad?" I would try to help you understand, using the words of Eva Hoffman, that "only a full imaginative confrontation with the past—however uncanny, however unknown—can bring the hauntings to an end," can help you register that the "awful events in whose spectral grip [you] have lived belong to another time," and the past is truly past (2004, 73, 74). What's it to you, you might say, at this point, feeling a little defensive. And I would try to explain as gently, clearly, and lovingly as I could, that as in the Greek myths, I think the sins of the fathers keep being revisited on the sons and daughters until someone finally breaks the cycle. That's what I'm trying to do here, Dad, break the cycle. I'm trying to produce a story of the trauma, not so much through a mastery of the facts, through the retrieval of everything that really happened, for that I genuinely believe is impossible, but rather to testify to what can be known, went wrong, to cause and effect, to appropriate affect around events, and to what could not and cannot be known; these are what Jodie Wigren calls the goals of constructing a narrative of trauma (1994, 415–16). I believe that the act of testifying to what cannot be known or to what could not have been known by you then itself testifies eloquently. You once said to me in a plaintive voice, "I'm trying to think who ever helped us." (chapter 2, section 5f) Through my recital here, I am also trying to point out a few people who actually did help you. Still, I regret deeply that my telling isn't likely to benefit you much at this stage in your life's journey. And yet, by bringing certain things to light, I believe my testimony, my cowitnessing to your story, begins to restore the social order, as Judith Herman (1997) has put it. How? you might ask. And I would answer, by implicitly proclaiming that no boy or girl should have to go through what you went through. This is the value of cowitnessing I tried to argue in my book *Talk Fiction* (2001), Dad. I know you were proud when I published it. But I also know you didn't read it. So, I have just repeated that point here.

What follows is my best guess about your activities to accommodate as many of your specific memories as possible to the historical record. Of course "history" is also a constructed narrative, but it's one that's held accountable to documentary evidence, documentary evidence that we don't have for most of the things you did. Then, too, the historical record on Greece during the occupation and the civil war is not nearly as complete as for other countries in Europe. Surprisingly, some official records are still inaccessible to historians, and not surprisingly, the political prism through which Greeks view everything produces continuing disagreement about what happened. And, Dad, the way the war, occupation, and civil war ran their courses in Greece is, plainly speaking, very complicated, as you know from a different perspective than I. The number of invasions and occupations, of groups organized for various types of resistance against and collaboration with the occupiers and the puppet governments, of shifting alliances of these groups among themselves and with foreign states, groups, and political parties is simply stunning. I don't know how you managed from day to day to figure out whom to trust or what to try to do. Using some concrete facts that are well established as an anchor, though, I have been able to gain a better sense of how things might have unfolded for you. There are many activities you recounted to me that I can't precisely date, so what follows has gaps and also presents multiple possibilities for some periods. What follows here is of course also another constructed narrative—my own.

On August 14, 1937, you, your mother, Chrysoúla George Kacandes, née Tsínga, your two younger brothers, Harry (Harálambos) and Nicholas, and your younger sister, Pearl (Panagioú) departed New York harbor on the steamship *Vulcania* for Greece. I found a photo of this boat in a book about ships that brought immigrants to America (Anuta 1983, 342) and my research assistant found advertisements for luxury cruises on the *Vulcania* in the *New York Times*; it was an elegant vessel, and you must have been excited, even as you must have also been fretting about leaving your father behind. You were only seven-and-a-half years old. Harry was to turn five that November, Pearl had turned three that May, and Nick was a mere four months old. Your mother was approaching her thirty-fourth birthday. She was traveling on a Greek passport, not yet having become an American citizen, though I discovered proof in your father's papers that she had applied for naturalization in 1936 and ironically, notification of her interview arrived shortly after your departure.

You siblings were Americans, having been born in the United States. I found the actual passport you used for this trip to Greece: Dark red, United States of America, Passport No. 461991, issued in Washington on July 16, 1937. You are the "bearer," and your brothers and sister— "Harry, Panagiou and Nicholas"—are listed as accompanying minors, "Brothers and Sister." There's that beautiful picture of the four of you that we all know from having seen copies. You and Harry are in white sailor suits with blue trim. Aunt Pearl and Uncle Nick are dressed in white. You're standing in the back, with Harry seated in front of you to your right and Pearl to your left. Baby Nick appears mysteriously propped between Harry and Pearl, looking a little shell-shocked from the flash, I assume. Pearl has a perfectly tied silk bow in her hair, and the three of you are gazing slightly to the left, which somehow gives you each an air of timid expectancy.

27. The Kacandes children's passport of June 1937.

The official language of the passport concerns you: Height 3 feet 6 inches; Hair LIGHT BROWN; Eyes BLUE; Distinguishing marks or features XXX XXX XXX; Place of birth NEWARK, N.J.; Date of birth DEC. 8, 1929; Occupation STUDENT XXX XXX. The passport communicates how little all of you are. You look young and vulnerable in that photo, and you are young and small: Three feet six inches. The standard travel plot and your alternate plot are both perceptible in the passport as well. In the "form language" of the passport, it's clear that the expectation is that a husband takes his wife and kids somewhere:

The bearer is accompanied by his
Wife, _____
Minor children, _____
_____
_____

"Wife" and "Minor children" are crossed out, the latter replaced by "Brothers and Sister." Still just a child yourself, the passport positions you as head of household, portending what you could not have known at the time would come true.

On August 25 your boat docked at Palermo, Italy, where your passport was stamped with an Italian transit visa. And on August 28 you were processed by Greek authorities in the port of Piraeus. I don't know much about the immediate aftermath of your arrival. Since your mother was eager to see her family, it seems likely that you went straight to Chryssó, the village where she had been born and gotten married and where her parents and her sister Loukía were still living. Did you immediately visit Delphi, the site of some of the most famous ancient ruins in Greece just north of your mother's village? You probably passed through it on your way to Chryssó, unless you took a boat from Piraeus to Itéa, the port village just south of Chryssó, on the Corinthian gulf.

I don't know if you also immediately visited Kolopetinítsa, the village in which your father had been born and which he had left as a child, up the mountain slightly to the west and south of Chryssó. Your father's oldest sister, Argyrí, had married Kóstas Tsakíris, a local man, receiving the tiny ancestral home as her dowry. You probably first encountered Panagioú, your widowed, half-blind paternal grandmother in Itéa. She appears to have moved there from Chryssó with her younger daughter, your aunt Kondílo, the younger of your father's two older sisters. Kondílo had married a man named Giórgios Baïzános from Chryssó, and they lived there with your grandmother and ever-growing family. In Itéa mother and daughter both worked in the Gerentés household to earn money. No one I talked to remembers your arrival precisely; however, the photographs your mother sent to your father show you all looking very young in the courtyard of the first house your mother rented from Efthémios Bourazánes in Itéa, so I'm thinking if you did initially reside in your maternal grandparents' home in Chryssó, as your sister Pearl seems to remember, it wasn't long before your mother installed you all in Itéa.

Your mother enrolled you for that very same fall in a private coed school called Chatzikonstantínou, where evidently quite a few Greek Americans studied. It was located in Palió Fáliro, one of the southern and nicer districts of Athens. You told me it was near the intersection of Neriídon and Terpsichóres, but those are parallel streets. I'm thinking you remembered Neriídon because the two sisters who ran the school lived there. Your enrollment in this school in fall 1937 means that within a month or two of having been separated from your father, you were then separated from your mother and siblings as well. It's hard for me to imagine that you didn't feel **abandoned**. Even though you were being told this was a wonderful school and you could get an excellent education there, you had registered your father's threats that if you didn't shape up, you would be sent to Greece. And there you were, not only in Greece, but alone.

You boarded at the school and were looked after by some Pétsas cousins of your mother's, originally from Itéa, then living in Piraeus, just to the west of Fáliro. You don't remember all their first names or how often you saw them, but it seems probable that it was on the weekends and during shorter holidays. You spent longer holidays and the summers themselves with your own family in Itéa. Your mother seems to have delighted in organizing activities and visits for you; she documented it well for your father, to whom she sent many photographs, inscribed with date, place, and loving greetings from you kids and her. From the look of your clothes, the money your father was sending was more than adequate.

Another moment you shared with your mother celebrated your triumph in the fifty-meter freestyle, in a swimming competition held at Stylída, near Lamía, on August 11, 1940, and sponsored by EON (H Εθνική Οργάνωσις Νεολαίας), the mandatory national youth organization instituted by Metaxás, the quasi-fascist but pro-British dictator of Greece. You were good at swimming. Your sister says your father had taught you how to swim at the YMCA in Newark before you left for Greece. Your

28. Celebrating the Greek national holiday, March 25, 1938, at a war memorial in Itéa. Left to right: Chrysoúla, Harry, Pearl, John.

29. John wins first prize in a swimming competition in Stylída, August 1940. Pictured with his medal and certificate and his mother Chrysoúla. Barely visible on John's head is the cap of EON, the national youth organization that sponsored the competition.

cousin Chrysoúla Kapsiáni, née Tsínga, and named after your mother by her at that time still beloved brother Giánnis, John, remembers that you used to swim in the sea off Itéa at night, something all the locals found remarkable. Stylída was quite a distance away on the road north toward Thessaloníki. Your traveling there and winning top prize must have been a big deal; the photo of you in your bathing suit with the pinned on gold medal and holding your award certificate made it to your father. Did the dictatorship impinge on your lives in any other ways? I don't know. You didn't mention anything else to me, though Chrysoúla told me that she was not allowed by her family to participate in any of the youth organization's activities; it wasn't clear to me if that was because like good Greek girls she was supposed to stay home or if her parents disapproved of the organization.

You have mainly fond memories of attending Chatzikonstantínou for three years. Your mother and your sister, Pearl, came to visit you often. According to Pearl, the two sisters who ran the place thought the world of you. You still remember that one of them was called "Pópi," a nickname for Penelópe. I found the other sister's name in your address book: Ioulía. You liked the way the school was situated. From the top of hill where it was perched you could see down to the church of Aghía Varvára and the sea. There was a lot of open land around there then. You remember seeing gliders taking off in the pastureland. Even though it seems like you were happy at the school and did well, you would take the opportunity to sneak away when you could. Giórgios, the politician Giórgios Papandréou's son by his second marriage to the actress Zoé Kavéli, also attended this school. Sometimes you and "Trelákis," the little crazy one, as he was known because he was so spoiled he behaved as if out of his mind, would head up Avenue Syngroú to the central part of Athens and try to visit his mother at the theater where she performed near Plateía Syntágmatos. There was a sweet shop nearby, and you two would feast on Greek pastries until someone from the school came to get you. How did you manage to negotiate that long trip by yourselves

30. Before the school gate, Chatzikonstantínou, Palió Fáliro,
on a rainy December day, 1938. Left to right: Miss Pópi,
unidentified boy, Pearl, Miss Ioulía, John, Chrysoúla.

at under age eleven? Was it he who knew the way? I was skeptical about
your claim to have walked from the school to the center of the city, so I
tried it myself in December 2006. It took me almost two hours, and I was
going in the downhill direction. Still, you might have been able to do it
faster back then, since there would have been significantly less traffic to
negotiate and you had good, strong legs. You say you were the one who

31. Kacandes children in traditional Greek dress, May 1938.
Left to right: John, Pearl, Nicholas, Harry.

always got punished for playing hooky. Was that because his parents were
rich and famous, or did he make you the scapegoat? Maybe you were the
instigator? After all, you had done plenty of sneaky things before leaving the United States. Be that as it may, in a letter to your father dated
March 20, 1940, the director reports that you are a fine student, though
a bit wild whenever you return from your stays in the countryside.

Neither your mother nor your father seems to have had a quick return to the United States on their minds. The excursions continued to
be documented at an impressive rate, with photos sent to your father.
Your passport should have been renewed in July 1939 and never was. My
grandparents also don't seem to have been overly concerned about the
initial hostilities in Europe. Did Europe seem very far away to Pappou,

as it did to most Americans in 1939? Was he so busy working and saving money that he didn't pay much attention to the news? For a long time I believed that we had no record of his thoughts. However, when I finally found a few of your father's papers in the attic of your house in White Plains, I located among them a telegram dated May 6, 1940. In a plea to the Commissioner of Immigration, your father inquires about your mother's petition for American citizenship, worrying that "delay in approval endangers my family and American born children who are with my wife in Greece and must get out before war breaks."

So, Pappou *was* worried about your welfare and specifically about when the war will spread to Greece. Other families were too. The outbreak of the war in other parts of Europe in 1939 caused quite a few of the Greek American families to send for their children at Chatzikonstantínou. And yet, as that letter from the director to your father and your promotion diploma from fourth grade attest, you continued at least through spring 1940. Did the school itself become unprofitable because of all the withdrawn Greek Americans and never reopen in fall 1940? Or did you begin school year 1940–41 and then experience a closing of the school precipitated by the country's quick and complete mobilization for war when the Italians invaded Greece from the Greek-Albanian border in late October 1940? You don't remember, however the version of "school closing" stored in my brain from my childhood makes me suspect it was the latter, emergency scenario. Still, you didn't have to find your way to your family alone; your mother came to get you and brought you back to Roúmeli, where she was living with your siblings. There was not yet any fighting in that part of Greece, which doesn't mean that you all weren't anxious.

I suspect your mother had already moved into the second house she rented in Itéa, one block closer to the waterfront and one block closer to the central street, this one owned by a family named Bíllios. You developed a close friendship with the son, Tákis, who became your swimming buddy, according to your cousin Thýmios, and whose illness at the end of the war worried you terribly.

Maybe the move had to do with changed financial circumstances, though according to your sister this house was nice, too, and your family stayed in it until you finally were able to depart from Greece in October 1945. The house was torn down before I went looking for it, but my cousin Dina said she was shown it by some locals when she visited in the 1980s.

One thing about your mother in those early years of your stay that seems certain is her own desire to contribute to the future financial stability of your family. She sat at her loom for hours weaving the sheets, blankets, and rugs she originally hoped to sell for a profit. You remember five or six trunkfuls, filled with items she eventually had to barter away piece by piece to keep food in her own and your and your siblings' mouths. She must have carried a lot of bitterness in her heart about this necessity; my cousin George remembers our grandmother's refusal to touch a loom later in her life, even when a sympathetic Greek American art teacher, a man originally from your father's village, as it turns out, asked her to give a demonstration to his pupils.

Whether it was directly at your father's instigation or at that of the American Embassy, as you remember, some time between the Italian invasion of Greece in late October 1940 and the German invasion of April 1941, your mother must have felt a heightened sense of danger and tried to take you all to Athens in preparation for a departure. You did not make it out of the country. In one account you gave me you made it to Athens but the American Embassy had withdrawn; in another, you never made it past Thebes because of the advance of the German army.

The war had begun well for the Greeks, who managed not only to push the Italians back over the Albanian border but also to occupy three major towns in southern Albania by early December 1940. It was one of very few military successes against any Axis power in the initial stages of the war. Most inside Greece could not or did not imagine then that Hitler would come to the rescue of his ally. The embarrassment to the Axis does not seem to have been nearly as important in his calculations, however, as the insecurity of having part of southern Europe under Allied control before or during his planned (and still secret) attack against the Soviet Union. Hitler certainly didn't want British planes within striking distance of the Romanian oil fields and refineries. The Wehrmacht invaded Greece and Yugoslavia simultaneously on April 6, 1941. The Greeks and their too few British allies held on slightly longer than their northern neighbor. Still, on April 21 General Tsalákoglu capitulated to the Germans. The Italians demanded a capitulation directly to them two days later, something that was obviously designed to humiliate the Greeks and rehabilitate the Italians' own sense of military prowess after the Albanian debacle the previous autumn and winter.

In one interview you insisted to me that you were an eyewitness to a German air offensive on Attica from the town of Thebes, and that it was the sight of German parachutists that halted your family's trip toward the capital. Thinking of Oedipus's fate, I marvel at the mythological resonances of you seeing such a dreadful display precisely from Thebes, but I found no corroborating evidence for it. I do believe you witnessed some terrible violence in Thebes, but I don't know what it was. More certain is your experience of the bombs dropped in the port of Itéa. History books report that the Luftwaffe used Stukas to attack ports and cities in mid-April 1941. Your friend Steve Zévas remembers the local attack coming on the Tuesday after Easter. That would have been April 22. Were you subject to the bombing in Itéa before fleeing to Athens, only to realize the Germans were about to take Attica? (Athens was officially handed over to the Wehrmacht on April 27.) Or had you tried to flee to Athens earlier and returned to Itéa only to experience bombs dropping there? Either way, you and your family were checked and then checkmated by the rapid German invasion of Greece. You experienced this not only as frightening, but also as an injustice; somehow you'd been cheated. You knew you held an American passport; you felt you shouldn't have to suffer in Greece. America was not (yet) part of this war. A sense stayed with you well into adulthood, as my sister Tina remembers from

32. Street in front of Kacandes ancestral home in Kolopetinítsa
as it appeared in summer 1984, with Lucie Kacandes
(foreground right) speaking to two unidentified villagers.

a conversation with you in 1992, that your mother should have known
to flaunt your American passport to get you all out.

trapped inside the country, your first real refuge from the fighting
seems to have been Kolopetinítsa, the village of your paternal family. It
is only a few kilometers from Itéa, but at that time had no real road leading to it; the steep ascent also protected it from at least certain kinds of
assaults. You're not sure how long you stayed in the small house in Kolopetinítsa, but if you fled there right after the bombs dropped in Itéa,
it may have been four months until school started in the fall. You told
me that you were sharing the space with your aunt Argyrí Tsakíri, née
Kakanté, your father's oldest sibling; her husband, your uncle Kóstas
Tsakíris; their three children, Andréas, Thýmios and Panagoúla; and,
of course, the sheep—though they would have been outside in the summer. It was a tiny place, a hovel, really. Your cousin Thýmios reports
that with the little house so crowded, you and your family didn't actually stay very long.

Roúmeli, your part of Greece, along with most of the mainland plus the Ionian and Cycladic Islands, were awarded to Mussolini's Italy, despite the Greeks' sound defeat of the Italians in the Albanian campaign. Over the course of May and June 1941 German troops withdrew from these areas and were replaced by Italians. Greece experienced a particularly hot and dry summer. That must have made it easier for the entering Italians to burn Tolophónas, the mountain village to which your oldest maternal first cousin, Zoé, and her family had fled from their home in the coastal town of Galaxídi. For the most part, though, things quieted down quickly and certain normal activities could be resumed. Schools reopened for the first time since the invasion at the Albanian border, for example. So I'm thinking that your mother probably wanted you and your brother Harry—by September 1941 you were eleven and a half and Harry was going on nine—to attend classes. You probably descended from Kolopetinítsa and took up residency in Itéa again that fall.

Even though you claim not to have gone to school during the Occupation, I found witnesses to the fact that you and Harry did attend at least sometimes. Your contemporary Evgenía Argyríou, who still resides in Itéa, told me that she was in your class. Evgenía further reported that because of the missed time during the Albanian campaign and the German invasion, the teachers tried to cover two years of the curriculum in the single school year of 1941–42. She also has a clear memory of how you looked at that stage: λεπτός, ξανθός, ωραίος (thin, blond, handsome). I see clearly from the photos sent to your father before the war began how blond your hair got in the summer. Evgénia said all the girls admired you, especially the way you walked. They associated your gait with your being an American. Your cousin Chrysoúla remarked on the way you walked too. She labeled it χορευτά (dancelike) and jumped up to give me a demonstration in her kitchen when I visited her in Athens in December 2006. The way she moved forward on the balls of her feet imitating you reminded me of my own brother Peter's childhood gait, and I wondered to myself if such things can be inherited.

Bóbis Talaroúgas, whom I met serendipitously on the quay when I visited Itéa in 2005, remembers being in Harry's class. Despite these eyewitnesses to your school attendance, how regularly you or your brother showed up would remain unclear to me, since in 1941–42 getting enough food was on the minds of many Greeks. Food was most certainly the major concern of your mother, who by this point had lost contact with and financial support from your father. I found a telegram from May 1941 in which Western Union tells your father to come collect a refund, since they could not deliver the money he had just tried to send.

To be sure, Itéa and environs did not experience the extremity of famine that Athens and other big cities did. You told me yourself that you did not witness people dropping in the streets from starvation as is documented in numerous reliable sources for Athens. Your contemporary Evgenía told me that a certain number of families came from Athens to Itéa as refugees from hunger, and that the area was "drowning in olive oil" because traditional export channels were cut off. Though your family might have been based there already, your situation did not differ much from that of "starvation refugees," since you did not own olive trees or have any other steady source of your own food. With each family worried about itself, your mother could not rely on her relatives or your father's to share what they had. Someone took pity on you and gave you a χωράφι, a small piece of land. You don't remember who it was, but you once told me that there were so many rocks it was impossible to grow anything there. So your mother mobilized the only resource she had. She began to travel to the surrounding villages to try to sell or barter for food the cloth she had been weaving and continued to produce. It wasn't enough. You began to work at any available job. You were twelve years old.

In this period you went out on the night boats from Itéa and assisted the fishermen. As your pay you would receive a tiny fraction of the catch. But instead of bringing the fish home, you would sell them in the surrounding villages to get money with which you could buy bread, a foodstuff

33. View of the *lóngos* from Delphi with Chryssó (foreground right) and Itéa (background left), summer 2005.

you all needed more urgently to fill your stomachs. The bread wasn't enough. You and Harry would go to the *lóngos*, the area between Itéa and Delphi that is filled with olive trees. One of you would stand watch while the other picked up fallen olives. You told me they caught you at it one night and you were put in the local collaborationist jail, installed after the Italians arrived on the second floor of the partly requisitioned Gerentés family home, one block up from the waterfront and one block east from the Bíllios home you were renting.

I don't know when construction on the road began, but Evgenía, your friend Elías Skarímbas, and you yourself report that you worked on the road the Italian occupiers started to build between Itéa and Ámphissa, the regional capital, where Elías was lucky enough to go to high school. He was three years older than you, and his father had a παντοπωλείο, a small grocery store. He would see you as he walked to school, and he assures me that it was backbreaking work if ever there was such a thing. I imagined you to myself in the hot sun sledgehammering rocks all day. In exchange you would receive a small amount of food. In the interview you gave to the local Asbury Park newspaper when you returned to the United States from Greece in 1945, you said that you received as pay one slice of bread and a cup of olives per day. I can't put precise dates for your work on the road. But I eventually received reports about it from several additional witnesses. Loukás Gerentés told me that your brother Harry got him a job working on the portion of the road near Chryssó in winter 1942. He said it was so cold that you would put newspaper under your shirts to cut the wind. Loukás was grateful to have the job, though. Even his family couldn't get enough food in that period. I heard too from the now quite elderly Démos Dimitríou from Chryssó, six years your senior. He distinctly remembers your mother working on the road. It was worse than I had thought. For your mother to do such manual labor not just in a public place, but in Chryssó, where everyone knew her, she must have become completely desperate. Démos and Loukás added the further detail that you all were working with your hands, smashing rocks against one another to get them to break, not using a hammer as I had originally envisioned to myself.

These primitive, painful, and humiliating conditions lead me to suspect that it was this road construction job that engendered that genuine hatred of the Italians you harbored then. Many Greeks experienced the Italian occupiers as relatively harmless, even charming. But you despised them and reported to me that they committed every kind of social violation during the occupation. In one of the talks you gave at the local JCC, you announced to the audience, "Let me surprise you a little bit by telling you that the greatest brutalities that were committed on the Greek populations were not by the Germans but by the Italians." You didn't offer any details to that audience nor to me. After viewing photos of the atrocities perpetrated by the Wehrmacht, I have trouble agreeing with your assessment in relation to the whole of Greece, but you have repeated this charge to me so often, I accept it as true of your own interactions with the Italians, even though I cannot figure out more about what those interactions were.

As far as I can put together, three dramatic events of rather different nature probably occurred in summer or early fall 1942 and changed the basic patterns of how you and your mother were trying to keep the family afloat. I really don't know in which order they transpired, but this is what I'm guessing.

Maybe it was due to your own knowledge of the terrain (from selling fish on foot in all the surrounding villages), maybe it was due to your cousin's involvement, but at some point your cousin Thýmios Tsakíris, one of the members of the family you had shared the paternal homestead with in Kolopetinítsa for part of 1941, appears to have taken you "to the mountains" to one of the newly formed Greek partisan groups. There seem to have been the first real efforts to organize resistance in your part of the country in May and July of that year (Kaïmáras 1988, 24, 31). I don't know where Thýmios took you exactly if you did go with him in 1942, but it probably wasn't initially to Colonel Demétrios Psarrós's 5/42 Sýntagma Evzónon, named after a celebrated fighting unit that had fought in the Asia Minor campaign decades before, since they didn't start to use the mountain Gióna as a base—a place that does appear in your accounts—until the following year, 1943. I also really don't know what kind of help they let a twelve-year-old boy render. However, since the resistance was in its infancy and the need for communication and coordination was high, it seems possible you were recruited to take messages from one spot to another. Many young people were. Someone your age and size—you were still small in stature in those days—presumably was less likely to be suspected of doing anything wrong. After the war you recounted hiding messages in donkeys' ears and making narrow escapes from being captured or even killed, but I don't know how to verify these stories. In one fleeting reference during an interview with me, you said you spent a lot of time in Athens "to prevent being recaptured."

34. John's cousin Thýmios Tsakíris pictured in his garden in Itéa with George H. Kacandes, son of John's brother Harry, December 2006.

The way that phrase slipped into your narration about something else makes me think it referred to a real event. My sister Maria reports hearing a story of a raid where you were so scared they would discover you, you shat in your pants. Near miss, or arrested, you must have been **terrified**. But again, I don't know how, when, where, or why you might have been caught. You never said anything to me directly about your guerrilla activities. Did Psarrós's men give you money? I know they were getting some supplies and gold sovereigns from the British. Did you do it for the adventure? Out of patriotism? Did you think of it as revenge against the Italians who had exploited you? I don't know.

I can connect you and the particular resistance group, the 5/42 as they were known, in the sense that Psarrós was a native of your mother's village Chryssó, born there in 1893, a decade before your mother. Your mother and he may have been distantly related; half the people I asked about this were skeptical; half indicated it was possible but said they didn't know for sure. I do know that your mother and father had used a notary public in Chryssó named Demétrios Psarrós. Was this the same person? It doesn't seem likely since the resister had been career military prior to the Greek defeat in 1941. Did you meet the local hero face to face? Perhaps. That you wanted to have a connection to him seems completely understandable to me. History has assessed his capabilities as a leader variously; still, the opinion of Giánnis Engonómou, a former EAM fighter who participated in the November 1942 blowing up of the Gorgopótamos viaduct and whom I met through the innkeeper when I stayed in Delphi in 2005, is shared by many: Ἦταν καλός χαρακτήρας. (He had a good character.) When I showed you a book about Psarrós and his partisans, you opened to the roster of known participants and immediately picked out two names you knew. I was surprised. How had you met them exactly? You didn't say.

What your cousin Thýmios reports is that he took you with him one time when he was supposed to transfer foodstuffs for resisters from one mountain location to another. It was night and you were traveling by foot, of course. In your case that meant barefoot. Thýmios let you fill a large sack with bread for your family and disguise it with weapons on top to make the journey. How did that strategem strike you? I note that at that time you were less likely to get in trouble pilfering weapons than bread. Such was the rarity of real—meaning wheat—bread in your region during the war. Most people ate a substitute made from cornmeal, but one had to have something to trade for the corn. Thýmios doesn't remember having you with him on more than this one occasion, but of course, this doesn't mean you didn't go try to help on your own.

Despite your still young age, you were the oldest male in the household, and it seems you incessantly felt a strong responsibility to try to provide for your family. Was it you or your mother who had the idea to cross over the Corinthian Gulf to work the raisin crop in the Pelepónnisos? If my calculations are correct it was probably harvest 1942 when you did so together. Your mother must have been pretty desperate by that time, because the endeavor would involve leaving the other children behind. Nick was now five years old. Did your mother entrust him to Harry and Pearl, or did a relative come to stay for the three weeks you were gone? Go, you did. Under the hot late summer sun, you and your mother cut the grapes and laid them out to dry. Looking back on it in 1945 you called it the hardest job you had ever done. You were paid in raisins. And according to something your mother many years later told her first daughter-in-law, my mother, you were stripped of those raisins by Greek resistance fighters traveling between where you had worked and the port in Aígio before you crossed back over the Corinthian Gulf and made it home. You didn't say anything about that to the American newspaper reporter in 1945. Were you ashamed to have to recount that it was fellow Greeks who robbed you? Was the futility of having worked so long and hard only to come home empty-handed so great that you wiped out the theft from your memory? It embittered your mother.

How and when exactly your maternal grandparents died remains contested among members of the family. I'm reckoning it may have been the straw that broke your backs in late 1942. There is agreement that they died in close succession, your grandmother Asymoúla first and then your grandfather Harálambos. Your sister says your grandparents died twenty-two days apart. Your first cousins Chrysoúla and Ólga both used the religiously symbolic period of "forty days." You never said much to me about your grandparents, though you once pronounced your grandfather an excellent shoemaker and told me that he would go to the festival of Saint John, your patron saint, on the outskirts of Itéa, to take orders. You retained the detail that many refugees from the Asia Minor Disaster would attend that festival and be fitted for shoes. Your cousin Zoé loved your grandfather very much, and he her. She cried out with delight when I showed her an unlabeled photo from your collection, and she immediately identified it as a portrait of herself as a young child with grandfather Harálambos. She also reported that he had a sign in his workshop in his home in Chryssó that read: Ένας είναι ο Τσίγγας! (There's only one Tsíngas!) Your cousin Chrysoúla remembers watching him make shoes in a second workshop he had set up in a corner of her father's store in Itéa. She recalls his concentration and the cigarette hanging from his lips, despite her father's demand that he not smoke there. Your brother Harry told his daughter, my cousin Dina, about stealing boots from the dock where a German soldier had temporarily left them. The story goes that he took them to your grandfather to have them cut down to his size. Your sister recalls both your grandparents with great affection. Did the sad events shut off your own emotions about them, Dad? You mentioned them so little and did not recognize your grandfather in the photos I showed you. And yet you made sure that your own children knew their grandparents as well as possible.

Your Tsíngas cousins report that your grandmother died of complications from minor surgery and your grandfather from grief. Zoé and your sister believe that they both **starved** to death. Pearl further reports that you were sent to beg food from your uncle John Tsíngas to give to your dying grandfather and that he refused you. Whatever the exact reasons for their premature deaths, your mother feared her parents' demise presaged your own. She decided to take the drastic and surely for her terrifying measure of separating you. She kept Nick with her in Itéa. Pearl was sent to a wealthy family in Livathiá who promised they could feed her, a family who had met her when she and your mother attended a wedding there in the prewar period.

Harry spent more and more time with your cousin Thýmios and the other shepherds. And I believe this is when you probably returned to Athens—this time not as a privileged boy reporting back to his private school after termbreak, but rather possibly originally as a mendicant. You hadn't quite turned thirteen. The Red Cross had expanded operations in Athens. I'm thinking this is the kind of news that spreads quickly. Perhaps you heard about it and figured you could get supplies for your family.

How did you travel to Athens? Gasoline was at such a premium that the buses used a wood burning attachment. My mother remembers that such buses were called *gazozén*. You report that it was so inefficient that it would sometimes take days to cover the 180 kilometers between Itéa and the capital, and that often the "passengers" had to not only get out and walk, but also to push the bus up the hills. Once you did make it to Athens, how did you find the Red Cross? I have no idea. You remember the specific detail that it was the Swedish Red Cross who helped you by feeding and clothing you. Children were a priority; you had always been thin, and I'm guessing you looked malnourished by then. Though the Red Cross workers were eager to feed you, they would not give you provisions you could take away and send to your family. So you started to work again.

It began with cigarettes. The Pétsas family, your relatives who had been your guardians during your schooldays before the war, lived somewhere in the proximity of the Papastrátou cigarette factory in Piraeus. They took you in again, and the obvious choice for supporting yourself was to sell cigarettes, along with dozens? hundreds? of other children who were doing so. The phenomenon of the child cigarette vendor during the war is well documented. You yourself were very moved by reading the diary of Néstoras Mátsas (1999), a Greek Jewish boy whose mother had died in the early war years and whose father was arrested and deported by the Germans from Athens in March 1944. It's one of the very few books I can remember you reading start to finish in recent decades. When I asked you what you liked most about it, you told me: he sold cigarettes to survive. I did that too.

You told me they were called *Chýma*— "Tsigára tou Bakálee *Chýma*," which means literally "the grocer's cigarettes." I suppose people could buy them at the grocer's, though I've only heard about you band of child street vendors. You would purchase two or three cartoons of one hundred and then sell them mainly individually. I went to see the factory myself one evening in December 2006. The imposing boxlike building still bears a gigantic neon sign that reads: PAPASTRATOU, even though the company has been bought out by Philip Morris. I suppose the waning winter light enhanced my ability to feel the desolation of the place, despite its location in the busy port. I stood there for as long as I could bear, trying to imagine all the little children walking these particular streets and paying out their precious money to get another carton of cigarettes. I got spooked and left.

You don't remember how much a single cigarette cost, and anyway, with the inflation as rampant as it was, the price must have kept changing. You recount walking all over Athens and Piraeus to sell your wares, day and night. If you got caught by fatigue or curfew too far from your base in Piraeus, you could sometimes stay at the dormitory of what you always referred to as the Third Police Precinct between Plateía Káningos and Leofóros Tríti Septembríou. I tried to locate this building, too, that was so important to you during your time in Athens, but I didn't manage to. The police I consulted insisted that the third precinct had been in Kolonáki during the war, a fair distance from the precise location you pointed me toward. I was able to confirm my suspicion that it was actually the fourth police precinct, Dad, when I finally tracked down, again with the help of my cousin George, your coworker from there, Pantelís Manoúsos. I'm thinking that "third" got lodged in your head because it was in fact located near the street Third September. The head of that precinct, Ioánnis? Demétrios? Sakellaríou—you weren't sure of his first name, but you do have a picture of him in your photo album—had a niece who had been enrolled in your school. When Sakellaríou found out that you hadn't managed to leave Greece before the war broke out, he more or less looked out for you when he could. Pantelís told me that the police chief walked in with you to the room the two brothers slept in and announced, from now on he sleeps here too, and you look after him. The brothers even assumed you were a relative of the chief. In any case, Pantelís told me he has a strong recollection even today of you with your tray of cigarettes and the strap that went around your neck to support the tray. So, you caught some sleep either at the police precinct dormitory or with your relatives in Piraeus when you'd finished selling the cigarettes you had. And the next day it would be more of the same. You have no recollection of how long you did this. But you seem to have vended cigarettes on and off for several years, and even after the official end of the war in Greece. In one interview with me you called it "my cigarette business." Whenever you had saved enough of the inflated Greek currency to make the cost of shipping worthwhile you'd send it to your mother. The paper bills took up so much space you had to put them into large potato sacks. Sometimes you must have bought things so the money wouldn't lose its value. Your sister Pearl remembers you sending packages from Athens to Itéa that "kept us alive."

One day, which I'm thinking might have been in early 1943, you were in Piraeus searching for an honest-looking caïque owner headed to Itéa with whom you could entrust the potato sacks of inflated occupation money intended for your mother, when you heard a voice call out your name. You were in the area close to the docks referred to as Το Ρολόι (the clock) because there was a large seaman's clock on a tower in front of the church there. It no longer exists, but some old timers can still point out where it once stood, and I went to see the spot for myself, the same day I located the cigarette factory. You followed the sound of the voice and saw the friendly face of Pétros Tsardákas, whom you'd met in Itéa before the war when he would come with his father's caïque, load up olives, and take them to various locations. By this time, of course, his boat, the *Vellisários*, had been requisitioned by the Germans. (In the Axis division of Greece, Germany had retained control over the ports of Piraeus and Thessaloníki, among other strategic areas.) Tsardákas was allowed to continue to skipper it, though. Captain Pétros was surprised to see you. Like Sakellaríou, he too had assumed you and your family had made it out of the country. When he heard how hard you were working to achieve basic survival, he said you should join him on the boat where you could make better money. Thus, for what I'm calculating might have been several months in early to past mid-1943 you were the μούτσος, the ship's gofer, doing any odd job that no one else cared to do. You sailed up and down the Ionian Sea between Piraeus and Kérkyra (Corfu) with Captain Pétros and a mixed Greek-German crew on the *Vellisários*. You still have one photo you had taken of yourself in Patrás to send to your mother, because according to the caption you put on it much later, she didn't know your whereabouts. In that same caption you mention the period of time on the boat as being "seven months," and the photo as being taken specifically on your third trip to Patrás. You don't relate what you were transporting, but you told me in an interview that it was German ammunition. I found one photo of a requisitioned Greek caïque in German service in a history book (Mazower 2001, 59); did the *Vellisários* have to fly the swastika as well? How did you feel about that?

When I asked you whether Tsardákas might have been considered by natives to be a collaborator, you vehemently protested, telling me that "he was trying to protect his own property and grabbing what he could like everybody else." You also insisted that you would deliver German ammunition to the Greek guerrillas when you could, but it's unclear to me how you did that if part of the crew was German. The presence of Germans on the boat is also one of the reasons I'm not sure how Captain Pétros could have risked an attempt to cross from Kérkyra to Italy to help in the Allied invasion, which had started in Sicily in June. Did the German crew want to defect too? Were there Germans on board only some days? You never made it across the Adriatic, you said, because the engines conked out. In any case, if you were trying to reach the Allied forces in Italy, it helps me roughly date this period to summer 1943.

The end of your own days on the *Vellisários* seems to have been dramatic enough. You said that Captain Pete's boat was anchored next to a larger boat in Piraeus when the Allies began bombing the port—or were they aiming specifically for that ship next to you? The force of the blast knocked you into the water. Your swimming skills saved you, and you managed to get to land, but only to discover that part of the third toe on your left foot was hanging. That you had no choice but to walk to the hospital seems probable to me, though I'm assuming you or someone near you must have done something to stop the blood flow first. You report that you went to Politikós, a hospital that was about ten kilometers away, because you knew that Tsardákas's brother Demétris was a surgeon there. Whether or not he actually operated on you, I cannot prove, but given how fond I myself know Pétros was of you, it certainly seems possible that he or his brother checked up on you, and that they arranged for you to make your convalescence at their parental home in Kallithéa. You remember doing errands for his mother, Elisávet Tsardáka, tasks like fetching groceries. When you recalled the fact in October 2006 for your friend Elías Skarímbas, you told him that you were working σαν υπηρέτης (like a servant). I'm not sure you liked that, since your "base," as you quickly added, continued to be in Piraeus, and you took up selling cigarettes once again.

Major military and political events were transpiring during your post-*Vellisários* period. On the 8th of September 1943 Italy surrendered to the Allies, and the Germans quickly reoccupied the whole of Greece. Having succeeded in deporting almost the entire Jewish population of Thessaloníki by August of that year, the Germans now tried to impose restrictions on the Jewish community of Athens, a goal the Italian cooccupiers had previously resisted. ELAS, the military arm of the left-wing underground organization EAM, kidnapped Grand Rabbi Barzilai of Athens to preempt what was assumed to be his imminent arrest by the Germans. This dramatic rescue served as a sign to the rest of the Athenian Jewish population to go into hiding if they could. EAM also circulated a tract specifically urging Greeks to help hide Jews, who "are Greeks just as much as we are" (quoted in Clogg ed. 2002, 107), though I'm told that not many people actually saw this noble message. That same tumultuous autumn is considered the first round of the Greek Civil War. Fighting broke out between EAM and EDES, and a British brokered armistice wasn't signed until late February 1944. In the meantime, the Germans were worried about increased attacks, and a decree on October 25, 1943, announced that "fifty Greeks will be executed for every murdered German soldier, and ten for every wounded German soldier" (quoted in Clogg ed. 2002, 101; see also Mazower 2001, 177).

You once related a story to me about finding such a flier in Kolopetinítsa. Were you back up there in fall 1943? I'm not sure, since you also have told me about getting a job as a guard at some kind of German property. You have referred to it as an ammunition dump and as a villa— in Néa Smýrni, just behind Avenue Syngroú in Athens. I was skeptical about this story until I saw a handsome portrait of you in your photo album that you captioned as a photo your German employers required. You note that you had to borrow the clothes "just for the picture from a wealthy friend of mine." I wonder if that friend wasn't Pete Tsardákas or someone in his family. I was thrilled when I discovered this photo; it is one of only two photos that I could locate from the years 1941 to early 1945, the other being the much more humble snapshot you had taken in Patrás while you were sailing on the *Vellisários*. What strikes me most looking at the studio portrait now is how apparent your light hair and blue eyes are, even though the photo is in black and white. Your light coloring couldn't have escaped the notice of your race obsessed German employers, and I wonder if that might not be why you were hired in the first place. You considered it one of your better jobs because they fed you so much that you could send for your brother Harry to share the food. You always thought to share when possible. You used the movie house Rosie Claire as a "babysitter" and worked while Harry watched movies. I heard that story from Uncle Harry directly sometime in the years before he died. He would recount watching the same movie over and over again in a very funny way to us, proclaiming at the end of the anecdote that despite that or maybe because of it he still loved the movies, as we all knew from his interest in and support of our sister Georgia's career in movie production. Tina remembers you having told her that one time Uncle Harry borrowed a bike you had access to; you were

35. Studio portrait of John used to secure employment
with the Germans in 1943, Athens.

furious when he crashed it on a steep hill. Did that mishap lead to your
being fired? Or was it the malaria that you reported in the interview you
gave in the United States after your return? Tina remembers hearing
you recount stories about body chills and attempts among you brothers to warm yourselves by lying on top of each other. Tina, who knows
a lot more about medicine than I do, says those chills are signs that you
might indeed have had malaria. But you never said anything to me about
becoming ill in Athens or why and when the job working as a guard for
the Germans ended.

Given the timing of the Germans' full reoccupation of Athens, I am thinking you worked as a guard in fall 1943, though other aspects of your accounts place you in Kolopetinítsa that fall. Maybe that job for the Germans didn't actually last long. If I discount the story about finding the reprisal flier in Kolopetinítsa just when I know the Germans to have dropped them, or if I assume that the fliers continued to be distributed long after their first appearances in late October 1943, this is what I would guess about your itinerary during this period of the war: You sailed on the *Vellisários* in the first half of 1943 and worked for the Tsardákas family and sold cigarettes in late summer 1943. At some point in early or perhaps in later fall, you got that job guarding the German property. Subsequently the arrangement fell apart—because of your own illness? because of your mother's? I don't know why—and you returned to the Itéa area.

No one seems able to date when your mother got so sick. I'm guessing it was winter 1943–44. Your cousins Chémo and Voúla, nées Gerenté, say that your mother contracted pleurisy. Your sister Pearl says that when the word reached her in Livathiá, the family she was staying with immediately sent her back to Itéa so that she could comfort her dying mother. Were you already in the area, or did you also return because of the bad news? I don't know. What I am certain of—because of all the miseries and indignities you suffered, this one marked you the most—is that you went to your mother's brother, your theio Giánnis, for help and he refused you. You felt **betrayed**. Bitterness and hatred wiped out all memory of what happened next. I've never heard from you how my grandmother managed to get better, but regain her health she did. Theia Chémo says that her older sister, Voúla, used βεντούζες (cupping glasses) on your mother and that that helped. People brought food. You wouldn't have left her side to go to Athens until you were certain she would recover.

Return to Athens you must have, and I believe it was probably sometime in late winter, early spring 1944. You seem to have relied on at least two ways to keep yourself afloat: you took up your cigarette business again, and at some point your stays in the police precinct dormitory led to a job in the kitchen. The assistant cooks were two brothers from Ándros—an island you would become connected to in another way when you met my mother's brother Alex Psomas in Ithaca, New York, about ten years later while you were studying at Cornell, and he then introduced you to his sister Loukía, who became your wife. My mother's family is from the port village of Ándros, Gávrio. The mother of the brothers in the police kitchen hailed from Messariá, near Chóra, the island capital. You have fond memories of Leonídas and Pantelís Manoúsos. You managed to keep in touch with them after the war and years later when they came to the States and were running a profitable diner in Hackensack, New Jersey.

Athens was a chaotic place in mid-1944—one historian described it as "approaching anarchy" (Mazower 2001). This is the period when your own life was perhaps most determined by the changing political situation around you. Dad, I really know don't if you were arrested by the Germans or not, nor if it was for stealing something or because someone who knew you were circumcised pointed you out to them. There were numerous raids in many neighborhoods for all kinds of reasons in 1944. I count it as possible that you were swept up in one of them and that being detained for even a short period of time must have been **terrifying**. How did you get that scar on the tender side of your left arm, Dad? Were you tortured, as you have claimed to others, but not to me? These days, anyway, your scar looks like it resulted from some kind of ripping action rather than a burn. Given where it is located on your body, that wounding must have been terribly painful no matter how inflicted. I want to recognize that pain, Dad, but I also want to emphasize here that if you were arrested, even if you were tortured, you were also released. You did not share the fate of so many political enemies and Jews—and for the Nazis Jews counted as political enemies—who were killed or deported to death camps. You survived.

The German occupiers began leaving in the summer, and the last of them are recorded as departing Athens on October 12. So, Thursday October 12, 1944, is celebrated as the liberation of Athens. I've seen pictures of the crowds that flooded the streets and squares. The banners people hung out carried statements like "We Believe in Your Justice" and "The Bulgarians Must Pay Dearly" (in English) and ΖΗΤΩ Η ΑΓΓΛΙΑ Η ΣΟΒΙΕΤΙΚΗ ΕΝΩΣΗ Η ΑΜΕΡΙΚΗ (Long live England, the Soviet Union, and America), while others displayed the name of the leftist underground organization EAM surrounded by images of the Soviet, British, American, and Greeks flags (Paraschos 1983, 64–66). The people in the photos look ecstatic. I hope you experienced that joy and relief, too, Dad. The Papandréou government of National Unity that was agreed to by all major resistance groups, the Greek government in exile, and the British, received an enthusiastic welcome in the city on Wednesday October 18, delaying by one day what could have been their arrival, because Greeks never commence important tasks on Tuesday, the day of the week when the Ottomans administered the death blow to the Byzantine Empire by invading Constantinople.

By early December the cooperation had broken down, EAM ministers resigned from the cabinet, and a protest gathering took place on December 3 in Sýntagma Square in anticipation of a general strike planned for the next day. There are many different versions of exactly what happened, but it appears that Greek police fired on the crowd and a number of people were killed. This unleashed terrible fighting in the city between those loyal to EAM and those supporting the Papandréou government. Churchill's infamous order to his general Scobie to destroy "all EAM-ELAS bands approaching the city" and his recommendation that the British commander act "as if you were in a conquered city where a local rebellion was in progress" bring British troops, some of whom had been deployed as early as mid-October, into full engagement. Churchill's imperialist attitude toward an ally and sovereign nation shocked many in Britain and the United States when the telegram from Churchill to Scobie was leaked shortly after being sent. The subsequent fighting is referred to by Greeks as Τα Δεκεμβριανά (the December events) because the struggle for control mainly occurred in December. In a document issued in February 1945 in your possession attesting to your own role fighting for the British, Captain Bond called it "the troubles."

Today this fighting is considered as the second stage of the Greek Civil War, and it had a number of immediate political consequences: Churchill and Eden actually flew to Athens on Christmas Day 1944 to assess the situation and try to broker a peace. During the visit Churchill finally registered how deep Greek antipathy ran toward a return of the monarch. Churchill then put pressure on King George to appoint Archbishop Damaskinós as regent, which he did, and General Plastíras replaced Papandréou as prime minister. The defeat of the left did not take long. A truce was signed between ELAS and the British on January 11, 1945, and a more far-reaching agreement referred to by the place it was negotiated, Várkiza, is signed by representatives of the Greek government and members of the central committee of EAM on February 12, 1945.

The way you described your own experience of liberation to me was that one night a few communists broke into the police precinct dormitory where you'd been living with the two brothers from Ándros, Leonídas and Pantelís, and these intruders? unexpected heroes? announced to you that Greece was liberated. They didn't bother you, you told me, they just wanted to know where the nationalists and the communists were. You also make reference to a theater across the street that was being used to store ammunition. Did they ask you where it was? Did they swear you to secrecy should anyone else ask you where it was? I'm not sure why you connect this storage place with that same night.

You have one other memory of liberation. You were selling cigarettes to the crowds watching a parade on or near Leofóros Alexándras, when all of a sudden you realized that your old schoolmate, Giórgios Papandréou, o Trelákes, the little Crazy One, was in one of the limousines driving by. Given that his father was now prime minister, it seems plausible that he might have been included in a caravan of the new government, though I couldn't find any images of this in the photos I studied of the liberation celebrations. You waved to him wildly and called his name; he saw you. He made the driver stop, you got in and rode along for a while. That limousine must have been quite a change from the buses you occasionally splurged on. You weren't able to tell me any additional details about this unexpected reunion with Crazy George. I'm thinking you immediately lost touch with your former schoolmate.

I don't know if you returned to the village at this point to celebrate the reality of liberation with your family and make plans for the future, or if you did, how long you stayed. But I strongly suspect that your family must have come to Athens at least briefly in November 1944, for on the 20th of that month, your passport from 1937 is cancelled by the "Foreign Service, American Embassy." It would make sense from today's perspective if that were done in tandem with issuing you a new one, but that's not the way it happened. You are wearing your British uniform in your new passport picture (which means the photo was taken in January 1945 at the earliest and probably much later). The passport has disappeared, but I was able to verify that you chose to wear your British uniform for the official photo, as I eventually located an extra copy and you identified it immediately as "our passport photo." I hope your family returned to Itéa after the interview related to the passport renewal, because otherwise they too were exposed to the daily dangers of "the troubles." No one in the family has ever volunteered any memories about that. I do know that you stayed, or at least came back to the capital sometime in December.

On December 8, 1944, you turned fifteen while central Athens was a battle zone. Were you able to celebrate your birthday in some fashion anyhow? Did you take stock of how much you had been through? Of how young you still were? You never said. But December and January were probably the most dangerous months of the entire eight years you were in Greece. This point was brought home to me not so much by the history books I studied, as by a small devotional image of a very Anglo-Saxon looking Jesus, the Good Shepherd, you carried on your person after it was given to you by a young woman you met one night in the

36. Talisman given to John by unknown woman in Athens in 1944.

streets of Athens. You wrote about it years later: "I never did find out her name. But I kept this because she has written on the back of it something nice." That something "nice" was a wish that you be saved from every calamity (από κάθε συμφορά). It was a wish that spoke deeply to you in those days. I see you through that woman's eyes. You look vulnerable and need all the protection you can get.

You have described more nocturnal visits to the kitchen: one night the communists, the next the British. Helping the British was self-evident to you. You told me that they were "the only people you would talk to." I'm not sure if you were referring to your actual joy at communicating in English or if you had a strong sense that the salvation of Greece or of your family lay in making sure the British triumphed against the communists. There are numerous pictures of you in your British uniform taken both during the time of your actual service and afterward. You

The bearer of this pass, John Kacandes, is
employed by the ½ Regt

J. Northover. Sgt.

50th R.T.R. — 19.1.45.

The above will probable be wearing items
of ½ military clothing.

TO WHOM IT MAY CONCERN

JOHN KACANDES has been with this son since 29 Dec 44 and
at all times has rendered good service.   In ATHENS
during the troubles, he risked his life on several
occasions in the forward positions occupied by British
troops.   Since that time he has been serving in various
capacities and he is honest and of good character.

I recommend for him any odd duties which may arise.

V. E. Bond.

Capt., R.T.R.

15 Feb 45.

37. Top: Military pass issued to John by Sergeant Northover, 50th
RTR, January 19, 1945. Bottom: Photostat of letter of reference
for John from Captain Bond, 50th RTR, February 15, 1945.

even had yourself photographed in it when you returned to the States. Your beret is still in the house in White Plains, though nobody has seen the badge that goes with it recently. When I was searching in your files I found documentary proof of your actual military service to the British. The earlier dated one is a small ivory piece of paper, about fourteen centimeters wide and ten centimeters high. The bottom edge is torn, and it is written on by hand in pencil. It reads, "The bearer of this pass, John Kacandas [sic] is employed by the H/M regt." I couldn't quite make out on my own the spelling of the name that signed this pass, but after consulting a published list of members of the regiment, I realized the name must be "J. Northover. Sgt. 50th. R.T.R." (See Hamilton 1996, 290). The pass is dated "19.1.45." Along the bottom torn edge the sergeant adds, "The above will probable [sic] be wearing items of H/M military clothing." You had this piece of paper in your hand, evidently, as you made your way through the streets of Athens in January 1945. Even though the truce had been signed, Athens was still a dangerous and factionalized place on January 19. The necessity for and particular wording of the pass make that clear.

A second document is typewritten and I could only locate a certified copy of a photostat of the original. The text declares,

TO WHOM IT MAY CONCERN

JOHN KACANDES has been with this sqn since 29 Dec 44 and at all times has rendered good service. In ATHENS during the troubles, he risked his life on several occasions in the forward positions occupied by British troops. Since that time he has been serving in various capacities and he is honest and of good character. I recommend for him any odd duties which may arise.

[signature U. E. Bond]
Capt., R.T.R.
15 *Feb* 45.

I'm wondering if this document might have been created in Patrás, since it refers to Athens as if you were already elsewhere. I have seen several photos of you with British tanks and with members of the 50th RTR in Patrás from February 1945. You had gone there, you told me, to keep chasing the communists.

For a long time, I felt like I didn't know anything and would never be able to document anything about the actual fighting you did. Your photo captions refer to working in the "kitchen." But I suspected that you must have done something more than help prepare food and wash dishes prior to the taking of those photos, since I doubted that a captain in the Royal Tank Regiment in February 1945 would have used the expression "risked his life on several occasions" if you hadn't made a genuine contribution from a military perspective. After all, the 50th RTR was mainly an advance assault force, and had fought at Alamein and in Sicily, among other places, and Captain Bond himself had been wounded three times, including during the night of December 10–11 in the early days of "the troubles" in Athens (see Hamilton 1996, 215, 272). I had difficulty imagining your soldierly role, never having myself been in an active war zone. Then, too, it's hard for me to remember a stage when you weren't ruled by fear of danger the way you have been for much of the last decades.

However, after I finally tracked down Pantelís, Peter, your roommate in the police precinct dormitory and compared what he said to the published account of the activities of the 50th RTR I finally have a better idea. It is as harrowing as anything else you might have gone through. For Omónoia Square, the approximate location of the police station, and Káningos Square, the location of the police canteen and the room you shared with the Manoúsos brothers literally formed the border between turf held by the British Regiment and turf controlled by EAM and ELAS (Hamilton 1996, 212–25, esp. map 10 on p. 213). Pete, who is two years your senior, remembers more details about your fateful encounter with the British. He said you all heard banging at the building's door and when he went to check it out, the British broke through. He raced back into the room and told you and Leonídas to hide under the beds. Moments later the British burst through that door too, pointing their guns. At that point, Pete told me, you started screaming in English, "Don't shoot! Don't shoot! I'm American!" and you came out from under the bed with your hands raised and continued to solicit the soldiers in English. One trained his gun on the brothers, and the other two took you to their commander. Pete didn't know exactly what transpired there, of course, but when you returned, you explained to the brothers that it would be okay. The soldier wouldn't stop pointing his gun, though, until the officer with whom you'd spoken actually appeared. Pete couldn't tell me how many days then elapsed with you three continuing to sleep in that spot as the battle for control raged around you. But the next thing he reports is that you boys discovered a large stash of Molotov cocktails in the Alhambra, the empty theater whose location across the street you did retain in your memory. You reported this to your British contacts, who in turn rolled a tank in and blew up the theater. The fire erupted so ferociously it jumped the street and set your building ablaze. At that point you raced out of the back of the building to try to save your lives, and the brothers went to the left toward some Greek police they recognized and you to the right toward the British. They didn't see you for a few weeks, but when you found each other again, you had a uniform and food and happily shared the latter with them.

Dad, this story would sound as fantastical as the one Tom heard from his schoolmates about your rescue in Yugoslavia—it is as fantastical—and yet I found corroboration in general histories of the December troubles, in the chronicle of the 50th RTR and in your letter from Captain Bond. For one thing, when the cooperation between the Left and the coalition government broke down in early December, it was police stations that the Left first attacked. So it makes sense that you might have gotten "visits" from communists and that the British would investigate the same locations as the month went on. Additionally, the Hamilton account of the 50th RTR in Athens in this period attributes numerous skirmishes to information from native sources; that you could have been, would have wanted to be, such a source makes sense to me. From what you've told me, you really didn't understand much about the politics of the battle for control of Athens and Greece, but at the very least, the British spoke a language that symbolized rescue from the hell you'd been living in for many years; in your own words: they were the only people you would talk to . . . Most importantly, on the night of December 29–30, a date specifically mentioned by Captain Bond in his testimonial for you, the A Squadron, of whom you have numerous photos, was facing fires in its sectors near Patissíon Street, fires that were preceded by a blast the British had instigated (Hamilton 1996, 223–24). Without being able to prove it for sure, I suspect the building dynamited was the theater, and the fire engulfed the place you fled from. Dad, the blast and conflagration killed at least three adult men that night; you ran in the right direction fast enough to save yourself.

You refer to the document signed by Captain Bond as your "discharge papers," by which I assume in your mind it marked the transition from actual fighting to peacetime. It reads to me more like a character reference, and I suspect you showed it in order to get hired as a "batman" or valet, and as an elevator operator in British headquarters in Athens, a job you did for several months in late spring and summer 1945. By that time, you told me, you had made contact with your father in the United States through the Swiss embassy and were waiting for money he had paid in the United States to reach Greece to pay for your departure. I'm not sure why you think your father negotiated with the Swiss, since the American embassy had reopened. In any case, your photo album documents this period richly. For instance, in addition to many snapshots of you walking the streets of central Athens in uniform, you have a picture of a pretty young Greek woman named Roúla Papathastopoúlou, whom you were asked by the British to train to operate the elevator, presumably in anticipation of your own departure. You have another photo of

38. Members of the A Squadron, 50th RTR, in Patrás, February 1945, in a photo taken by John, who identifies the man in the center of the first row as "Sergeant Sheppard."

an American woman whom you identify as helping you file your papers with the American Embassy. I found it curious that you had her photo but didn't note her name. Or maybe you simply had forgotten it by the time you put the photo album together. I'm glad you felt other people were finally helping you.

There is one other piece of evidence for your connection to the British that I found late in my own research: correspondence after the war, or rather, proof of correspondence exchanged after you returned to the United States. You kept a small bound notebook in which you kept track of addresses and recorded each letter you sent and each letter you received from late October 1945 to late 1948. I relied on this log heavily to retrieve names your memory no longer could. You were a prolific correspondent, Dad. According to the long list, you seemed to have managed to stay in touch with a C. M. Sheppard of the A Squad of the 50th

39. Menélaos Costís pictured at his desk in Alexandria. Inscription reads: "That you might remember me and write to me."

RTR (according to your records you received a letter from him on May 23, 1946, for example) and a Private N. A. Ashwell, to whom you wrote at the "H.Q. Land Forces, Greece" (letters from him arrived on November 23, 1946, and July 1, 1947). The first initials don't quite match, or maybe I can't make out your handwriting, but I did find a "Sheppard" and an "Ashwell" in the roster of the 50th RTR members.

Your correspondence log also reveals numerous letters sent to and received from a Janette F. Magley who worked for the Greek UNRRA mission. In the newspaper interview you gave after your return to the States, you mentioned UNRRA as being "the most helpful organization in the country," but you didn't cite the specific aid they might have given you. Your most regular exchanges were with Menélaos Costís. The photo album you put together in the late 1940s includes numerous pictures of this Menélaos. You noted he was born in Alexandria, Egypt, and that he worked as a translator for the British. In one caption you write, "We became the best friends ever existed in this world." It makes me happy to think you felt that way about somebody. At the same time, I note that you never said a word to me about any of these nice people. They obviously made an impression on you, and I'm assuming that was at least partly because they had a profound impact on your daily life; they must have helped you improve your emotional as well as your material well-being.

You went back and forth between Athens and Itéa several times in those last months of your eight-year stay; the trip must have gotten somewhat easier after the war's end and the ceasefire between the communists and the British. Your photo album gives me some help with your whereabouts and your activities, if not with an exact chronology; it contains several pictures of you with British soldiers in Patísia on the outskirts of Athens, two of which include your brother Nick, whom I'm assuming you brought to the city for the same reason you had brought Harry a year and a half earlier: you could feed him. Your concern for others is also apparent in your aid to your hometown friend Steve Zévas. As a former ELAS member, life got dangerous for him in royalist Itéa after the

40. Friends pictured on grounds of requisitioned convalescent home
used for British soldiers in spring 1945. Nicholas (left, standing),
John (center, reclining), unidentified soldiers.

war was officially over. You found him a job with the British in Athens
and appear to have roomed with him for at least a few months. He described to me your moneymaking operations exchanging currency and
your attempts at socializing with women. He says one night you managed to get hold of an officer's uniform that facilitated your entrance to
the British officer's club. The sense I have of your personality and cleverness lends credence to this story, but the photographic record makes
me wonder how you convinced anyone you were old enough to be an
officer—or an eligible bachelor.

You obviously celebrated Easter 1945 in Itéa; the photos of your roast-
ing lamb in the streets, as is still the custom today, verifies that. When
and how did you acquire the three sheep and Kítsos, the ram who com-
manded steady stud fees and whom you decided to entrust to your theio

41. John (left) with hometown friend Steve Zévas, on errand
for the British, downtown Athens, spring 1945.

Kóstas Tsakíris in Kolopetinítsa rather than sell or have slaughtered before you departed? I've seen pictures of you in your British uniform hugging those sheep. Leaving them and Itéa behind, despite all you had suffered, couldn't have been easy. Loukás Gerentés remembers vividly your last night there. He says you all cried in each other's arms, eventually falling asleep on one big mattress before the truck came in the early morning to load the things you would take with you to Athens and on to the United States.

What was the "magic click" that unlocked the prison door and led to you finally being **saved**, departing Greece on the ship *Gripsholm* on September 13, 1945, and arriving in New York harbor on October 9—more than eight full years after you had left? In a contextless blurting-out to me one day in October 2006, you said that with a gun you still had from the resistance you had threatened an employee of the American Embassy to get you and your family on the next ship to the United States for Americans. You had missed the first one, your sister believes, because it was restricted to U.S. citizens and your mother still had only her Greek passport. Or rather, your mother may have had no passport at all for a time, as I eventually found one that was obviously issued specifically for her departure in September 1945. You have a Robert W. Cauldwell identified in one of your address books as the "Vice Counsular in Greece that helped us to come here." Though I do not know all the types of assistance he offered you and your family, I deciphered his signature on the American visa in your mother's new Greek passport. Whatever it took, whoever helped, I feel like I owe my own existence to the lucky timing of that departure. For with it, you and your family avoided the third, the longest, and the bloodiest stage of the Greek Civil War. Mercifully for us, and tragically for them, those are stories for another family to tell.

Dad, you taught Greek roots to everyone you could: your children, your students, the young ones, and those in your adult education classes, your acquaintances, anyone who would stay still long enough for you to get

42. The Greek passport on which Chrysoúla was
able to leave Greece in September 1945.

your flashcards out. You considered it the best vocabulary builder possible. Here's a good Greek word: "enigma," from the Greek verb *ainissesthai*, "to speak in riddles." Its contemporary meaning in English includes "obscure speech or writing," "something hard to understand or explain," and "an inscrutable or mysterious person." It's distinguished from its synonyms in that it applies particularly to an "utterance or behavior that is very difficult to interpret" (see *Merriam-Webster's Collegiate Dictionary*, 11th ed., s.v. "mystery"). All these meanings are relevant to one degree or another to the topics I want to take up briefly before I conclude my attempt to cowitness to your war, a few subjects that puzzled me, even drove me to ask certain questions while I was doing my research, and yet were not addressed overtly in the previous pages. In my view, these topics shed light on, if not directly explain, some aspects of what you went through. I'll move from a more concrete and decipherable mystery to two areas for which the connections to your war necessarily remain more tenuous. In a sense, I want to create a series of concentric circles around your war; while each is farther removed, each adds to our understanding of it.

The most unexpected discovery in my whole enterprise was to locate an envelope stuffed with Greek documents from the 1930s related to The House in Chryssó. As I tried to communicate in earlier parts of this book, the idea that your mother had been cheated out of a house in her native village was so deeply embedded in my consciousness that such a **betrayal** was perhaps the most sinister part of my childhood memories. As a result, I think it never occurred to me that something as mundane as a paper trail could exist. I found these documents truly by accident. Not only was I searching for Pappou's letters to the State Department at the time I picked up the envelope, but also I took the envelope back to my house in New Hampshire without even realizing I had it. When I started examining what I'd found in your filing cabinets, I noticed a business-size envelope crammed full of yellowed papers. I opened it, and the sheets were so tightly folded and had obviously been in that position for so long that I couldn't get them to stay flat enough to pry them apart or to peruse them. I did notice, though, that they were all in Greek, many were handwritten, and to my frustration they were in *katharévousa*, that artificial bureaucratic language in which most business was conducted until late in the twentieth century. After a couple of weeks under some heavy books, the papers were flat enough for me to try reading. I quickly realized they were related to your parents sending money to Greece in the 1930s and to the status of your maternal grandparents' house in Chryssó. My first thought concerned how Yiayia managed to keep these documents throughout the war and even to return to the States with them, given all she had gone through, including physical displacements. Though Mom tried helping me decipher the documents over the phone, it wasn't until I poured over them with a lawyer friend in Greece that I got a sense of what they meant in relation to our family history.

The short version is that your mother's parents, Harálambos and Asymoúla Tsínga borrowed a large amount of money from some loan sharks in fall 1928, the very year your parents had married. They put up the house in Chryssó, which was in Asymoúla's name (it was probably her dowry, but I couldn't find proof of that) as collateral. In 1931 your father, George Kacandes, sent money from the United States to Greece to buy the loan from the loan company, and in turn, the house as collateral came to him. Something happened in 1935 that makes your father wonder if his investment is safe, for he asks a bank in Greece to determine whether the value of the house is enough to cover the loan and the interest owed on it. No existing documents indicate what could have triggered his concern at that particular time. My two best guesses are either the floods of 1935 that do much damage in the area of Chryssó or news that your mother's parents were going to give the house as dowry for their youngest daughter, Loukía. In any case, the reply does not allay your father's fears, and in 1937 he gives his wife, your mother, Chrysoúla, power of attorney. As soon as she has recovered from childbirth (remember, your brother Nick is born in April 1937), she goes to Greece, arriving with you and her other three children in tow by end of August 1937. Just a few months later, in January of 1938 your mother files a request to the local court to determine whether or not her mother, Asymoúla, is to be considered a farmer (αγρότισσα) or a housewife (νοικοκυρά). The reason this designation was important is because of a law that had been passed in 1937 declaring that creditors could not collect by confiscating houses that belonged to farmers; the government feared a collapse of the indebted agricultural sector if a large number of farmers became homeless. And that's where the paper trail ends; I could find no document indicating that the court had ruled on your mother's request or if they had, what their determination had been.

All this could seem rather irrelevant to what happened to you personally, Dad, but to my mind it is central. For starters, it explains why your mother took you to Greece in 1937 better than any reason any currently living relative has given. Sure, it's believable and even probable that she missed her family, and sure, it's likely that you really were a troublemaker and that your father figured a visit like this could straighten you out. But this loan was the biggest investment your parents had made in their married lives to date, and given that they appear to have kept it an open issue between them of whether or not they would return to Greece to live more permanently, having a house there or collecting on the loan would have been key. Dad, what I want you to realize is that your behavior probably had very little to do with why you all ended up in Greece, and of course it had nothing to do with how you got **trapped** there. The complexity of the legal and financial issues involved makes it perfectly understandable to me why neither you nor anyone else alive today had this story and why you were given, rather, other reasons for your departure instead.

In addition to providing an explanation for why you went to Greece in the first place, these papers provide clues to the tensions you witnessed and to a large extent yourself experienced between your mother and her brother Giánnis and younger sister, Loukía. The strife with Loukía had long been rumored to be attributable to the fact that the house was being given to Loukía as a dowry. But I was shocked to hear Giánnis's oldest daughter, your cousin Chrysoúla, explain to me in 2006 that because your common grandfather Harálambos owed a lot of money (the loan taken out in 1928), the father basically made his son marry a seamstress with a lot of cash for a dowry, the woman who became Giánnis's wife, Ánna, from the town of Desphína. Chrysoúla's story was corroborated in a way by a strange source. Before Chrysoúla told me this story, Zoé, your oldest cousin on that side of the family, had related to me that Giánnis was a gorgeous young man (she had a photo of him to prove it) and that his wife, who was not considered attractive, was always jealous and kept close watch on him.

I was surprised that no one I talked to seems to know the exact years of the weddings of Giánnis or his sister Loukía. I'm calculating that Giánnis's must have occurred around the time your father took over his in-laws' loan, 1931, since their first daughter was born in 1933. And Loukía's betrothal may well have been, as I suggested above, in 1935, around the time your father inquires about the value of the house. Your mother's presence in Greece from 1937 on must have been a constant reminder to her younger siblings of outcomes to important events in their own lives that they did not fully control. If Giánnis, for example, kept this "injustice" done to him alive enough to pass it onto his daughter, and then she to me more than seventy years after the fact, it must have really stung, even if he did end up having a long and, as far as I have heard, happy marriage to Ánna. Maybe Giánnis figured he could finally get his revenge during the war when his father was expiring and his sister, your mother, got so ill she needed medication only he could afford to buy. His behavior had little to do with you and perhaps not even that much to do with his sister, your mother, who had become the scapegoat, in a sense for their father's decisions and poor financial management.

The enigmatic piece that remains is why there are no papers after the request to the court of 1938. Did the court tarry and in the meantime the war broke out, postponing indefinitely such civil matters? Did your mother figure out some other way to reconcile herself to the state of affairs? Did she decide she simply did not want to take her own mother to court? Did she negotiate a payment in kind for the loan? According to your cousin Chrysoúla, your maternal grandmother did quite a bit of housework in your mother's rental home and grumbled about it to her daughter-in-law, Ánna. Chémo Gerenté does not recall this to have been the case. I do not know the truth of this matter. Still, what I want most to communicate to you, Dad, is that deciphering these papers shifted my view of your parents and of their fates—and even of yours. To begin with, for individuals who had had very little formal schooling, they were quite smart with their financial affairs—or at least tried to be. The lawyer in Greece who helped me decipher the papers was impressed with your father's savvy when he read the two documents from 1935 related to evaluating whether the collateral covered the size of the loan and interest. Also, the paper record shows that there was a high degree of cooperation between the two spouses, your parents. While I don't think that cooperation stems all the rumors about the quality of their intimate life that have circulated over the years, it does provide a counterweight to them, as does my discovery that your father bought the house in Neptune even before your return, putting it only in your mother's name. Finally, the recoverable facts indicate that your parents were never compensated for a huge favor they did your mother's parents. A sense of injustice, indeed **betrayal**, like fear, I'd suggest, was bequeathed to you and to at least some of us as a result. I recognize that I, for one, am sensitive almost to a degree of paranoia about being **cheated** and about each individual receiving his or her fair share in just about any situation from the most trivial to the most consequential.

The next enigma concerns dead babies, a sad subject to consider, but one that it turns out permeates your family's history: your infamous theio Giánnis/uncle John had a twin sibling who died in childhood, and all of your aunts and uncles lost at least one child, sometimes more than one, during the course of those children's first or early years of life. Of course, infant and child mortality have been major dimensions of earlier time periods for essentially all societies; it's more the experience of my generation and later ones in the West for whom infant and child deaths have become the exception. Still, ubiquity doesn't erase the potential pain and indeed tragedy of losing progeny or siblings. Mythologies and folk tales of many eras and cultures are filled with such stories.

I've heard say that surviving twins grieve lost twin siblings their whole lives, even when the other twin had died in utero. If there is even a grain of truth in that, it seems important to me to know that Uncle John had a twin who died young. Perhaps, too, the loss of their infant son Harálambos compounded your theia Loukía's husband's rage at finding out his wife was pregnant by another man and contributed to his decision to take their remaining son Giánnis/John and abandon his wife, Loukía, and their daughter, Asymoúla. Obviously, I can't prove this loss was a factor in how their later lives played out, and yet I feel compelled to document here that they had a son who died in infancy. I had never heard this child mentioned by anyone before I spoke with the elderly Giorgía Polítou, née Dimitríou, Démos's older sister, in Chryssó in 2006. It was she who baptized the baby and told me he died as a nursling. Is it my own infertility that has led me to these lost children? Perhaps.

When I began to research your family, Dad, I had heard vague rumors that your mother had lost a child, a daughter born after you. I asked about her to whomever I could, and finding her traces registered deeply within me. Your sister informed me of her name, Asýmo or its diminutive, which seems more appropriate here, Asymoúla. You having been named after your paternal grandfather, it makes cultural sense that your parents gave their second child your maternal grandmother's name. I had already heard from other Kacandes relatives, Aunt Stella, I'm fairly certain, of the manner in which Asymoúla died: an overdose of medication. Your sister Pearl insisted it was the doctor's mistake, not your mother's or that of a questionably motivated Greek neighbor, as rumor had it. No one seemed to know when the baby was born, though. There's an obvious gap between the births of you and your brother Harry, December 1929 to November 1932, but what was Asymoúla's place in that gap? I became transfixed by a photo I found of your parents with you as an infant, transfixed by the resplendent joy on their faces—I have never seen another photo of them looking so youthful and beautiful—and by your mother's stomach. Oh my, she is pregnant, I realized, and you were still

43. The young Kacandes couple, George and Chrysoúla, with
their baby son John, New Jersey, early summer 1930.

an infant yourself. I finally found her, Dad. Not in the cemetery, as I had sometimes imagined myself searching and locating her headstone, but rather in the church files. Her baptismal record. Asymoúla was born on December 3, 1930, slightly less than one calendar year after you. Some people call siblings born so closely together "Irish twins." I hope it gave your mother some comfort that Asymoúla made it to her baptism in early February. I don't know how soon after that she died. Somehow, having documented her birth, I don't feel as strong a need anymore to know exactly when she left this world. Pearl says she lived to be three months old; that would put her death in early March.

When I told you about these discoveries, Dad, you didn't seem very interested. Granted, there's not much that captures your attention these days. Or maybe you felt something, but just could not express the emotion to me. I'm writing about Asymoúla's short life and death here anyway, because to my mind it explains part of the shadow cast on those young parents' joy and how they positioned themselves in relation to each other and to you. I had always assumed that you were treated royally as the first son of Greek immigrant parents. And the photographic record shows a certain truth to that: the quality and size of your wardrobe, the toys, the frequency with which you were photographed, all lavished on you despite your father's modest income.

In this scenario, you must have felt the separation from your father and the deprivation of the war even more deeply because of the affection and plenty that preceded it. However, there also exists the possibility of an additional or different scenario, one that explains better those claims you made in fleeting remarks to me that you were the "scapegoat"; that being sent to Greece was the threatened punishment for your misbehavior; the guilt that I believe deepened the sense of responsibility you felt for your family's predicament during the years in Greece. Seen through the lens of your parents losing a daughter, you were protected and cherished too, to be sure. Yet that adoration, I'm hypothesizing, had an ambivalent quality to it caused by your own joyful noise in being

44. Studio portrait of Chrysoúla, George, and their son John,
Newark, New Jersey, 1931. Marjorie Studios.

alive sounding a sullen echo in your mother's, perhaps both your parents' hearts. You, the animate child, were living in the shadow cast by
the perfect, because deceased, child. I am fascinated that you married
a woman who lived a very similar scenario. In Mom's case, though, she
was born soon after the death of her four-year-old sister to leukemia.
And in her own mother's view, my mother was never good enough, beautiful and smart though she was. My siblings and I are all witnesses to
the persistence of such an attitude, since that grandmother lived with
us for more than twenty years. My maternal grandmother's criticism
of my mother was incomprehensible to me until my Greek improved

45. John in his playpen with toys, Newark, New Jersey.

enough to ask her about her life, and I learned from her directly about that loss and the profound sorrow it still caused her as an old woman. Maybe my own special interest in the "afterlife" of these dead children is due not only to my mourning my never born children, but also to the fact that I was given that lost sister's name: Irene.

I hope you can forgive me for staying with the topic of the dead. I know you have long abhorred talking about death. I had heard rumored that your father had another brother, someone who was never talked about and with whom our family had obviously had no contact whatsoever. I think it started with that first visit I made to your father's village where the old ladies with blue eyes told me their mother had had brothers that went to the States with your father and uncle, and that they had fought and separated. At some subsequent point to my hearing this story in the village, you showed me the book you had found in your father's desk after his death, a book in Greek with advice for new immigrants to the United States. I was fascinated by its content and most especially by the scrawled cursive inscription in black ink on its cover: James Ef. Kakandes. And on the inside:

December = 12 = 18 = 1918 =
James Ef. Kakand
No. 437 = sumákin stree
stockton, cal

There are no "Jameses" in our family, I immediately remarked. It would take me years before I could trace the mystery of this inscription. Your sister, too, would eventually locate in her library a volume with similar content to the one you had discovered, this one focusing on writing proper business and personal letters in English, and also owned by James Kakandes. I recognized the signature immediately when she sent me the book, along with a note stating, "The enclosed was found in my books and I have no idea where it came from or when it was given to me." The book in Pearl's possession was dated one year later, and James's English had gotten a little better; the "sumákin street" was there decipherable as "San Joaquin," for instance. With the help of Gayle Maduros, someone I introduced myself to at the Greek church in Stockton, California; two local librarians there; and my cousin George and his Internet skills, I found James (Demétrios) Kakandes in 2006. And Steven (Efstáthios), too. Their story deserves its own book; it would be at least as colorful as the popular Greek account *The Synaxis of Andréas Kordopátis* by Valtinós (2007), which details a Greek's persistent attempts to emigrate to and work in America in the early twentieth century. Some aspects of such a narrative might take us away from, not toward your war, Dad. Still, some facts belong here.

James and Steven appear to have been older first cousins to your father

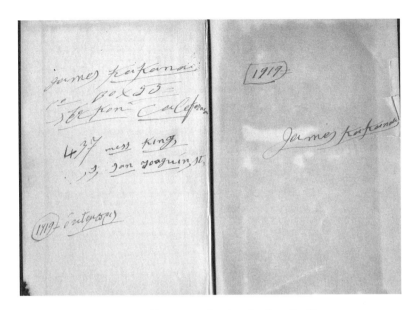

46. Inside of book owned by James Ef. Kakandes, inscribed by owner, 1919.

and uncle, and they preceded them to the United States (they in 1907, your uncle Tom in 1912, your father most likely an undocumented arrival in 1918). As did so many Greek immigrants of the period, they traveled widely seeking employment and trying to integrate themselves into American culture, as the books attest. Like your uncle and father, they started out in Orange, New Jersey, helped by Efstáthios Zévas, the same man, I'm fairly certain, who was your parents' koumbáros and your godfather. James and his younger brother traveled on to St. Louis, and there they may have fought. In any case, they appear to have separated by 1911, since only James is listed in the naturalization records of St. Louis for 1911. He then continued westward to California, where he had settled in Stockton by 1918; I'm not sure where Steve went in that period. James registered for the draft in 1918, as all men were required to do, but at age thirty-four did not serve in World War I; I've traced him in Stockton for 1918 and 1919, at which time he disappears from the record for a while, reappearing in the San Francisco directory in 1922. Steven appears to have been nine years younger than James and did serve in the U.S. Army from April 8, 1919, to April 7, 1920. I don't know where he was prior to military service nor where the army sent him, since the Great War was officially over. Steven and his older brother, as it turns out, both ended up institutionalized. It's not clear to me what caused James to be committed to the New Jersey Hospital for the Insane in Parsippany, as it was called at the time, better remembered today as Greystone Park. Your friend Steve Zévas—to my knowledge not from the same branch of the large Zévas clan as your godfather—says that his own father had served in the military with Steven Kakades, as that individual ended up spelling our family name in English. Steve Zévas reports too that Kakades's service caused him mental distress that required professional treatment. Steve's father, confusingly also named Steve, became his guardian. He lived until the end of his days, 1965, in the veterans hospital in Lyons, New Jersey, and lies buried in the veterans' cemetery in nearby Beverly. I hope to visit his grave one day soon. I do not know the year of James's death, but two of his books, as we know, end up in your father's and then your and your sister's possession. So, the enigmas multiply. However, so do the connections to your War, in my eyes. While the blue-eyed old ladies in Kolopetinítsa did not have the story quite right, some pieces of it can be confirmed by the information I have newly unearthed. The four Kacandes men of the generation before you did not arrive together, but they all ended up in the same state of New Jersey—indeed, within a fifty-mile range of each other by at the latest 1930, just after your birth. I can't determine that they had a single falling out. I'm thinking it may have been James and Steven who decided to part ways; maybe that explains, too, why Steven ended up spelling our last name differently. In any case, the four cousins kept their relatedness and the nature of their contact hidden from the rest of the family. Of course it is also possible that each thought the others dead, as the story about a Prohibition era shootout from the nieces in the village would indicate. James's books in your father's possession point at the very minimum to the hospital authorities' or your father's awareness that James and your father were relatives.

Here's where I make the connection to you, Dad, and obliquely to me and my siblings. On the most obvious level, secrets in the family are known to children, often having insidious affects because they are known only as secretive and not in their factuality. More directly, it seems to me that the story of James and Steven is the counterpart of the immigrant story of Tom and George, your uncle and father. All four come to this country and work hard. Tom and George end up making money, creating families, enjoying children and grandchildren. James and Steven, for reasons not fully known, end up abandoned and alone. In most Greek clans—such as in our own—first cousins are intimates, often almost indistinguishable from siblings. Did Tom and George reject or at least ignore their cousins because they didn't want the taint of their failed integration? Did James and Steven not contact your uncle and father because of their incapacity or their shame at lack of success? For sure, their fates make it clearer to me how precarious achieving "success" was for individual immigrants. The bogey of his cousins' lives might have reinforced your father's own determination to become "so, so Americanized," as your sister described him to me, and his aspirations for you, and even your aspirations for us. The words imprinted in my brain about my own childhood indicate a connection:

My father was worried we might have trouble in school, so when my eldest sister, Maria, reached school age, he told my mother to switch completely to speaking English to us.

So, here's something else you need to hear, Dad. You did succeed by many measures the world sets. Despite your inability to attend school regularly as a young teen, when you returned to the United States you learned English well enough to be accepted at Cornell University, where you earned two degrees. You acquired more advanced degrees by continuing to enroll in classes at other universities for an additional dozen years. You had a long and successful career as a teacher in an excellent public school system. Your children all learned English properly. You provided for your six children into adulthood. All six graduated from college. They hold among them more than a dozen undergraduate and advanced degrees. All have become productive citizens. Why could you never take that in? Was the fear of immigrant failure too strongly imprinted from your birth? Was it impossible to embrace your own dual cultural identity after the war? After all, America was a much more xenophobic place as you grew up than in my own lifetime.

Let's recognize it explicitly here: during the war, your mixed identity almost cost you your life. Here's how I would renarrate parts of your story through the lens of what I now want to call the family identity crisis around assimilation and biculturality. Having learned about James and Steven, I am no longer as surprised as I was when you first insisted to me that as a young child you thought of yourself as American, not Greek. When you went to Greece you insisted everyone call you Τζον (John), not Giánnis. Even your mother transliterated your name this way in her commentaries on the backs of photos she sent from Greece to your father in the United States. For you, being an "American" had some positive sides. I repeat here Evgenía Argyríou's comment that the girls in Itéa admired your strut and associated it with your American origins. My cousin Katrina Kacandes related to me that one of the few memories of Greece her father, your youngest brother, Nick, ever shared with her was how he liked the locals calling him "American." In your own memory, Dad, being from America had many liabilities, too. In the story that I am least able to document, about your possible arrest and misidentification as a Jew, being from America was decisive. Most obviously, you would not have been circumcised if you had not been born in the United States. Beyond that, your status as American citizens itself also affected your attitudes and fates. I have already mentioned earlier my hypothesis that your profound sense of being **trapped** may be attributable to your knowledge that as an American you should have been able to get out of Greece before the "European war" started. Once America enters the war, there's a different risk. "Should Yiayia tell or shouldn't she?" is the way I remember my brother Pete recounted it to me once. He related our grandmother's dilemma to her knowledge that the United States had entered the war against Germany. Pete's "memory" is ultimately traceable to you and your attitudes, of course. In another version, you were **betrayed** by fellow villagers as "Americans." In other words, you were "passing" as Greeks, but you were "really," or rather were "held to be," Americans. And that threatened your lives. Contradictions remain, to be sure, for in other versions it was precisely the opposite: it was your American passport that **saved** you from deportation.

What I was even less familiar with until we finally talked directly is how you perceived your American citizenship and your ability (or not) to speak English playing out in the end stages of the war. I can't read through the effects of audience and time well enough to decode when and how things began to change in your story about what happened. The Newspaper Article of 1945 states that you had learned Italian and forgotten your English while working in the "Italian Fascists' kitchen." I'm not sure whether that phrase derives from the journalist or you at the time. As far as I can deduce, it refers to the canteen kitchen in the Fourth Police Precinct, where there may have been some Italians until fall 1943 but probably not after that, and, again, though you may well have been there frequently earlier, my reconstruction of events has you also there at liberation in September–October 1944, just before or as you encounter the British. A few paragraphs later, the article—which is very pro-American and fairly anti-British in its slant—reports indirectly that you were perceived by the British as a Greek, not an American. As part of the 50th Royal Tank Regiment "he was poorly fed and poorly paid" because "the British observed a distinction between themselves and the Greeks, throwing away quantities of food rather than feed it to the Greeks, to whom they rationed soup." My cousin George Kacandes has an expression of this sentiment from you also; according to George, the fact that the Germans gave leftover rations to the Greeks, whereas the British threw them on the streets, explains why we John Kacandes kids were allowed to learn German. That's an enigmatic line of reasoning that can perhaps only make sense in a context of war.

When I asked you about your attitudes toward the British when you and I first spoke directly about the war, you expressed a strong Anglophilia, telling me, for example, that "they were good guys because they were the only guys that you would talk to" (chapter 2, section 9a). The very next thing you said to me concerns the Allied agreement to assign Greece to a British sphere of influence in postwar Europe. I pointed out to you during the interview that you could not have known about that political decision at the time. Did you "smell" which way the wind was blowing? After all, your intuitions had probably saved your life several times already. It is certainly a skill you continued to cultivate and draw on throughout your adult life.

This issue of supporting the British came up in a very quick exchange during our conversation of July 7, 2005, something that did not register with me at the time but resonated when I studied the interview much later and particularly in light of my new knowledge about James and Steven. You told me, "No one would pay attention to me with an American passport." I believe I heard you say that sentence more than one time; in any case, I found it repeatedly in my notes. Did you literally run around with your American passport in hand, trying to find the person who would put you on the next boat back to America as a result? Your hometown friends Elias Skarímbas and Steve Zévas, both of whom had grown up in Greece but who, like you, also had American passports—in their cases due to their fathers' naturalization in the United States—spoke of you and themselves as a little pack, waiting to get out of the country. My image fits with a feeling Tina had while watching you tell your war stories to the hospital chaplain in January 2005: "I was so struck by his desire to be somebody; that desire to be this unknown prince. It was as if he were saying, 'I was born into the wrong family. I actually belong in that castle'" (July 2006).

What fascinates me even more than the excusable self-pity and desperation that your comment that "no one would pay attention to me with an American passport" implies is how, during that interview, anyway, you connected your individual fate with a major decision of the Allies:

IRENE: Do you remember anything about what those guys were like? Were they very British? Or in your perception—

JOHN: Well, it was a British regiment. Fiftieth Royal Tank Regiment— are you kidding? They were the ones that fought up the Italian peninsula and liberated and came into Greece first 'cause that was the agreement Roosevelt had made. He had seceded [sic] Greece to the British.

IRENE: Yeah, I need to find out more about that. I mean I knew that was the case generally, but you think that was one of the things that happened at Yalta or maybe Potsdam?

JOHN: Oh yeah, because, uhh, no one would pay attention to me with an American passport . . .

IRENE: Uh huh . . .

JOHN: . . . but uh, being in the British Army was different. [Your voice is quiet by the time you end this sentence and neither you nor I pursue the topic.]

So you connected in 2005, if not in 1944 or at some point shortly after the events, something you experienced individually with the largest type of decisions made about the World War and its outcomes. . . . You've got your history a bit wrong, as usual—as do I at the time. There was, however, a negotiation started in May 1944 between Churchill and Stalin referred to as the "percentages agreement," which sets British preponderance in Greece and Soviet influence in Romania at 90 percent; the agreement reaffirmed and extended terms from Greece and Romania to Yugoslavia, Bulgaria, Hungary in October 1944. I'm so sorry I did not pick up on the importance of what you were saying here; I would have wanted to ask you more about your perception that major, secret negotiations were felt at the most local level, influencing if not determining individual fates. That is to say, I wish I had asked you to name a concrete instance of you declaring your American citizenship and being ignored. At the very least, I wish I had asked more about what it felt like to you to be part of the British Army; I've been told by experts that the British did not let locals join in this "informal" way, and yet, you do have a uniform that proves your participation.

Dad, this language and identity issue is important in a number of contexts, including in the political realm. Most of your contemporaries were fighting with ELAS, not with Psarrós or later with the British. As far as I can tell, you communicated well enough in English to save your life in December 1944, and later to make friends, some good friends among the British. In my mind I make a connection to your mother befriending her Jewish neighbors in Newark before the war, despite her limited English language skills. In any case, presumably you communicated better and better the longer you worked with the British. Then there's the elevator story (chapter 2, section 9c). It seems completely possible to me that you just didn't know the word "ambassador" and that's how that delicious miscommunication took place. But when you tell the story, you use it to show that your English was bad. I wonder to myself if you didn't need that excuse to get yourself off the hook at the time, and it stuck, indeed became magnified over the years. Knowing English and being American when it suited you and not when it didn't was a survival strategy. I recognize that, and I salute you for it. I'm certainly glad you figured out how to use your identity to your advantage, Dad. What I need to add, though, is that you continued to emphasize your Greekness or your Americanness to suit your own purposes as a father in ways that were not always beneficial to your children.

Did you realize that you "pulled out" the Greekness and the war mainly when you wanted to reprimand or punish us? I cited in a previous section my own memories of your admonishments to clean my plate because people had starved in the war and Maria's memories of being harangued about the value of greens you can locate yourself in the wild. A phrase that has stayed in my memory is: "We are not like the neighbors; we do things differently, we're Greek." That might have been deployed when you wanted to instill pride in us, but it was not. It was always sounded when you wanted us to do work around the house or in the garden, or we made a request to do something and you refused us, our Greekness being the only reason proffered for the refusal. I remember when you told us Mom was expecting another child. This could have been a happy announcement, but you barked at us, "Mom is expecting another baby. You all need to do more around here from now on. That's how a Greek family does it." I remember exactly where I was standing in the kitchen. The four of us were doing the dishes in the manner we had devised: the first child on a stool washing at the sink, the next two drying and passing to the last child, also on a stool, placing the dishes in the cabinet. Similarly, when our mother found out her father had died, a sad occasion indeed, you yelled at us, "There will be no parties or going out. We are Greek." I remember my mother crying, and I was sad for her, but I had never met my maternal grandfather and this was my first experience with a death in the family. You know, Dad, with the passage of so many years, these situations almost seem like comical cultural caricatures. We could debate whether or not physical discipline should be considered a culturally acceptable norm for the period. But when you inflicted corporal punishment on my siblings, it was nothing to laugh about. Certainly not for them and certainly not for me, the fearful and guilty witness to your beatings. Why was I spared the beatings themselves? Because I looked so much like my mother? This, too, puzzles me. But we each were supposed to endure our roles because we were Greek and, as we were told, you loved us.

To come back, then, one last time to the idea of enigma: The biggest riddle for me has been that of your personality: how you could be so lively and cheerful with others and so withdrawn and despondent at home; obsequious to external authority and tyrannical to your students and family; extravagantly generous with your hard earned material resources to loved ones and strangers, and withholding of your affection and praise from your children; my tormentor and a few critical times, my savior. While I was doing this research, Tina once asked me, so of all the things that happened to him, what do you think traumatized him the most? what made him the way we knew him? I balked; I felt like I had and did not have an answer. I don't, in the final analysis, believe there was a single trauma that made you the way you are. People are much more complicated than that. War is much more multifaceted. Our histories begin before our births, as I've tried to show in previous pages.

What facets of your personality do I now connect more directly to your War than to your genes or to your other life experiences? Well, Dad, you worked harder in your adult life than anyone else I have ever met: teaching day school, coaching, teaching night school, waiting on tables on the weekend. You barely stopped to sleep. This work ethic was forged in the war, I sense: just keep moving, trying, striving. Sell fish, sell cigarettes. Work on the boats. Guard the German property. Wash the dishes in the police precinct. Peel the potatoes in the English mess tent. Somehow it will come out okay; if you just keep moving nobody can catch you.

You bear the marks, physical and emotional, of someone who was victimized. I don't know if it was an actual Nazi or some other brute, but someone hurt you physically on purpose. Maybe more than once. Maybe more than one person. You learned to do the same. The worst beating you ever administered, Dad, to my sister Tina, for failing to go on stage at the correct moment in a baton twirling show when she was seven years old points back to your war, in my estimation. Seven, the age you were when you left for Greece, the age you used for yourself in so many of your stories—for example, to my brother Tom, for you dodging the Nazis in the hills. It was dangerous not to move at the right time. As luck had it, you usually did. Diving off the burning ship. Racing out

47. The three oldest Kacandes girls swimming at Lakenridge Swimming Club, White Plains, New York, summer 1961.

the back of the dormitory. But children don't always get it right, as Tina once didn't, and you as well when they caught you and Uncle Harry in the olive grove.

In playing out past scenes of you ridiculing me, I can now hear not just you, Dad, but also the person who was ridiculing you, a child, trying to do any one of a man's tasks during the war and struggling. Someone watched and laughed instead of helping. In my own experience of teaching, ridicule does more harm than good. It surprises me that I still like to swim. I didn't mind being thrown in the water as a toddler, but your taunts to close my fingers because I looked like an octopus felt like whiplashes. It was something in your tone of voice. Now I know that you were desperate for me to learn a skill that had saved your own life.

I trace your difficulty with accepting responsibility for your actions and decisions to the War, too. I now can see you with your American passport in your hand trying to persuade someone, anyone, that you didn't belong in this war zone. And you were right. No one belongs in a war zone. Most especially not children, for they do not make the decisions that lead to the conflicts nor to their presence in wars' midst. I was proud of you, Dad, for that one brief moment in the hospital after your heart surgery when you admitted to getting yourself into the bad state that put you there, and you shared with my brothers your hope that they would take care of themselves so that the same fate did not await them.

For years I have thought and even written about the closing scene of Albert Camus's *La Chute / The Fall*. I don't know if you had to read this when you studied French or world literature, Dad. The protagonist, Jean-Baptiste Clamence—you were named after John the Baptist, too—is dying in bed, and he speaks to the same interlocutor he's been addressing throughout the book. He asks this confrere to narrate his own story and to "utter the words that for years have never ceased echoing through my nights and that I shall at last say through your mouth" (Camus 1991, 147). Words that would change the past, reverse a bad decision, save a drowning woman's life. Clamence, however, quickly changes his will to reverse the past, succumbing to the position that "it's too late now. It will always be too late. Fortunately!" I think I interpret this scene a little differently than some readers. For me the point is not that the dying man cannot actually change the past or that he cynically changes his mind from wanting to. In my view, the personal moral triumph is that he has finally succeeded in articulating—even if only for one brief moment—that he wishes it had been different. That he had acted differently. Dad, one tragedy of our relationship is that I do not know exactly what you would wish to say through my mouth right now if you could.

I do know what I want to say through my own mouth—or hand—and I've been trying to say it over and over. Let me try once more.

I am sorry for what happened to you, for the pain, the fear, the hunger, the loneliness, the humiliation. I wish it had been different for you; I wish you had had a glorious, carefree, nurturing childhood surrounded by people who cherished you and whom you adored. I know, too, what I wish for you to say to me: that you are sorry you could not keep your War out of our lives. And I would say, I know that now, Dad. Thanks for wishing it had been otherwise.

I love you,

Irene

[Epilogue]

Surviving Daddy's War

H ere I sit. It has been about three years from the moment I finally asked my siblings what they knew about our father's war experiences and how they thought they had learned what they knew, until this moment: post-research, post-interviewing, and on the verge of finishing a final draft of this book. And I am different. I can chuckle at the memory of the self-righteous demand I felt at the outset of this project, that I had a right to know what had happened to my father, expressed in my working title at that point: "I Need to Know Your Story." It was as if a child is sure the parent has a piece of candy in his or her fist and is withholding it even though the child has behaved and has asked for it properly. I laugh because I understood so poorly then how inapt the metaphor. There was no story like the one I sought: a single, coherent narrative that could be held accountable to a documented public historical record. I have found terra firma neither in my pursuit of family nor of Greek history, the narrative in the previous section not withstanding. Yet I have received much more than a piece of candy.

For one thing, I learned about myself. The interview transcripts became unexpected mirrors where I saw myself reflected, not always as attractively as imagined. To be sure, I expressed interest, support, excitement.

But I also interrupted, corrected, and worst of all, sometimes failed to listen. I'm reminded of a trenchant passage in Sebald's magisterial *Austerlitz*, where the protagonist recounts something his high school history teacher had once told him: "Our concern with history is a concern with preformed images already imprinted on our brains, images at which we keep staring while the truth lies elsewhere, away from it all, somewhere as yet undiscovered" (Sebald 2001, 72). Sometimes I was so preoccupied with the images already imprinted on my brain that I didn't hear the cues to precisely that history I wanted so much to learn: for instance, my father's passing comment that he returned to Athens "because of the fear of being recaptured." Where was that first arrest? When? Why? I feel certain and sad that I will never know. And that's partly my fault. Because for the brief moment when my father's brain had access to that memory, I was "staring" elsewhere and didn't ask. Perhaps due to the nature of traumatic memories, perhaps due to his increasing dementia, to my knowledge he has never had willed access to that past event since.

Being confronted with my inability to reconstruct the personal pasts of my parents, aunts and uncles, and grandparents and other ancestors produced a certain humility I'm thankful for acquiring. It, along with the privilege of in fact being able to learn some things, countered the rage I had felt so strongly for so long about emotional baggage my father had saddled his children with. I can remember that I hated him in the hospital that day in January 2005, but I do not feel hatred anymore. Similarly, by learning more about what my father went through, I feel like I have become more able to simply accept him the way he is rather than to judge him. For example, my fuller understanding of the physical cost of the war on him, the bodily suffering he experienced himself and watched others submit to has helped me extend my comprehension of his eating disorder to his intolerance of any pain. I remember my whole childhood thinking that he was a sissy for making such a fuss when my mother would comb his hair or cut his toenails. I had taken a certain perhaps misguided pride in being able to tolerate pain myself, partly in reaction to his behavior. Now the diabetes has created havoc with his nerve endings. While I recognize that his own actions played a huge role in his developing this terrible disease, it makes me sad that he is back in a situation like the war of never knowing when or from where the next "blow" will come. Furthermore, learning how complicated and ever-shifting the power politics were in Greece during the period of the war and occupation has helped me gain some tolerance for my father's lying and his paranoid and catastrophic thinking. It can still be hard to stay calm when he cries out, "Be careful, someone is going to go through the red light" when I pull out of my parents' street, but I am determined to try to be more patient. I'm reminded of a powerful statement by Anthony Eden toward the end of the epic documentary *The Sorrow and the Pity.* Marcel Ophuls, the interviewer, asks the Englishman's view of how Pétain and the French behaved during the Second World War, and specifically about decisions made after the war to punish collaborators. Eden in turn responds, "Our people did not go through the horror of an occupation by a foreign power, you have no right to pronounce upon what a country does which has been through all that" (Ophuls 1975, 168). Well, I have never lived in a war zone, unless you count the time my sister Georgia, my mother, and I spent in Greece during the brief coup on Cyprus in July 1974. For a few hours, the colonels did try to mobilize the country for war. That was scary enough for me to not have any illusions about individual decision making in such an environment or the real costs of war.

There's a poem by my favorite Greek poet, Constantine P. Cavafy, called "Ithaka" that comes to mind now. Though it is not his best, it carries a message that applies to me and this project. The poem's persona admonishes the addressee not to expect too much from Ithaka herself, but to enjoy the trip there. To quote the last stanzas:

Keep Ithaka always in your mind.
Arriving there is what you are destined for.

But do not hurry the journey at all.
Better if it lasts for years,
so you are old by the time you reach the island,
wealthy with all you've gained on the way,
not expecting Ithaka to make you rich.

Ithaka gave you the marvelous journey.
Without her you would not have set out.
She has nothing left to give you now.

And if you find her poor, Ithaka won't have fooled you.
Wise as you will have become, so full of experience,
You will have understood by then what these Ithakas mean.

   (Cavafy 1992, 36–37)

In many ways, I found "my Ithaka" of family history and family stories quite barren. But along the way, like Odysseus, and like gleaners everywhere, I found many hidden treasures. Beyond the diminution of negative feelings about my father, I developed relationships to and loving feelings about several of his relatives whom I had previously not known.

I contrasted earlier my comfort with going to the island of my mother's birth with my apprehension about traveling to my father's region (chapter 4). In a section of my travel journal I have not yet quoted, I recorded for myself that walking around the town of Itéa is "like being locked out of a room where a party is going on. I can't even find the lock on the door, much less open it with the key I don't have" (August 17, 2005). Just one week later, after having met my father's first cousins Chrysoúla and Ólga, two daughters of his problematic Uncle Giánnis/John, my journal entry reads,

> I left Greece feeling not triumphant exactly, but very, very grateful. Somehow I felt like some great reconciliation had happened. Ólga and Chrysoúla's tears and mine at the end. I couldn't help trying to keep my eyes on Chrysoúla as long as possible when my

48. Kóstas Gialelís and Ólga Gialelí, née Tsínga, on either
side of Irene, in their home in Itéa, December 2006.

subway car was pulling away from the platform she was standing on. The feeling of "reconciliation" can only? mostly? have
been on my side in the sense that I don't think they were really
told about what Uncle John did to my father and his family. They
kept repeating stories of how their father loved my family (giving my grandmother's name to his first daughter, for instance,
or giving my family the money for the tickets to leave in 1945).
But I, knowing what hatred my dad felt all those years, was re-
evaluating his effort to stay in touch with Ólga, for example,
when my mom and dad were in Dimitrópoulo (when they tried
living in Greece in the mid-1990s). I kept thinking to myself:

49. John's first cousin Panagoúla Zéva, née Tsakíri,
with Irene, in Itéa, December 2006.

we are a different generation. We get to make different choices.
It is not those children who kept food or medicines from my
family. I don't know if my own desire to forgive and put it behind us would have been as strong if I had not had the physical
proof in their bodies of the kinship. I felt so happy to just look
at them for the joy of "seeing again" my grandmother, whom
they resembled. (August 24, 2005)

So, for me, work on this project restored one "concomitant loss" of
the war, the rupture of our larger family. I had not anticipated one bit my
father's cousins' strong physical resemblance to my beloved paternal

50. Chrysoúla Kapsiáni, née Tsínga, with husband Giórgios Kapsiánis on the balcony of their home in Athens the day Irene first met them in August 2005.

grandmother, who died in 1983. Indeed, helped along by the fact that Ólga and Chrysoúla are now themselves in the age range my grandmother was when I spent a lot of time with her, the family resemblance was so strong that I truly did feel as if the impossible gift of seeing my Yiayia again had been bestowed on me. It was like some barely earned reward for having made the effort to find Ólga and Chrysoúla.

This sense of triumph was to be challenged when I met with Ólga and Chrysoúla again the following year, for in 2006 we had more time to spend with one another, and I knew a lot more family history. Still, as difficult as the second visit seemed, it taught me another valuable lesson about family stories. This time, both sisters, but especially the older, told me a whole series of negative things about my grandmother, some of which I knew could not have been true and some of which I simply couldn't know the truth of. For example, Chrysoúla told me that when my grandmother left Itéa in 1945, she didn't even say good-bye to her

51. The funeral procession of Panagioú Kakandé in Itéa, May 10, 1947.

mother-in-law, and that Panagioú took it very badly, and all the other villagers looked on it as a mean-spirited gesture. It is impossible to be sure whether my grandmother had or had not failed to take leave of her mother-in-law; I have little basis for evaluating their relationship myself, and there exists no neutral witness to consult. When my aunt Pearl heard this tale, she immediately protested and said that she remembered distinctly the whole family going to say good-bye to their only surviving grandmother and being told by her mother to kiss her hand and ask for her forgiveness and blessing.

When I discovered photos of Panagioú's funeral in my father's collection, I realized that at least some people in Greece assumed his family would want to know about the event and made the effort to send inscribed photos to them. Even this of course could not prove whether or not the two women parted angry at one another.

In contrast, when Chrysoúla told me that my grandmother always had enough to eat during the war because she knew foreign languages and had worked as a translator for the Germans, who gave her lots of food, I knew that that contention was absurd. I had spent the first twenty-five years of my life seeing my grandmother regularly, and having occasionally interpreted for her, I knew she couldn't even speak English adequately after living in the States for decades, much less speak German. When first listening to these pieces of what I took in at the time as slander, I got very, very upset. Then it dawned on me: Chrysoúla, born only in 1933, couldn't really know the truth of these things. She did seem to believe them, though, and that, I realized, must be because she had heard them so many times from others, presumably from her father. So, I reasoned further, Chrysoúla, too, has a Daddy's War, even if she doesn't look at it that way. After all, I had spent the last years discovering that many of the things I had heard all my life were either not historically verifiable or simply not true. Through this experience of being forced to listen to Chrysoúla's versions of her father's stories about my grandmother, I resolved to try even harder to embrace all my family, and to judge them on the basis of our interaction, not on the roles our ancestors had cast us in. I became even more respectful of those Greeks, family and not, who had refused to pronounce judgment or even give information about issues I had raised with which they did not have personal experience.

This thought led to another realization: that of the serious responsibility I had in publishing this book. Writing changes memories. I had already experienced during the process of researching and writing this book how my sharing what I was learning would instantly transform the stories of my nuclear family. When Maria learned that I was seeking information about the possibility of concentration camps or transit camps in Macedonia, for instance, her story of my father's imprisonment in Mesopotamia changed to detention in Macedonia. She didn't register the switch, but I did, immediately. My published versions of others' stories will carry a huge weight for future versions of family history, merely by virtue of being in print.

Another less emotionally laden, but still surprising realization for me was that in the process of conducting my research I was also teaching. As I learned things myself—for example, about the course of the war and occupation in Greece—I would share them with others. I have already discussed in chapters 1 and 4 my dilemmas about overly easy comparisons between traumatic experiences, particularly between persecution in general, war, and genocide. However, in the course of explaining my project, I often found myself imparting years' worth of my own learning about antisemitism and the course of the Nazi Judeocide. I experienced this opportunity too as a felicitous accident.

Other benefits were anticipated, but nonetheless welcome as a result. Members of my own nuclear family and the aunts, uncles, and cousins I grew up with in the United States are now so spread apart geographically that, while there were no major emotional ruptures between me and them, I simply don't get to see my siblings very often, much less my other relatives. So, the decision to interview many family members led to numerous reunions that brought me, and I believe them, much joy. I quoted above the metaphor of the key to get into the room where the party was on, but here I'm thinking that that family contact as adults during my research contributed to my sense of being able to lock the door on the haunted household of our childhood while simultaneously opening a door to more mature and pleasurable new adult interactions. This project certainly created countless hours of conversation with my father at a stage in his life when little interests him.

I cannot necessarily pass on to others the benefit to me of those relationships and experiences that helped me exit from my bondage to Daddy's War, but I note here that the steps I took are widely accessible, even if the particular analytical tools I used in chapters 3 and 4 were available to me mainly through my specific education. I began by trying to name the ghosts for myself. Then I tried to capture the stories behind the ghosts by interviewing people involved in the original events and those who also experienced the ghosts. Identifying holes, gaps, and silences in the stories led me to consider which persons might have been ignored or mainly absent from the stories. Educating myself about the relevant geographical, cultural, political, and historical contexts was critical, as was mining those few family documents that have survived. Passports, address books, newspaper articles, photo albums, and baptismal certificates were particularly helpful to me. As were "marked" books: I have mentioned the information James Kakandes inked onto two of his books that made their way into our family. I also mined my father's marginalia in books he owned on the Holocaust and the war and occupation in Greece. Other families might have surviving correspondence, naturalization or death certificates, tombstones, family bibles or other devotional texts to consult.

I think the most critical step for me concerned abandoning my attempt to reconstruct the historical record and trying to deduce instead how certain stories came into being or why they continued to be told. This attitude eased my frustration at the same time that my attenuated affect allowed me to "hear" better and to actually learn some history in the process. In terms of my own sense of managing to leave our enchanted household behind, I think the decision to try to stand next to my father instead of to stand in judgment of him was key. At least as important was the decision to use the knowledge I had acquired to make certain decisions about my own behavior and what position I wanted to take to the family history that had now come down to me and to the family members who are still alive. Recognizing the "friendly" ghosts the War had brought into our home also aided me, for **generosity** to strangers, **commitment** to family, and **resilience, persistence**, and **adaptability** also resided at our house, and I believe I and my siblings managed to take them with us when we moved out.

As for writing up my experiences, I realized what I had become the most qualified to do was to pass on the stories. Other people, relatives and not, other generations will do different things with these narrative fragments from what I have done in creating this "paramemoir." Still, since stories and storytelling dominate my professional and personal worlds, I will close with another story. Here is one told by my theia Chémo Glynos, née Gerenté, whose mother, Efstathía Varkoúta, was a first cousin of my paternal grandmother's father, Harálambos Tsíngas (see chapter 2, section 1c). Of course, I could not have explained that relationship until recently, since one of the stupid consequences of never asking certain questions as a child was that I never quite knew who Chémo was to us, even though we have seen her and her family fairly regularly our whole lives. The following story, though, isn't directly about my family. In some ways, it's about all families in war, which is why I want to end this journey here. Chémo had been speaking in response to my query about whether the Germans or the Italians were the harsher occupiers. I was still trying to account for my father's hatred of the Italians. Chémo told me neither group caused her any suffering. The Italians were like us Greeks, she felt, and the Germans didn't bother us. She then shared several anecdotes, one about a German developing a crush on a friend's sister. Another about the Italians teasing her mother that she and her sister weren't allowed to go to the beach like the other girls in Itéa. Then, as if to make sure I understood that the teasing was no more than that, she looked at me and recounted the following incident that must have occurred shortly after the Italian capitulation in fall 1943:

CHÉMO: Αλλά ήταν καλοί μαζί μας. Θυμάμαι που ερχότανε στο σπίτι και η μαμά τους έδινε καφέ. Τους έδινε ότι θέλανε και τη φωνάζανε Mama. Ήταν special ένα παιδί που το λέγανε Ορλάντο. Είναι μερικά περιστατικά που δε τα ξεχνάς. So, ερχεται όταν έπρεπε να φύγει, όταν φύγανε οι Ιταλοί. Όταν φύγανε οι Ιταλοί έπρεπε να περάσουν από τον ισθμό της Κορίνθου για να φύγουν. So, ήρθε στο σπίτι. Μας αποχαιρέτισε όλους. Μας φύλησε όλους. Και έφυγε. Και το καράβι το βουλιάξανε οι Αγγλέζοι στον ισθμό της Κορίνθου. Και σκοτόθηκε. Μαζί με όλους τους άλλους. Γιατί μπορεί να ήτανε κατοκτηταί, αλλά ήταν κι'αυτοί άνθρωποι. Τα παιδιά δεν φταίνε ποτέ.

But, they were good to us. I remember they would come to our house, and my mother would make them coffee. She gave them whatever they wanted, and they called her "mama." One boy was special, his name was Orlando. There are some events you just never forget. So, he comes when they're supposed to leave, when the Italians left. When the Italians left, they had to pass through the isthmus of Corinth in order to leave. So, he came to our house. He said good-bye to everyone. He kissed everyone. And he left. And the ship, the British sank the ship near the Corinthian isthmus. And he was killed. With all the others. Maybe they were occupiers, but they too were people. It's never the kids' fault.

[Acknowledgments]

There would have been no book without those members and friends of my family who agreed to share their memories with me, above all, those who survived the war and lived to tell about it. My profound gratitude to my father, John G. Kacandes, my mother, Lucie N. Kacandes, my aunt Pearl Veronis, my aunt Stella Kacandes, and my adopted godmother Chémo Glynos. I consulted with my mother about almost every stage of my work, and she constantly aided me with translations. This project was also inconceivable without the profound insights and encouragement of my siblings, Maria, Tina, Georgia, Tom, and Pete, not just in the last years, but over our lifetimes. Several cousins told me stories or helped me solicit them; I thank especially George, Dina, Nick, and Katrina Kacandes, and Luke Veronis.

There are many relatives and friends of the family who helped me figure out what might have actually transpired in Occupied Greece. My thanks to Zoé Paphíli and Amalía Tsakíri, who have passed on since speaking with me, to Ólga and Kóstas Gialelís, Chrysoúla and Giórgios Kapsiális, Thýmios and Alexándra Tsakíris, Voúla and Loukás Gerentés, Elías and Carol Skarímbas, Pantelís and Váso Manoúsos, Steven Zévas, George Hatgen, Bóbis Talaroúgas, and Evgenía Argyríou. My gratitude goes also to several then-strangers who agreed to speak to me about wartime events in Roúmeli: Giánnis Engonómou, Démos Dimitríou and his sister Georgía, Pagonítsa Skoúra, and Chrístos Kontogiórgios and his family. Tákis Papangelópoulos receives my deep thanks for his generosity in time and spirit in helping me decipher the documents related to the Tsíngas family home in Chryssó, as does Demétris Diamantópoulos for showing interest and connecting me with so many individuals who knew about the region of my ancestors. Fellow schoolteachers of my father, Arthur Howard and Ted Simon, confirmed information about my father's storytelling.

These family stories would never have made much sense if I had not been pointed to the right sources and facts by several experts on Greek and European history. I cannot thank enough John Iatrides, Gerhard Weinberg, Mark Mazower, Dagmar Herzog, Manuel Borutta, and Zanét Battínou and Aléxis Menexiádes of the Jewish Museum of Greece. For some key information on American popular culture, I thank Michael Brodski. Helen Gerzon Goransson generously shared her own family stories.

I can never properly acknowledge the critical aid of all the trained librarians and archivists who have played a role in producing this book, for alas, so many remain anonymous. Through those whose names are known to me, I offer thanks to all: Christine Sundby of the National Archives of Sweden and Håkan P. Tell, who helped me understand the reports; Daniel Palmieri and Nicholas Pachu, who searched for my father in the archives of the International Committee of the Red Cross; Gayle Maduros and other members of Saint Basil's Greek Orthodox Church in Stockton, California, the research librarians at the Stockton Public Library, and my cousin Linda Psomas, who enthusiastically helped me navigate my way to the Stockton church and library; Reverend K. Makrinos of Saint Nicholas, and Constantine and Helen Church, Roseland, all formerly Newark, New Jersey, who helped me find proof of my father's baby sister's short life; and Lois Stogel of Congregation Kol Ami (formerly Jewish Community Center) of White Plains, New York, who searched for signs of my father's talks there.

As there would have been no book without my informants, there would have been no publishable book without the aid of some energetic research assistants. Thank you Yevgenya Strakovsky, Despoina Sideri, and Katerina Stojcevska; additional assistance at critical stages came from Jason Spellmire and Pam Ploeger. The visual dimension of these stories exists due to the expertise of members of the Humanities Computing staff of Dartmouth College: Susan Bibeau, Otmar Foelsche, Tom Garbelotti, and Jason Nash. My gratitude to Dean Carol Folt, Associate Deans Lenore Grenoble and Kate Conley, and Dartmouth College for making research funds and writing time available.

I have been fortunate enough to have many readers of earlier drafts of this project. I thank first of all those who participated in a seminar sponsored by the Dickey Center for International Understanding at Dartmouth College: Susan Brison, Ada Cohen, Mona Domosh, Atina Grossmann, Susannah Heschel, Marianne Hirsch, Amy Lawrence, Annelise Orleck, Ivy Schweitzer, Leo Spitzer, Allan Stam, and Chris Wohlforth; my gratitude also to organizers and members of the Feminist Inquiry Seminar at Dartmouth College, and to members of Holy Resurrection Orthodox Church in Claremont, New Hampshire, who heard the very first snippet of this book and have sustained me throughout. Margaret Powell and Ladette Randolph encouraged me to just start writing! Special thanks go to voluntary and expert readers and interlocutors Bettina Gerischer, Nancy K. Miller, Jeffrey M. Peck, Karen Remmler, Galina Rylkova, Susan R. Suleiman, and Peter Trachtenberg, who offered excellent concrete suggestions. The first person to read the entire manuscript was Philippe Carrard, whose sense that this actually was a book made all the difference to me.

Despite the extraordinarily enthusiastic and expert advice I was fortunate enough to receive, flaws remain, and I am solely responsible for those, as I am responsible for forgetting to thank some people. Memory would not have it any other way.

Portions of chapters 1 and 4 have been paraphrased from Leon S. Holocaust Testimony (T-45) and Eleftherios S. Holocaust Testimony (T-1429). Fortunoff Video Archive for Holocaust Testimonies, Yale University Library.

Stanzas of "Ithaka" are from C. P. Cavafy, *Collected Poems*, translated by Edmund Keeley and Philip Sherrard, edited by George Savidis. Translation © 1975, 1992 by Edmund Keeley and Philip Sherrard. Reprinted by permission of Princeton University Press.

"'Never Leave the United States'" originally appeared in *Asbury Park Sunday Press*, October 28, 1945.

[Appendix A]

A Note on Greek Names and Naming

It might help to know before studying the family trees that follow that Greek Christian tradition dictates that parents will name their children after those children's grandparents, usually starting with the paternal grandfather. This is the way my own father was named: John George Kacandes; his paternal grandfather's first name was John and his own father's name was George. Even if you are not Greek, you may have guessed at this tradition from a comical scene in the hit movie *My Big Fat Greek Wedding*. At one point the parents of the non-Greek boyfriend are being introduced to the family of the Greek American protagonist. All the males—brother, cousins, uncles—appear to be named Nick. My Swiss husband found that scene hilarious. He thinks most males—and a fair number of females—in my family are named Nick. He's almost right. We have a lot of Georges, too. All children are supposed to receive their father's first name as their own middle name. Wives normally change their middle names to that of their husbands. Yes, these are definite markers to the patriarchal nature of Greek culture. And, yes, that means that even female children and married women have male middle names. Sometimes, of course, parents (and wives) choose to buck both these sets of rules. And, of course, if parents don't give birth to two boys and two girls and/or bear more than four children, they have to come up with additional names no matter how they feel about the traditions.

Here are a few other tips to avoid being confused by the names in this book: Greek masculine names, first or sur, and titles frequently end in *s*;

however, this letter is dropped when the person is addressed directly (the vocative case) or when the person is talked about (anything other than the nominative case). Greek Americans do not always follow this rule consistently and often drop the *s* no matter what grammatical role the name or title is playing. Thus "the grandfather," ο παππούς (phonetically: *o pappoós*), usually comes out as "Pappoú," no terminal *s* and accented on the second syllable, or even the more Americanized "Páppou," no terminal *s* and accented on the first syllable. The word for "uncle," ο θείος (phonetically: *o theéos*), actually follows a rule where the direct address form turns into θείε (phonetically: *theé—e*, long *ee* accented, followed by short *e*). But again, Greek Americans usually say *theé—o* (long *ee* accented, followed by long *o*), no matter what the exact grammatical role of the word in the sentence they are uttering. You'll see "uncle" in this book as "Theio" and "grandfather" as "Pappou." Other Greek words you will see often in this book are the words for "grandmother," γιαγιά (phonetically: *yiayia*, two glides *ia*; as in the idiomatic "ya," for example, in the phrase "meet ya there at six"), like the word for "grandfather," accented on the second syllable in Greek but often accented on the first by Greek Americans: "Yíyia"; and θεία (phonetically: *theé-a*), meaning "aunt." You will see these words in this book spelled respectively "Yiayia" and "Theia."

One final explanation about names that appear here: the last name of Greek women is put into the genitive form—yes, another sign of patriarchal culture—and thus while the American form of our name is "Kacandes," in Greece I, for example, would be referred to as Κακαντέ (phonetically: *Kakandé*, last syllable short *e*, accented). Most Greek Americans don't make this distinction at all, and I do not make this distinction in the book while referring to any individual who lived her life mostly in the United States, but I do when referring to names of people more closely attached to Greece. Thus I refer to my paternal grandmother as Chrysoúla George Kacandes, née Tsínga: *s* on the "Kacandes," but not on the name "Tsínga." I apologize if this inconsistency seems confusing, but I feel compelled to express cultural traditions through it.

My paternal grandfather was born in a village with the name Kolopet-initsa or Kalopetinitsa or even Kolapetinitsa. I explain in chapter 1 why this name itself—regardless of its spelling—is problematic. I note here that multiple spellings can be seen in official and unofficial references to this village. Probably because the idea of *kaló*, meaning "good," is appealing, I came to always say Kalopetinitsa, whereas my father and most of his relatives say Kolopetinitsa. However, in an effort not to confuse readers, I have homogenized the spelling and use in this book "Kolopetinitsa." A very common surname in this village is Τζίβας (phonetically: *Tzeevas*, accented on the first syllable). When various individuals with this name came to the United States, they gave a plethora of spellings in English: Gevas, Givas, Tzevas, Tzivas, and Zevas. I have adopted the spelling here for any member of this large family of the one person whom I actually interviewed with this surname, my father's childhood friend, Steven Zévas.

All transcriptions from the Greek follow the system adopted by the Library of Congress. For the place names that are particularly well known in the United States, I use the standard American spelling: Athens, Piraeus, Delphi, Corinth, Thebes; whereas for lesser-known places, I transliterate from the Greek: Itéa, Chryssó, Gávrio, and so forth.

[Appendix B]

Family Trees

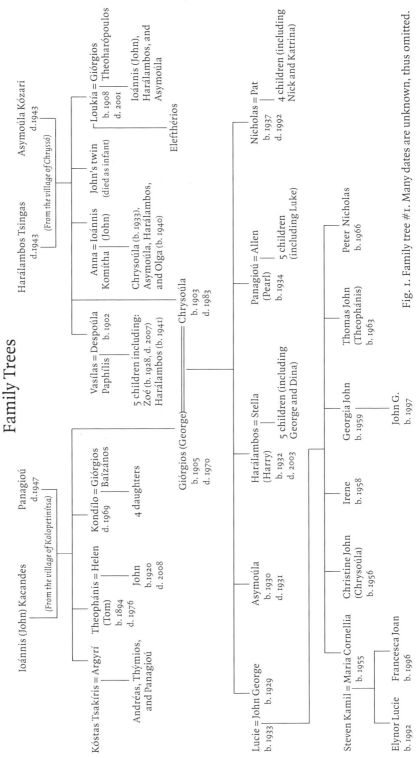

Fig. 1. Family tree #1. Many dates are unknown, thus omitted.

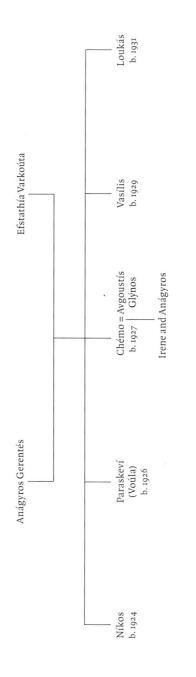

Fig. 2. Family tree #2. Efstathía Gerenté, née Varkoúta, and Harálambos Tsíngas (see family tree #1), my grandmother's father, were first cousins. Her mother and his father were siblings.

[Appendix C]

Maps

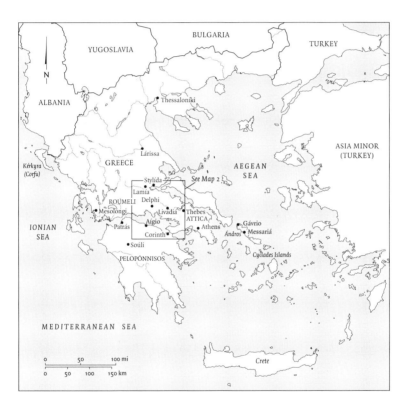

Map 1. Greece

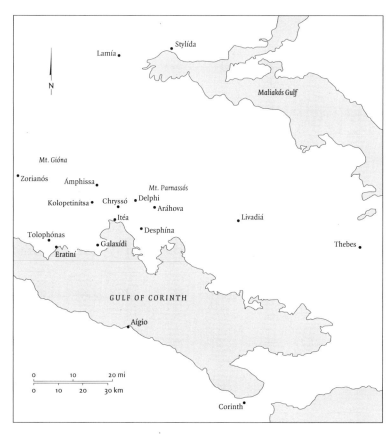

Map 2. Roúmeli

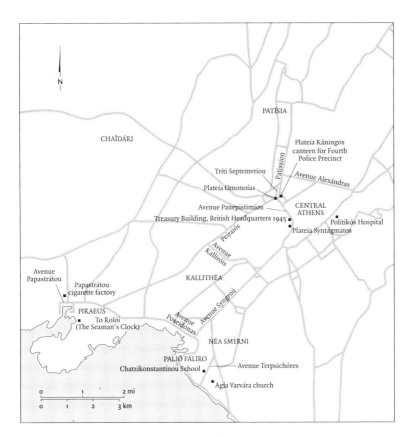

Map 3. Athens

[Appendix D]

"Never Leave the United States"

I have reproduced the Newspaper Article the way it originally appeared—
that is to say, I include spelling or other typographical errors and facts
I know to be incorrectly stated. There was no byline.

ASBURY PARK SUNDAY PRESS (The Shore Press)

October 28, 1945

"Never Leave the United States"

*That's the Advice of 15-Year-Old John Kacandes, Neptune Schoolboy,
After Years of Terror and Back-Breaking Labor Under the Yoke of the
Germans and Italians in Greece*

"Never leave the United States," advises John Kacandes, 15-year-old lad
who has just returned from a harrowing eight years in Greece. "I tell everyone that this country is far better than any other. People are friendly
here and have everything they need. I'll never leave the United States."

John is the son of Mr. and Mrs. George Kacandes of 1351 Eighth avenue, Neptune. His adventures, which rival those of "Terry" or "Jack
Armstrong," began in 1937 when Mrs. Kacandes took her three children to Greece for a stay of two of two or three years. While John attended school in Athens, the family stayed with their grandparents in
Etea, a small town about two miles outside Delphi.

In 1939 John's father wrote from America that war was imminent and
advised John to join his mother. A year later the American consul called

the family to return to the United States, but the Germans entered so rapidly that when the Kacandes' had reached Athens the American embassy had withdrawn.

Making the best of a bad situation, the family returned to Etea. Because of the currency situation John's father was unable to help financially. Mrs. Kacandes walked 60 miles to sell some home made clothing for food. Inflation had gripped the country and the value of the drachma had dropped so that two truck-loads of drachmas could not equal two British pounds. "It took a car to move your money," explained John.

Greece returned to the ancient barter system, the basis of which became olive oil. One oki (about three pounds) of oil bought five okis of wheat. John described a family forced to sell 70 olive trees for a little wheat, olive oil and soap. The trees had cost $1,500 before the war and they were traded at a staggering loss.

John bought three little lambs which he carefully tended until he was able to sell them a year later to feed the family.

BREAKS STONES FOR ROADS

John and his brother found a job breaking rocks for the roads being built by the Italians. Working all day without shoes and with scant clothing, they were paid only a piece of bread and a cup of olives. Every 15 days the Germans gave John six pounds of flour, two pounds of beans and three pounds of dirty raisins. That was all.

Later the boy worked in an Italian Fascists kitchen cleaning kettles in exchange for bread and macaroni. Here he rapidly forgot his English and learned the Italian language. His hardest job, however, was working on a grape farm in the Peleponnesus, where he spent all day in the hot sun cutting the grapes and setting them out to dry into raisins. John explained that between 1941 and 1942 raisins were the only form of cheap food for the Greek people. He was paid six pounds of fruit for five days' work.

For three months John worked on a night fishing boat. In the dawn he would come ashore and walk five miles to the mountains to sell the two pounds of fish he had received for his night's labor. Altho they might have eaten the fish, his family preferred to exchange it for bread which they needed even more. John was lucky to snatch two hours sleep before the ship set sail again at dusk.

In 1942 he walked to Athens to ask help from the Red Cross. There the Swedish Red Cross welcomed him. He was well fed and clothed and could have remained to continue his schooling, but the thought of his starving brothers and sister goaded him to return to work. The Red Cross could send no help to his family.

SHIP SUNK

John became a sailor on a German ship and was able to save two sacks full of money. During an American air raid, however, the ship was sunk and he lost money and clothing, saving his life only by swimming ashore. Wounded and exhausted, John walked 50 miles to a hospital. In Athens he was arrested by the Gestapo but released on the recommendation of the Swedish Red Cross.

Soon afterwards the boy became a guard for a German ammunition dump but was forced to return to Etea when he contracted malaria. Upon recovery he joined the Greek "King" guerillas fighting in the mountains about 100 miles from Etea. Only occasionally reinforced by British airplanes, the band endured constant exposure to the cold and rainy weather. They worked ceaselessly night and day under the most rigorous conditions.

In one engagement the guerillas ambushed and killed five German soldiers. In retaliation the Germans machinegunned a whole town of 2,500 people including 60 children. A priest who refused to reveal the whereabouts of the guerillas was hanged. Others were terribly tortured.

Later John went once more to Athens where he sold cigarets in the streets and during a period of three months was able to save one British pound. Changing it into Greek currency he sent it to his mother, but before it arrived the Germans had issued new money and John's earnings were worthless. His mother burned the money in the stove for fuel.

JOINS BRITISH

At the outbreak of the civil war John joined the 50th Royal Tank regiment, "A" squadron, where he worked as a "bat-man" or valet to British officers. He states that he was poorly fed and poorly paid and that the British observed a distinction between themselves and the Greeks, throwing away quantities of food rather than feed it to the Greeks, to whom they rationed soup.

In testimony to his services with the tank regiment John received an official recommendation which reads: "John Kacandes has been with this squadron since 29 December 1944 and at all times has rendered good service. In Athens during the troubles he risked his life on several occasions in the forward positions occupied by British troops. Since that time he has been serving in various capacities and he is honest and of good character. I recommend him for any odd duties which may arise." The document is signed "V. E. Bond. Capt., Royal Tank Regiment."

John's family was greatly helped by American representatives from UNRRA, who brought sugar, rice, macaroni and meat to the Greek people. They provided wagons for transportation and were the most helpful organization in the country, according to John.

Late this year the Kacandes family sold their possessions in Athens, reported to the American embassy and obtained passage to the United States on the liner Gripsholm, arriving Oct. 9.

During the five years before their return, no member of John's family had any shoes. The luxuries they saw here almost overwhelmed them. For instance eight-year-old Nick could not believe that his father actually owned a car and was astonished at the variety of forks and spoons set at his plate. "I have not four hands," he cried.

The children are attending Bradley Park school in Neptune, where the younger ones must first learn to speak, read and write in English.

John is now in the seventh grade at the school, where he recently told of his experiences abroad in assembly and showed many snapshots taken in Greece. "I tell everyone I know," he says, "that America is the best country."

[There is an accompanying photo of my father with his school principal. The caption reads, "BOY TELLS WAR STORY—John Kacandes, caught in Greece during the war, tells his adventures to Raymond Warwick, Bradley Park school principal. John fought with the Greek guerillas and kept his family from starvation. He returned on the Gripsholm Oct. 9. (Press photo)"]

[Appendix E]

My Grandfather's Wartime File on His Family

It appears that all these documents were originally taped to something, perhaps a wall, and that they were later attached, often with glue, sometimes with tape, to a heavier piece of paper, perhaps into an album of some kind. I have never heard reports of my father finding an album—though he himself often glued his correspondence into albums—just a "stack of letters." My first cousin George, eldest son of my father's brother Harry, claims to have himself seen a thick stack of papers that related to our grandfather trying to find his family during the war. In my own memory of my father's original discovery of these letters after his father's death, there were reportedly letters to the State Department and to the Red Cross. However, I found no correspondence with the Red Cross and only the meager quantity of correspondence reproduced below. I did myself check with the International Red Cross and the Swedish Red Cross to request they search for anything that might indicate involvement with my family, but they reported no such paper trail.

At the time I found these documents (October 2006) in the attic of my parents' home, I had been searching for them for about two years. On a tip from my brother to look in the attic, I found them in the bottom drawer of a filing cabinet filled with my father's notes from graduate school and with outdated articles about the pedagogy of reading—just before I was about to give up the search. The label on the drawer said "READING MATERIALS," and these letters were in a file folder labeled in my father's handwriting as "DAD's Letters to State Dept." Also in the same folder were some lined pieces of paper written on by hand on topics such as "TENDER TIES OF FAMILY" and "THE WORTH OF MAN." These appear to be favorite quotes from famous persons such as Homer, Sophocles, Callimachus. I recognize the handwriting as my grandfather's. Note that his English was not excellent; I am assuming he had help with the letters reproduced below. They are shown here in chronological order; spelling, capitalization, and punctuation are as in the originals.

I.

Postal Telegraph
Night letter
5/16/40
Hon. Commissioner of Immigration and Naturalization
Washington, D.C.

Please wire collect whether my petition has been approved stop petition was filed February 20 in favor of my wife Chryssoula Kacandes pressently residing at Itea, Greece And I was examined at Ellis Island [crossed out May 5] April 5 stop [another word crossed out but can't read] delay in approval endangers my family and American born children who are with my wife in Greece. and must get out before war breaks

George Kacandes
89a Court street, Newark, N.J.

2.

Western Union (right side cut off)

LD5 AG DH

NK NEWARK NJ MAY 3 1941

GEO KACANDES

89A COURT ST NEWARK NJ

YOUR CABLE TO GREECE CANCELLED AS THERE IS NO
COMMUNICATIONS

PLEASE CALL FOR REFUND

WESTERN UNION TEL CO

[number I can't read]

[in handwriting in pencil; cut off; can't see all] "cancelled and
refund

mone

$4.

3. [Copy of letter from my grandfather to Secretary of State]

October 1st, 1941
Honorable Cordell Hull
Secretary of State
Washington, D.C.

Honorable Sir:—

I am an American citizen, being naturalized in 1927 and reside in Newark, N.J. In 1937 I sent my wife and four children who are also residents to Greece and have been in communication with them since and up to March 11th, 1941. They last resided at Itea, Amphissa, Greece.

I have not heard from them since that date and I do not know of their whereabouts. I have heard that through your offices contact can be made with American Citizens stranded in Greece.

My wife's name is Chryssoula G. Kacandes and the children are: John 12, Harry 10, Panagrou 8 and Nicholas 5.

Any effort that can be made to find out if they are alive and in need will be greatly appreciated by a frantic husband and father.

Very truly yours,

George Kacandes
17 Academy St.
Newark, N. J.

[Note that the ages of the children are wrong: John was still 11, Harry was 8, Pearl 7, and Nick 4. Pearl's legal name is spelled wrong; it should be Panagiou.]

4. [Typed letter from Dept. of State to my grandfather]

Department of State

Washington

October 6, 1941

In reply refer to SD 368.6815/385

My dear Mr. Kacandes:

I have received your letter of October 1, 1941 regarding your desire to obtain information concerning the whereabouts and welfare of your wife, Chryssoula G. Kacandes, and your four children, John, Harry, Panagrou, and Nicholas Kacandes, who were last known to be residing at Amphissa, Greece.

The Department no longer has representatives in Greece. However, the American embassy at Rome has been requested by telegraph at Government expense to endeavor to ascertain the desired information through such Italian channels as may be available. I am sure you will readily appreciate that owing to existing conditions abroad it may prove impossible to obtain the desired information.

Mr. George Kacandes,

17 Academy Street,

Newark, New Jersey

[It appears the letter had a second page; looks like there may have been a staple in it and also a paper clip; no second page to be found now.]

5. [Typed letter from Dept. of State to my grandfather]

Department of State
Washington
November 17, 1941
In reply refer to SD 368.6815/442

My dear Mr. Kacandes:

Reference is made to the Department's letter of October 6, 1941 stating that a telegraphic inquiry was being made concerning the whereabouts and welfare of your four children, John, Harry, Panagrou, and Nicholas Kacandes, who were last known to be residing with their mother, Chryssoula G. Kacandes, at Itea, Amphissa, Greece.

In reply to its inquiry the Department has received a telegram dated November 14, 1941 from the American Embassy at Rome, communicating the following message for you:

"Mrs. Chryssoula G. Kacandes, same address, reports family in good health but in urgent need of money."

The Department understands that banks dealing in foreign exchange and having Italian correspondents, such

Mr. George Kacandes,
17 Academy Street,
Newark, New Jersey

[This letter obviously did have a continuation; there is a staple still in upper left; but there is no second page now.]

6. [Carbon copy of typed letter from my grandfather to the Dept. of State]

17 Academy St.
Newark, N.J.
July 6, 1942
Department of State
Washington, D.C.
Attention: Mr. F. Van-den Arend
Asst. Chief, Special Division
S.D 368 1115/1640

Dear Sir:

My wife Chryssoula Kacandes sailed from New York August 14, 1937 on steamship Volcania for Athens Greece. She had a Greek passport.

She applied for her citizenship papers and got several cards since she left for Greece to report at B 89 New Post office building, Newark, New Jersey. When she first went for her examination she was post-poned and before the second call came she had left for Greece with her four children, all born in the United States, birth certificates for each child enclosed. I am also enclosing a post card from United States Department of Justice, Naturalization service #36740, dated July 22, 1940 to report for examination.

All this material is enclosed and I would appreciate your returning whatever you do not require.

Please accept my thanks for your kindness.

Respectfully yours,
George Kacandes
My citizen papers #24,76721

[Appendix F]

Chronology

Main sources for this timeline are Clogg ed. 2002, esp. "Introduction" pp. 1–21, and Mazower 2001, passim.

1919–22
Greek campaign in Asia Minor; ends in rout of Greek army. Influx into Greece of more than 1 million mainly destitute refugees. Often referred to as the Asia Minor Disaster.

1936
Parliament dissolved by King George II.

April 1936
Elefthérios Venizélos (former prime minister, then in exile) dies in Paris; funeral in Chaniá, Crete.

August 4, 1936
Prime Minister Giánnis Metaxás declares martial law.

September 1, 1939
Germans invade Poland; Greece remains neutral.

October 28, 1940
Ultimatum from Mussolini to Metaxás about Italian occupation of Greece; Metaxás responds, "OXI, NO!" or, according to other accounts, "Donc, c'est la guerre."

Winter 1940–41
Fighting between Greeks and Italians; Greeks push Italians back into Albania; British offer limited air support.

December 1940

Hitler orders Operation Marita—Germans attack from Bulgarian border.

January 1941

Metaxás dies. Alexander Koryzís succeeds him as prime minister; Koryzís agrees to dispatch of British expeditionary force (mainly Australian and New Zealand troops).

April 6, 1941

Wehrmacht launches attack on Greece and Yugoslavia.

April 9, 1941

Wehrmacht enters Thessaloníki.

Mid-April 1941

Luftwaffe attacks ports and cities.

April 21, 1941

Gen. Giórgios Tsolákoglou capitulates to Germans.

April 23, 1941

Second Greek surrender, at demand of Italians.

April 26, 1941

Germans use parachutists to try to secure Corinth canal.

April 27, 1941

German troops enter Athens; city handed over. Germans occupy Patrás.

May 1941

Division of Greece among three Axis powers: Bulgaria receives Western Thrace (area directly south of Bulgaria) and part of Macedonia; Germany takes Crete, Piraeus, Thessaloníki, and areas bordering strip with Turkey, as well as islands of Lémnos, Lésbos, Chíos; Italy gets the mainland (including Roúmeli), Ionian islands, Cyclades. Himmler briefly visits Greece. Some Greek forces escape to Middle East; fight with Allies in North Africa.

May 18, 1941

Germans launch massive air and sea campaign against British and Greeks on island of Crete.

May–June 1941

Italians replace Germans as occupying forces in designated Italian areas.

June 22, 1941

German attack on Soviet Union.

End June 1941

Italians having trouble managing bread rations in Athens.

July 1, 1941

Greek Communist Party (Kommounistikó Kómma Elládos, or KKE) secretly resolves to organize defense of Soviet Union and overthrow foreign fascist yoke in Greece.

Summer 1941

Weather is hot and very dry.

Harvest 1941

Smaller than usual; Greek puppet government unable to manage bread distribution. Seizures of foodstuffs by Germans and Italians.

September 9, 1941

Antiroyalist National Republican Greek League (EDES) organized; Gen. Nikólaos Plastíras, in exile in unoccupied France, made its titular head.

September 27, 1941

Formation of National Liberation Front (EAM) by the communists with its military arm, the Greek People's Liberation Army (ELAS). Republican National and Social Liberation (EKKA) under Col. Demétrios Psarrós formed somewhat later. Rivalries among resistance groups begin almost immediately.

November 1941–April 1942

Severe famine, especially in Athens.

December 7, 1941
Bombing of Pearl Harbor.

July 20, 1942
Mussolini makes stop in Athens on way back from North Africa.

Autumn 1942
Red Cross begins shipping food into Greece. British Special Operations Executive (SOE) parachutes into central Greece; "Harling" mission to disrupt railway line between Thessaloníki and Athens; led by Lt. Col. E. C. W. Myers and his deputy, Maj. C. M. Woodhouse.

November 25, 1942
Gorgopótamos viaduct blown up by British with assistance of ELAS unit under Áres Veloukhiótis and EDES under Napoléon Zérvas. British Military Mission stays on as result of success.

Early February 1943
SS commander Dieter Wisliceny arrives in Thessaloníki. Jewish community of Thessaloníki ordered into ghettos. EKKA forcibly disbanded by ELAS; later EKKA regroups with sanction of British Military Mission.

March 1943
Greek government in exile moves from London to Cairo.

March 15, 1943
First deportation of Salonikan Jews to Auschwitz.

March 23, 1943
Archbishop Demétrios Damaskinós and large group of business and professional people send letter to Konstantínos Logothetópoulos (collaborationist prime minister) protesting deportation of Salonikan Jews.

March–June 1943
Majority of Salonikan Jews deported to Auschwitz.

April 6, 1943
Germans orchestrate Logothetópoulos's replacement by Giánnis Rállis.

April 7, 1943

Rállis government announces formation of Security Battalions.

May–July 1943

National Band Agreement negotiated by British: EDES, EKKA put themselves under Allied command with EAM-ELAS agreeing to adhere to agreement in July, concluding what retrospectively became recognized as first round of Greek Civil War.

May 1943

Axis forces surrender in North Africa.

May 20, 1943

Hitler orders plan for German takeover in Balkans.

June 1943

Allies land in Sicily. Rommel sent to Thessaloníki.

End June 1943

Mussolini toppled in palace coup in Rome. German tanks roll into position in Amerikís Street in Athens; gun barrels point at Italian HQ.

August 1943

Last transport of Jews from Thessaloníki to Auschwitz. Delegation of Greek guerillas (4 EAM, 1 EDES, 1 EKKA) accompanied by British Maj. David Wallace fly to Cairo for negotiations about postvictory fate of Greece; British surprised at demand that king not return to Greece until referendum held on constitutional issue.

September 8, 1943

Italy surrenders.

September 1943

Germans reoccupy whole of Greece.

September 23–25, 1943

ELAS kidnaps Grand Rabbi Elías Barzilái of Athens to prevent his capture by Germans.

Autumn 1943

EAM circulates tract in Athens urging Greeks to help and hide Greek Jews: "The Jews are Greeks just as much as we are" (quoted in Clogg ed. 2002, 107).

October 4, 1943

Germans decree registration of Jews of Athens, with limited success: of estimated 8,000 Jews in Athens, only 1,200 register (Mazower 2001, 251).

Early October 1943

Fighting breaks out between EAM and EDES.

October 25, 1943

German decree announcing reprisals: "Fifty Greeks will be executed for every murdered German soldier, and ten for every wounded German soldier" (as quoted in Clogg ed. 2002, 101).

Christmas 1943

Britain, United States, Soviet Union back appeal by Emmanouíl Tsouderós, prime minister of Greek government in exile, for an armistice and withdrawal of ELAS and EDES to clearly defined areas.

February 29, 1944

Signing of resistance groups' armistice negotiated by Major Woodhouse; referred to as "Plaka agreement."

March 10, 1944

EAM announces establishment of Political Committee of National Liberation (PEEA); seen as challenge to armistice and to authority of Greek government in exile; large-scale mutinies break out among Greek forces in Middle East, harshly suppressed on orders of Churchill.

March 23, 1944

Germans arrest Athenian Jews at routine registration check-in; sent to Haïdári, then Auschwitz; no exact deportation lists of the perhaps 1,000 deported at this time.

April 17, 1944

Leader of EKKA, Colonel Psarrós, assassinated by ELAS. EKKA dissolved; many members go south to Patrás and join collaborationist government's Security Battalions.

May 1944

Churchill and British foreign secretary Anthony Eden start negotiating "percentages agreement" with Stalin on respective spheres of interest in Balkans; British preponderance in Greece set at 90 percent; Soviet in Romania 90 percent; agreement reaffirmed and extended terms from Greece and Romania to Yugoslavia, Bulgaria, Hungary in October 1944.

May 20, 1944

"Lebanon Agreement" results from conference among seventeen political parties and resistance organizations; condemnation of recent mutinies within Greek army in exile; establishment of new Government of National Unity headed by Giórgios Papandréou: all resistance organizations to be under its authority, five posts foreseen for left; EAM not in agreement with negotiations of its representatives in Lebanon.

June 8, 1944

Germans arrest Jews of Kérkyra (Corfu) and begin protracted process of deportation via Patrás, Haïdári to Auschwitz; of approx. 1,700 deported, less than 1 percent survive.

End July 1944

Soviet Military Mission led by Col. Grigori Popov visits ELAS mountain headquarters; results in dramatic shift in EAM's position toward Papandréou government: they accept terms in Lebanon agreement.

Summer 1944

Athens city life approaching anarchy. Germans start to evacuate.

September 26, 1944

Agreement at Caserta, Italy, of ELAS, EDES to place their armed forced under authority of Government of National Unity, which in turn places all its forces under command of Lt. Gen. Ronald Scobie, who is to accompany government in exile back to Greece; includes among other pledges to prevent "civil war and killing of Greeks by Greeks" (Clogg ed. 2002, 175).

October 12, 1944
Last Germans leave Athens.

October 18, 1944
Papandréou Government of National Unity receives enthusiastic welcome in Athens.

November 1944
Papandréou government sets up new national-guard battalions.

End November 1944
Agreement among government, ELAS, and EDES that all military units, including regular Greek army units will disband on December 10; new national army to be constituted.

December 2, 1944
EAM ministers resign from Papandréou government.

December 1944
Ta Dekemvrianá: "the December troubles"; fighting between British and Greek communists in Athens (British troops in Thessaloníki and Vólos not attacked during fighting in Athens [Clogg ed. 2002, 17]). British strafe Athenian suburbs.

December 3, 1944
EAM protest in Sýntagma (Constitution) Square. Police fire on crowd.

December 5, 1944
Churchill orders Lieutenant General Scobie to neutralize or destroy "all EAM-ELAS bands approaching the city" and suggests he act "as if you were in a conquered city where a local rebellion was in progress" (Clogg ed. 2002, 187). Leak of telegram causes outrage in Britain and United States; no reaction from Soviet Union.

Christmas Day 1944

Churchill and Eden journey to Athens; Churchill finally registers broad Greek opposition to return of King George without plebiscite on issue.

End December 1944

King, at Churchill's request, appoints Archbishop Damaskinós as regent. General Plastíras replaces Papandréou as prime minister.

Early January 1945

Defeat of Greek left.

January 11, 1945

Truce signed between ELAS and British.

February 1945

Yalta conference commits Great Britain, United States, and Soviet Union to "ensuring free elections and democratic governments in the liberated countries" (Clogg ed. 2002, 19).

February 12, 1945

Várkiza agreement between representatives of the Greek government and members of the central committee of EAM; commits, among other things, ELAS to laying down weapons and the government to purging civil service, granting amnesty for "political" crimes, and holding "within the current year" plebiscite on monarchy with elections thereafter. Right-wing backlash follows; Plastíras government carries out few provisions of Várkiza agreement (Clogg ed. 2002, 188–90).

May 8, 1945

Germans sign capitulation at Karlshorst, outskirts of Berlin.

September 2, 1945

Japanese sign armistice, ending the Second World War.

Late 1945

Themistoklés Sophoúlis, a Liberal, becomes prime minister. Proclaims new amnesty; announces elections for March 31, 1946, reversing order of plebiscite and elections agreed to in February 1945.

Early 1946

Allied Mission for Observing the Greek Elections (AMFOGE) established; Americans, British, French participate; Soviets abstain on grounds of not meddling in internal affairs. KKE plans to abstain.

March 31, 1946

191 of 354 seats in parliament go to royalist bloc. AMFOGE estimates politically motivated abstentions at 9.4 percent votes cast; figure "almost certainly too low" (Clogg ed. 2002, 19).

September 1, 1946

Plebiscite on monarchy; 68 percent votes cast in favor of king's return. King George returns. Severe hostilities get under way.

November 1946

King George dies; succeeded by brother, Prince Paul.

1947

Attempts by communist Democratic Army of Greece (DSE), led by Márkos Vafiádis, to capture Kónitsa, near Albanian border, for use as seat of provisional (alternate) government.

March 1947

Britain pulls direct financial and military support from Greece.

March 12, 1947

President Harry Truman gives speech to U.S. Congress, announces along with other principles of the Truman Doctrine that "Greece must have assistance if it is to become a self-supporting and self-respecting democracy. The United States must supply that assistance" (Clogg ed. 2002, 199). Aid begins to flow from United States to Greece on massive scale.

October 1947

Communist press banned.

December 1947

KKE declared illegal organization.

December 24, 1947

Proclamation of Provisional Democratic Government (PDK) by communists with Giánnis Ioannídis as deputy prime minister and minister of interior. PDK not recognized by Soviet Union nor any of newly established governments in Eastern Europe nor Cominform (Communist Information Bureau, an international but Soviet-dominated organization of Communist parties). Flow of arms to communists through Yugoslavia, Albania, Bulgaria continues.

1948

Despite aid from United States, situation of national government in Greece remains unstable; martial law declared throughout the country. Dissension between Vafiádis and Zakhariádis over how to conduct war. Vafiádis favors traditional guerrilla tactics; Zakhariádis wants Democratic Army to fight as regular army.

Summer 1948

Expulsion of Yugoslavia from Cominform. Greek communists remain loyal to Moscow.

November 1948

Vafiádis declared anathema by KKE. Zakhariádis takes control of DSE.

Early 1949

Self-determination for Macedonians espoused. Slavic-language speakers compose as much as 50 percent of fighting strength of Democratic Army by this point.

March 1949

KKE seeks to clarify its position regarding the Macedonian question. Greek government portrays KKE as "unpatriotic" (Clogg ed. 2002, 20–21).

Summer 1949

Yugoslavs close frontier to Greek Democratic Army. Series of fierce battles in Grámmos and Vítsi mountains near Albanian frontier; much of leadership and rank and file go into exile in Eastern Europe.

October 1949

Democratic Army declares "'a temporary cessation of hostilities'" (Clogg ed. 2002, 21), which turns out to be permanent.

1967–74

Rightist military junta rules Greece.

1974

KKE legalized once again.

[Glossary]

demotikí (δημοτική): the demotic form of Greek

demotikó (δημοτικό): elementary school

eleftheria (ελευθερία): freedom

hórta (χόρτα): any form of green leafy plants, boiled and eaten, such as dandelion leaves

kaḯki, kaḯkia (καΐκι): caïque, small boat

katharévousa (καθαρεύουσα): the "purified" form of Greek, artificially created and introduced in nineteenth century

kótso (κότσο): plait (of hair)

koumbáros, koumbára (κουμπάρος / α): best man/woman, witness of a wedding; usually becomes the godfather or godmother of first child born to couple

lóngos (λόγγος): grove, wood, thicket

Pappoú (παππούς): grandfather

plateía (πλατεία): square (as in public place in a city or town)

proíka (προίκα): dowry

rolóï (ρολόι): clock; in my father's story it refers to a specific place where there was a clock tower in the port of Piraeus

Theía (θεία): aunt

Theío (θείος): uncle

Yiayiá (γιαγιά): grandmother

[Reference List]

Abatzopoúlou, Frangíski [Φραγκίσκη Αμπατζοπούλου]. 1983. *The Holocaust in the testimony of Greek Jews* [Το Ολοκαύτωμα στις Μαρτυρίες των Ελλήνων Εβραίων]. Thessaloníki: Paratirítis.

American Psychiatric Association (APA). 1994. *Diagnostic and statistical manual of mental disorders.* 4th ed. Washington DC: American Psychiatric Association.

Anuta, Michael J. 1983. *Ships of our ancestors.* Menominee MI: Genealogical Publishing Co.

Appignanesi, Lisa. 1999. *Losing the dead: A family memoir.* London: Chatto and Windus.

Assmann, Aleida. Forthcoming. Four formats of memory: From individual to collective forms of constructing the past. In *Performing the past*, ed. Karin Tilmans, Jay Winter, and F. P. I. M. van Vrec. New Haven: Yale University Press.

Berger, Alan L., and Naomi Berger, eds. 2001. *Second generation voices: Reflections by children of Holocaust survivors and perpetrators.* Syracuse: Syracuse University Press.

Bergman, Martin S., and Milton E. Jucovy, eds. 1990. *Generations of the Holocaust.* New York: Columbia University Press. (Orig. pub. 1982.)

Camus, Albert. 1991. *La chute: Récit.* Paris: Gallimard. Translated by Justin O'Brien as *The fall.* New York: Vintage. (Prev. pub. 1956, 1984.)

Caruth, Cathy, ed. 1995. *Trauma: Explorations in memory.* Baltimore: Johns Hopkins University Press.

Cavafy, C. P. 1992. *Collected poems.* Rev. ed. Trans. Edmund Keeley and Philip Sherrard. Ed. George P. Savidis. Princeton: Princeton University Press. (Orig. pub. 1975.)

Chambers, Ross. 2002. Orphaned memories, foster-writing, phantom pain: The fragments affair. In *Extremities: Trauma, testimony, and community*, ed. Nancy K. Miller and Jason Tougaw, 92–111. Urbana: University of Illinois Press.

Clogg, Richard. 2002. *A concise history of Greece*. Cambridge: Cambridge University Press. (Orig. pub. 1992.)

———, ed. and trans. 2002. *Greece 1940–1949: Occupation, resistance, and civil war; A documentary history*. Basingstoke: Palgrave MacMillan.

Danieli, Yael, ed. 1998. *International handbook of multigenerational legacies of trauma*. New York: Plenum.

Duranti, A., and D. Brenneis, eds. 1986. The audience as co-author. Special issue, *Text: An Interdisciplinary Journal for the Study of Discourse* 6, no. 3.

Epstein, Helen. 1979. *Children of the Holocaust: Conversations with sons and daughters of survivors*. New York: Bantam.

Felman, Shoshana, and Dori Laub. 1992. *Testimony: Crises of witnessing in literature, psychoanalysis, and history*. New York: Routledge.

Fresco, Nadine. 1984. Remembering the unknown. *International Review of Psycho-Analysis* 11:417–27. (Orig. pub. as La diaspora des cendres. *Nouvelle Revue de Psychanalyse* 24 [1981]: 205–20).

Gage, Nicholas. 1983. *Eleni*. New York: Random House.

Galea, Sandro, et al. 2002. Psychological sequelae of the September 11 terrorist attacks in New York City. *New England Journal of Medicine* 346 (13): 982–87.

Genette, Gérard. 1980. *Narrative discourse: An essay in method*. Trans. Jane E. Lewin. Foreword by Jonathan Culler. Ithaca NY: Cornell University Press. (Orig. pub. 1972.)

Gerzon, George, and Helen Gerzon Goransson. 2003. *The hand of fate: Memoirs of George Gerzon as told by him to his daughter*. Dover NH: Odyssey Press. (Orig. pub. 1999.)

Gilbert, Martin. 1988. *Atlas of the Holocaust*. Oxford: Pergamon Press.

Goransson, Helen Gerzon. 2004. Interview by Irene Kacandes. Transcript. March 22.

Halbwachs, Maurice. 1992. *On collective memory*. Ed. and trans. Lewis A. Coser. Chicago: University of Chicago Press.

Hamilton, Stephen D. 1996. *50th Royal Tank Regiment: The complete history.* Cambridge: Lutterworth Press.

Haviaras, Stratis. 1984. *The heroic age.* New York: Simon and Schuster.

Herman, Judith Lewis. 1997. *Trauma and recovery.* New York: Basic. (Orig. pub. 1992.)

Hirsch, Marianne. 1997. *Family frames: Photography, narrative, and postmemory.* Cambridge MA: Harvard University Press.

———. 2008. The generations of postmemory. *Poetics Today* 29:103–28.

Hirsch, Marianne, and Irene Kacandes. 2004. Introd. to *Teaching the representation of the Holocaust.* New York: MLA Publications.

Hirsch, Marianne, and Leo Spitzer. Forthcoming. *Ghosts of home: The afterlife of Czernowitz in Jewish memory.* Berkeley: University of California Press.

Hoffman, Eva. 2004. *After such knowledge: Memory, history, and the legacy of the Holocaust.* New York: PublicAffairs.

Hong Kingston, Maxine. 1989. *China men.* New York: Vintage. (Orig. pub. 1977.)

Kacandes, Irene. 1990. Orality, reader address, and anonymous "you." On translating second person references from modern Greek prose. *Journal of Modern Greek Studies* 8 (2): 223–43.

———. 1992. The oral tradition and modern Greek literature. *Laografia: A Newsletter of the International Greek Folklore Society* 9 (5): 3–8.

———. 1994. "You who live safe in your warm houses": Your role in the production of Holocaust testimony. In *Insiders and outsiders: Jewish and gentile culture in Germany and Austria,* ed. Dagmar C. G. Lorenz and Gabriele Weinberger, 189–213. Detroit: Wayne State University Press.

———. 2001. *Talk fiction: Literature and the talk explosion.* Lincoln: University of Nebraska Press.

———. 2003. 9/11/01 = 1/27/01: The changed posttraumatic self. In *Trauma at home: After 9/11,* ed. Judith Greenberg, 168–83. Lincoln: University of Nebraska Press.

Kaïmáras, Giórgios [Γεώργιος Δ. Καϊμάρα]. 1988. *The chronicle of a sacrifice: Demétrios Psarrós and the 5/42 Evzone Regiment* [Το Χρονικό μιας θυσίας. Δημ. Ψαρρός και το 5/42 σύνταγμα ευζώνων]. Athens: I. Sitheris.

Kalaphátis, Thanásis [Θανάσης Καλαφάτης]. 2001. *The Jews of Kerkyra and their passage from Lefkada to the road to Auschwitz, June 1944* [Οι Εβραίοι της Κέρκυρας και το πέρασμά τους από τη Λευκάδα στο Δρόμο προς το Άουσβιτς, Ιούνιος 1944]. Athens: Center of the Jewish Council of Greece.

Karpf, Anne. 1997. *The war after: Living with the Holocaust.* London: Minerva. (Orig. pub. 1996.)

Kogan, Ilany. 1995. *The cry of mute children: A psychoanalytic perspective of the second generation of the Holocaust.* London: Free Association Books.

LaCapra Dominick. 2001. *Writing history, writing trauma.* Ithaca: Cornell University Press.

Langer, Lawrence L. 1991. *Holocaust testimonies: The ruins of memory.* New Haven: Yale University Press.

Lanzmann, Claude. 1985. *Shoah: An oral history of the Holocaust; The complete text of the film.* Preface by Simone de Beauvoir. New York: Pantheon Books.

Levi, Primo. 1961. *Survival in Auschwitz: The Nazi assault on humanity.* Trans. Stuart Woolf. New York: Macmillan. (Orig. pub. 1958.)

Loftus, Elizabeth. 1996. *Eyewitness testimony.* Cambridge MA: Harvard University Press. (Orig. pub. 1979.)

Mandelbaum, Jenny. 1989. Interpersonal activities in conversational storytelling. *Western Journal of Speech Communication* 53:114–26.

Mátsas, Néstor [Νέστορας Μάτσας]. 1999. *This child died tomorrow: An occupation journal* [Αυτό το παιδί πέθανε αύριο. Ημερολόγιο Κατοχής]. Athens: Eleftheroudákis.

Mazower, Mark. 2001. *Inside Hitler's Greece: The experience of occupation, 1941–44.* New Haven: Yale University Press. (Orig. pub. 1993.)

McGlothlin, Erin. 2006. *Second-generation Holocaust literature: Legacies of survival and perpetration.* Rochester NY: Camden House.

Nesaule, Agate. 1997. *A woman in amber: Healing the trauma of war and exile.* New York: Penguin Books. (Orig. pub. 1995.)

Nofsinger, Robert E. 1991. *Everyday conversation.* Newbury Park CA: Sage.

Ong, Walter J. 1982. *Orality and literacy: The technologizing of the word.* London: Methuen.

Ophuls, Marcel. 1975. *The sorrow and the pity: The complete script.* New York: Berkley. (Orig. pub. 1972.)

Paráschos, Kóstas [Κώστας Παράσχος]. 1983. *The liberation* [H Απελευθέρωση]. Athens: Ermes.

Proust, Marcel. 2003. *In search of lost time.* 6 vols. Trans. C. K. Scott Moncrieff and Terence Kolmartin. Ed. D. J. Enright. Introduction by Richard Howard. New York: Modern Library. (Orig. pub. 1992; orig. French pub. 1913–27.)

Root, Maria P. 1996. Women of color and traumatic stress in "domestic captivity": Gender and race as disempowering statuses. In *Ethnocultural aspects of posttraumatic stress disorder: Issues, research, and clinical applications,* ed. Anthony J. Marsella et al., 363–87. Washington DC: American Psychological Association.

Sacks, Harvey, Emanuel Schegloff, and Gail Jefferson. 1974. A simplest systematics for the organization of turn-taking for conversation. *Language* 50 (4): 696–735.

Sebald, W. G. 2001. *Austerlitz.* Trans. Anthea Bell. New York: Modern Library.

Sicher, Efraim, ed. 1998. *Breaking crystal: Writing and memory after Auschwitz.* Urbana: University of Illinois Press.

Skakun, Michael. 1999. *On burning ground: A son's memoir.* New York: St. Martin's Griffin.

Solkoff, Norman. 1981. Children of survivors of the Nazi Holocaust: A critical review of the literature. *American Journal of Orthopsychiatry* 51 (1): 29–42.

Spence, Donald P. 1982. *Narrative truth and historical truth: Meaning and interpretation in psychoanalysis.* New York: Norton.

Spiegelman, Art. 1991. *Maus: A survivor's tale.* Vols. 1 and 2. New York: Pantheon Books.

Suleiman, Susan Rubin. 2004. The 1.5 generation. In *Teaching the representation of the holocaust,* ed. Marianne Hirsch and Irene Kacandes, 372–85. New York: MLA Publications.

———. 2006. *Crises of memory and the Second World War.* Cambridge MA: Harvard University Press.

Tannen, Deborah. 1980. A comparative analysis of oral narrative strategies:

Athenian Greek and American English. In *The pear stories: Cognitive, cultural, and linguistic aspects of narrative production*, ed. Wallace L. Chafe, 51–87. Norwood NJ: Ablex.

Time-Life Editors. 1982. *La luftwaffe*. Amsterdam: Time-Life.

Valtinós, Thanásis [Θανάσης Βαλτινός]. 2007. *The synaxis of Andréas Korthopátis. First book: America* [Συναξάρι Ανδρέα Κορδοπάτη. Βιβλίο Πρώτο: Αμερική]. Athens: Estia. (Prev. pub. 1964, 1972.)

Van der Kolk, B. A., and Onno van der Hart. 1995. The intrusive past: The flexibility of memory and the engraving of trauma. In *Trauma: Explorations in memory*, ed. Cathy Caruth, 158–82. Baltimore: Johns Hopkins University Press. (Orig. pub. in *American Imago* 48, no. 4 [1991]: 425–54.)

Weissman, Gary. 2004. *Fantasies of witnessing: Postwar efforts to experience the Holocaust*. Ithaca: Cornell University Press.

Wigren, Jodie. 1994. Narrative completion in the treatment of trauma. *Psychotherapy* 31 (3): 415–23.

Wilkomirski, Binjamin. 1996. *Fragments: Memories of a wartime childhood*. Trans. Carol Brown Janeway. New York: Schocken Books. (Orig. pub. 1995.)